THE CAMBRIDGE COMPANION
OF LOS ANGE

M000223036

Los Angeles has a tantalizing hold on the American imagination. Its self-magnifying myths encompass Hollywood glamour, Arcadian landscapes, and endless summer, but also the apocalyptic undertow of riots, environmental depredation, and natural disaster. This *Companion* traces the evolution of Los Angeles as the most public staging of the American Dream – and American nightmares. The expert contributors make exciting, innovative connections among the authors and texts inspired by the city, covering the early Spanish settlers, African-American writers, the British and German expatriates of the 1930s and 1940s, Latino and Asian LA literature. The genres discussed include crime novels, science fiction, Hollywood novels, literary responses to urban rebellion, the poetry scene, nature writing, and the most influential non-fiction accounts of the region. Diverse, vibrant, and challenging as the city itself, this *Companion* is the definitive guide to Los Angeles in literature.

KEVIN R. McNAMARA is Professor of Literature and American Studies at the University of Houston–Clear Lake.

THE CAMBRIDGE
COMPANION TO
THE LITERATURE OF LOS ANGELES

KEVIN R. McNAMARA

CAMBRIDGE
UNIVERSITY PRESS

CAMBRIDGE UNIVERSITY PRESS
Cambridge, New York, Melbourne, Madrid, Cape Town, Singapore,
São Paulo, Delhi, Dubai, Tokyo

Cambridge University Press
The Edinburgh Building, Cambridge CB2 8RU, UK

Published in the United States of America by Cambridge University Press, New York

www.cambridge.org
Information on this title: www.cambridge.org/9780521735544

First published 2010

Printed in the United Kingdom at the University Press, Cambridge

A catalogue record for this publication is available from the British Library

Library of Congress Cataloguing in Publication data
The Cambridge companion to the literature of Los Angeles / [edited by] Kevin R. McNamara.
p.   cm. – (Cambridge companions to literature)
ISBN 978-0-521-51470-5 (hardback)
1. American literature – California – Los Angeles – History and criticism.   2. Los Angeles
(Calif.) – In literature.   I. McNamara, Kevin R., 1958–
PS285.L7C36 2010
810.9′979494–dc21
2009050511

ISBN 978-0-521-51470-5 Hardback
ISBN 978-0-521-73554-4 Paperback

CONTENTS

NOTES ON CONTRIBUTORS

ERIC AVILA is the author of *Popular Culture in the Age of White Flight: Fear and Fantasy in Suburban Los Angeles* (2004) and is currently working on a second book project that considers the cultural history of urban highway construction in postwar America. He is Associate professor of History, Chicano Studies, and Urban Planning at University of California, Los Angeles.

J. SCOTT BRYSON is Professor of English at Mount St. Mary's College in Los Angeles. He is the author of *The West Side of Any Mountain: Place, Space, and Ecopoetry* (2005). He has also edited or co-edited several collections of criticism on nature writing, including *Ecopoetry: A Critical Introduction* (2002). His current scholarship focuses on urban theory and culture, primarily as it relates to Los Angeles literature.

RUSSELL A. BERMAN is the Walter A. Haas Professor in the Humanities at Stanford University, with appointments in the Departments of Comparative Literature and German Studies. He is also Senior Fellow at the Hoover Institution and editor of *Telos*. He has written widely on modern literature, culture, and critical theory. His books include *Enlightenment or Empire: Colonial Discourse in German Culture* (1998) and *Fiction Sets You Free: Literature, Liberty, and Western Culture* (2007).

JAMES KYUNG-JIN LEE is Associate Professor of Asian American Studies and English at the University of California, Irvine. He is the author of *Urban Triage: Race and the Fictions of Multiculturalism* (2004). He sits on the editorial board of the *Heath Anthology of American Literature*, and serves as an associate editor of *American Quarterly*.

WILLIAM MARLING is Professor of English at Case Western Reserve University in Cleveland, Ohio. A scholar of American literature and popular culture, he is the author of five books, including *Dashiell Hammett* (1983), *Raymond Chandler* (1986), and *The American Roman Noir* (1995).

WILLIAM ALEXANDER McCLUNG is the author of *Landscapes of Desire: Anglo Mythologies of Los Angeles* (2000), a *Los Angeles Times* Best Nonfiction Book of the Year. His other publications on Los Angeles include "L.A. 1900" in *Land of Sunshine: An Environmental History of Metropolitan Los Angeles*, ed. William Deverell and Greg Hise (2005). His other books include *The Architecture of Paradise: Survivals of Eden and Jerusalem* (1983) and *The Country House in English Renaissance Poetry* (1977).

KEVIN R. McNAMARA is the author of *Urban Verbs: Arts and Discourses of American Cities* (1996), and other essays on American cities, literature, film, and culture. The first literature seminar he taught was on Los Angeles, and his interest never waned. He has taught in the Czech Republic and Turkey and is Professor of Literature and American Studies at the University of Houston–Clear Lake.

BILL MOHR'S first book of poems, *hidden proofs*, was published in 1982; his most recent collection is *Bittersweet Kaleidoscope* (2006). A personal essay, "Headway," was included in *Best of the Web 2008*. His history of Southern California poetry, *Backlit Renaissance: Los Angeles Poets during the Cold War*, will be published in 2010. He is Assistant Professor in the Department of English at California State University, Long Beach.

JULIAN MURPHET is Professor of Modern Film and Literature at the University of New South Wales. He is the author of *Literature and Race in Los Angeles* (2001), and *Multimedia Modernism* (2009), both from Cambridge University Press.

PATRICK O'DONNELL is Professor of English and American Literature at Michigan State University. He is the author of several books on modern and contemporary fiction, including *John Hawkes*; *Passionate Doubts: Designs of Interpretation in Contemporary American Fiction*; *Echo Chambers: Reading Voice in Modern Narrative*; *Latent Destinies: Cultural Paranoia in Contemporary U.S Narrative*, and forthcoming, *The American Novel Now: Reading American Fiction Since 1980*. He is co-editor of *Intertextuality and Contemporary American Fiction*, editor of *New Essays on* The Crying of Lot 49, and an associate editor of *The Columbia History of the American Novel*. He has provided the introduction and notes to the Penguin Twentieth Century Classics editions of two works by F. Scott Fitzgerald, *This Side of Paradise* and *The Curious Case of Benjamin Button and Other Jazz Age Stories*.

BEATRICE PITA teaches in the Spanish Section of the Department of Literature at the University of California, San Diego. With Rosaura Sánchez, she co-edited and wrote the introduction to *The Squatter and the Don*, and *Who Would Have Thought It? Conflicts of Interest: The Letters of Maria Amparo Ruiz de Burton*, also written in collaboration with Rosaura Sánchez, appeared in 2001.

CHIP RHODES is Associate Professor and Chair of the English Department at Western New England College. He is the author of two books, *Structures of the Jazz Age: Mass Culture, Progressive Education and Racial Discourse in American Modernism* (1998) and *Politics, Desire and the Hollywood Novel* (2008).

ROSAURA SÁNCHEZ is Professor in the Department of Literature at the University of California, San Diego. She is the author of *Chicano Discourse* (1994) and *Telling Identities: The Californio Testimonios* (1995), and co-editor of the Arte Público Press editions of Maria Amparo Ruiz de Burton's novels, *The Squatter and the Don* and *Who Would Have Thought It?* Her work in critical theory, literary analysis, and sociolinguistics, as well as her fiction, has appeared in numerous journals and anthologies.

CHARLES SCRUGGS is Professor of American Literature at the University of Arizona. He is the author of *The Sage in Harlem: H. L. Mencken and the Black Writers of the 1920s* (1984) and *Sweet Home: Invisible Cities in the Afro-American Novel* (1993), and the co-author of *Jean Toomer and the Terrors of American History* (1998). He has also published essays on film noir, Phillis Wheatley, Carl Van Vechten, John Fante, Richard Wright, Ralph Ellison, James Baldwin, and Toni Morrison.

DAVID SEED is Professor of American Literature at Liverpool University. He has published books on Joseph Heller, Thomas Pynchon, and brainwashing, among other subjects, and has edited the *Blackwell Companion to Science Fiction* (2005). He works primarily in the fields of Cold War culture, science fiction, and the relation between fiction and film.

MARK SHIEL is Senior Lecturer in Film Studies, King's College London, author of *Italian Neorealism: Rebuilding the Cinematic City* (2005), and co-editor with Tony Fitzmaurice of *Screening the City* (2003), and *Cinema and the City* (2001). He is presently writing *The Real Los Angeles: Hollywood, Cinema, and the City of Angels*.

DAVID WYATT is Professor of English at the University of Maryland. He is the author of *Five Fires: Race, Catastrophe, and the Shaping of California* (1999) and *The Fall into Eden: Landscape and Imagination in California* (Cambridge University Press, 1990).

CHRONOLOGY

1769   Spanish explorers discover the Los Angeles River.

1781   September 4. Settlers from the San Gabriel Mission found the
         city as El Pueblo de Nuestra Señora la Reina de los Angeles del
         Río de Porciúncula (the Village of Our Lady the Queen of the
         Angels of the Porciúncula River).

1784   Rancho period begins with grant of three land concessions.

1804   First local orange grove, six acres and 400 trees, planted on the
         grounds of the San Gabriel Mission.

1820   Population of the Pueblo of Los Angeles is 650.

1821   *Diary of Captain Luis Antonio Argüello: The Last Spanish
         Expedition in California, October 17–November 17, 1820.*
         Mexico achieves independence at conclusion of armed conflict
         that began in 1810.

1832   Hugo Reid arrives in California.

1833   First printing press in California.

1834   Disestablishment (secularization) of the missions.

1836   First official census records a population of 2,228 in Los
         Angeles and its environs, including 603 men, 421 women, 651
         children, and 553 Indians, 29 Americans among them.

1841   The Workman–Rowland party, the first transcontinental
         wagon train, arrives in Southern California.
         William Wolfskill plants first commercial orange groves near
         Los Angeles.

1845   Los Angeles becomes the new capital of California.

1846   Alfred Robinson, *Life in California*.
July 29. The USS *Cyane* sails into San Diego Bay, soldiers plant American flag in the Plaza. After their departure, local citizens restore the Mexican flag.
August 6. Landing party under Lt. Jacob Zeilin, United States Marine Corps, seizes San Pedro.
August 13. Los Angeles taken by Lt. Archibald Gillespie and fifty marines.
September. Counter-revolt in Los Angeles. California retaken by the Mexicans.

1847   January 13. Treaty of Cahuenga calls for Californios to surrender their artillery, and provides that all Mexican and American prisoners be immediately freed.

1848   Treaty of Guadalupe Hidalgo cedes 525,000 square miles of Mexican territory, including California, to the United States.

1850   California admitted to the United States.
April 4. City of Los Angeles incorporated.
Federal census records Los Angeles population of 1,610. LA County population is 3,530.

1851   *Los Angeles Star/Estrella* begins publishing (suspends 1864–8 and ceases in 1879).

1854   John Rollin Ridge ("Yellow Bird"), *The Life and Adventures of Joaquín Murieta, the Celebrated California Bandit*.

1860   Population: City 4,385; County 11,333.

1870   Population: City 5,728; County 15,309.

1870s   Land boom follows completion of rail lines to Long Beach, Riverside, Pasadena, and Pomona.

1871   First bookstore in Los Angeles opens.
Vigilantes kill nineteen Chinese ("coolie riots").

1872   Charles Nordhoff, *California: For Health, Pleasure, and Residence. A Book for Travellers and Settlers*.
Los Angeles Public Library Association founded; library established 1878.

1876	Southern Pacific completes its railroad line to Los Angeles from San Francisco.
1877	William Mulholland, an Irish immigrant, rides into Los Angeles on horseback.
1880	University of Southern California founded. Population: City 11,183; County 33,281.
1881	Southern Pacific link to the East completed. December 4. The *Los Angeles Daily Times* is published for the first time.
1882	Chinese Exclusion Act prohibits Chinese laborers from entering the United States and makes reentry for Chinese who leave the US and return more difficult.
1884	Helen Hunt Jackson, *Ramona*. Charles Fletcher Lummis arrives in Los Angeles after 143-day walk from Cincinnati, Ohio. General Harrison Gray Otis takes over the bankrupt *Los Angeles Times*; the paper will reflect his extreme conservative views.
1885	María Amparo Ruiz de Burton, *The Squatter and the Don*. Santa Fe Railroad completes second rail line from the East; resulting fare wars spark land boom.
1887	Peak year of the 1880s boom brings 120,000 visitors to Los Angeles. Boom collapses the next year. The boom is fictionalized in Theodore Strong Van Dyke's *Millionaires of a Day: An Inside Story of the Great Southern California "Boom"* (1890). First electric streetcar lines in Los Angeles.
1888	Scott Act prohibits Chinese from reentering the United States if they leave.
1890	Tournament of Roses founded in Pasadena to promote the mild climate; it is patterned on the Battle of the Flowers in Nice, France. Population: City 50,395; County 101,454.
1891	California Institute of Technology (Caltech) founded.
1892	Edward Doheny discovers oil in Los Angeles. Angeles National Forest established by executive order.

1893   Bradbury Building (George H. Wyman, architect) opens.

1894   Lummis begins publishing his magazine, *Land of Sunshine*, which he renames *Out West* in 1901.

1896   Griffith J. Griffith donates the land for present-day Griffith Park to the city.

1897   December. Film crew employed by Thomas Edison's Edison Manufacturing Company arrives.

1898   *South Spring Street, Los Angeles, California* (Frederick Blechynden), a twenty-five second "actuality" film shot on location in downtown Los Angeles.

1900   Population: City 102,479; County 170,298.

1901   Pacific Electric Railway (streetcars) incorporated by Henry E. Huntington, nephew of the Southern Pacific Railroad's Collis P. Huntington.
Angels Flight Funicular Railway opens on Bunker Hill (dismantled, 1969; restored, 1996).

1902   First Rose Bowl college football game in Pasadena; becomes an annual event in 1916.

1904   Abbot Kinney founds Venice, Calif., begins development of Venice of America as home sites along a lagoon, Grand Canal, and six smaller canals.
First Border Patrol started to prevent migration of Asians through Mexico.

1905   Pleistocene fossils discovered in La Brea Tar Pits.

1907   Mary Austin, *The Ford*.
Charles Fletcher Lummis establishes the Southwest Museum.
Watts incorporated as a municipality.

1910   Mexican Revolution increases immigration.
October 1. McNamara Brothers blow up the offices of the *Los Angeles Times* and the home of General Otis.
Population: City 319,198; County 504,131.

1911   Nestor Film Company, Hollywood's first film studio.
Southern Pacific consolidates nearly all streetcar lines in Los Angeles region.

Raymond Chandler returns to the US, settles in Los Angeles.

1912   First performance of John Steven McGroarty's *Mission Play*.
Hubert Eaton becomes a salesman for Forest Lawn Cemetery.

1913   Construction of the first Los Angeles Aqueduct from the Owens Valley is completed.
Southwest Museum moves into permanent residence at Arroyo Seco.

1915   *Birth of a Nation* (D. W. Griffith).

1917   Charles Franklin Carter, *Stories of the Old Missions of California*.
Los Angeles Shipbuilding and Dry Dock Company established.
General Otis dies; he is succeeded at the *Times* by his son-in-law, Harry Chandler.
January 1. Hubert Eaton writes "The Builder's Creed," his vision for Forest Lawn Memorial Park.

1919   University of California, Los Angeles founded.
October 2. Raid on Industrial Workers of the World hall as part of Los Angeles Police Department "Red scare" tactics.

1920   First annual performance of a twelve-part *Pilgrimage Play* depicting the life and death of Christ, later moved to the Hollywood Bowl.
Davis-Douglas Aircraft Company founded; renamed Douglas Aircraft Company in 1921.
Population: City 576,673; County 936,455.

1921   Sabato ("Simon") Rodia begins building the Watts Towers in his spare time; completed in 1954.

1922   Harry Leon Wilson, *Merton of the Movies*.
Carey McWilliams arrives.
Hollywood Bowl opens.

1923   Rose Bowl stadium opens.
January 1. Evangelist Aimee Semple McPherson dedicates her 5,300 seat Angelus Temple; broadcasting on radio station KFSG (Foursquare Gospel) begins February 6, 1924.
July 13. "Hollywoodland" sign dedicated to promote a subdivision; last four letters removed in 1949.

1924	Mark Lee Luther, *The Boosters.* Federal Asian Exclusion Act prohibits immigration of Asian peoples; Immigration Act of 1924 limits immigration from Mexico.
1925	Sarah Bixby Smith, *Adobe Days.*
1926	February 18: LAPD vice squad shuts down a performance of Eugene O'Neill's *Desire under the Elms*, arrests seventeen actors.
1927	Horace Bell, *Reminiscences of a Ranger, or, Early Times in Southern California.* Upton Sinclair, *Oil!* Collapse of Julian Oil, a $150-million counterfeit stock and pyramid scheme. Financier Motley Flint gunned down in court by a ruined investor; C. C. Julian drinks poison in China. May 18. Grauman's Chinese Theatre has its grand opening in Hollywood. A riot breaks out as onlookers try to see the stars entering the theater for the premiere of Cecil B. DeMille's *King of Kings.*
1928	March 12: St. Francis Dam (near present-day Santa Clarita) bursts; estimated death toll as high as 600.
1929	Watts annexed to Los Angeles.
1930	Olvera Street converted to a Mexican marketplace by Christine Sterling. The Production Code (Hays Code or Breen Office) governing the moral content of movies initiated; abandoned in 1968 in favor of a film-rating system that designates "appropriate" audiences and restricts admission based on age. Population: City 1,238,048; County 2,208,492.
1930s	Dust Bowl drives Oklahoma and Arkansas migrants ("Okies" and "Arkies") to California; many settle in the LA region.
1931	Arna Bontemps, *God Sends Sunday.* James M. Cain arrives in Hollywood.
1932	Los Angeles hosts the Summer Olympics. William Faulkner arrives in Los Angeles for first of many sojourns as screenwriter.

1933   James M. Cain's "Paradise," an essay about Los Angeles, published in *American Mercury*.
Long Beach earthquake kills one hundred.

1934   James M. Cain, *The Postman Always Rings Twice*.
Upton Sinclair runs unsuccessfully for governor as candidate of the EPIC (End Poverty in California) Party.
Los Angeles Science Fiction Society founded.

1935   Horace McCoy, *They Shoot Horses, Don't They?*
Nathanael West settles in Los Angeles after an earlier trip in 1933.
Griffith Observatory opens.

1936   Jet Propulsion Laboratory founded at Caltech.

1937   Aldous Huxley, on a speaking tour in California, decides to remain in Los Angeles.
California's "Anti-Okie" law provides that "Every person, firm or corporation, or officer or agent thereof that brings or assists in bringing into the State any indigent person who is not a resident of the State, knowing him to be an indigent person, is guilty of a misdemeanor."

1938   Ray Bradbury's first science fiction stories published.

1939   Raymond Chandler, *The Big Sleep*.
John Fante, *Ask the Dust*.
Aldous Huxley, *After Many a Summer Dies the Swan*.
Nathanael West, *The Day of the Locust*.

1940   Raymond Chandler, *Farewell, My Lovely*.
LA aqueduct system extended to bring water from the Mono Basin.
Arroyo Seco Parkway (Pasadena Freeway) completed, first freeway in the West.
Population: City 1,504,277; County 2,785,643.

1940s   Second Great Migration brings African Americans to Los Angeles in large numbers; Watts becomes predominantly African American.

1941   James M. Cain, *Mildred Pierce*.
Budd Schulberg, *What Makes Sammy Run?*

Bertolt Brecht, Theodor Adorno, and Max Horkheimer arrive in Los Angeles.
Colorado River Aqueduct completed.

1942   Bertolt Brecht, "Hollywood Elegies."
Thomas Mann moves to Pacific Palisades.
"Sleepy Lagoon Murder." Discovery of the body of José Diaz at Sleepy Lagoon reservoir leads to arrest of more than 600 Latino youths and trial of twenty-two. Three convicted of first-degree murder, nine of second-degree murder, and five of assault; all convictions reversed on appeal.
Executive Order 9066 decrees that all Japanese Americans and Japanese nationals be evacuated from the West Coast.
Bracero Program establishes temporary worker status for Mexican laborers in the Southwestern United States.

1943   James M. Cain, *Double Indemnity*.
Pachuco (or Zoot Suit) Riots.
Magnuson Act repeals Chinese Exclusion Laws.
Long Beach Naval Shipyard established.

1944   Serviceman's Readjustment Act passed, will help fuel postwar housing purchases.

1945   Chester Himes, *If He Hollers Let Him Go*.

1946   Carey McWilliams, *Southern California Country: An Island on the Land*.
Carlos Bulosan, *America Is in the Heart*.

1947   Hollywood Ten refuse to testify before House Committee on Un-American Affairs.
Black Dahlia murder case.
Evelyn Waugh comes to Hollywood to explore a film version of *Brideshead Revisited*; the film is not made, but Waugh uses the experience to write *The Loved One*, published the next year.
First Los Angeles television station, KTLA, goes on the air.
Federal Ninth Circuit Court of Appeals affirms *Mendez* v. *Westminster (California) School District* case that outlaws segregation of Mexican and Mexican-American students.

1948   Paramount Decision ends the studio system that enabled movie studios to control production and distribution.

1949   Aldous Huxley, *Ape and Essence*.

1950   *Sunset Boulevard* (Billy Wilder).
        Mattachine Society founded in Los Angeles; oldest US homo-
        phile association.
        Population: City 1,970,358; County 4,151,687.

1950s   Beat poets in Venice.

1953   Ray Bradbury, *Fahrenheit 451*.
        El Pueblo de Los Angeles State Monument dedicated.

1954   *Dragnet* (Jack Webb).

1955   Norman Mailer, *The Deer Park*.
        Rebel without a Cause (Nicholas Ray).
        Disneyland opens in Anaheim.

1957   Frederick Kohner, *Gidget* (film version, 1959).

1958   Allen Ginsberg reading hosted by the editors of *Coastlines*
        magazine.
        Brooklyn Dodgers' first season in Los Angeles, where they play
        in the LA Coliseum.

1959   José Antonio Villarreal, *Pocho*.
        The Crimson Kimono (Samuel Fuller).

1960   Otis Chandler becomes *Los Angeles Times* publisher and makes
        it a major newspaper; he will be the final publisher from the
        Otis-Chandler family.
        Population: City 2,479,015; County, 6,038,771.

1961   Closure of the Los Angeles–Long Beach line marks the end of
        electric streetcar service in Los Angeles.

1962   The Beach Boys formed.
        Opening of Dodger Stadium in Chavez Ravine, formerly a
        Mexican American barrio.
        Cesar Chavez organizes the National Farm Workers
        Association.

1963   *It Catches My Heart in Its Hands*, Charles Bukowski's first full-
        length collection, published by Loujon Press; *New York Times*
        review by Kenneth Rexroth, July 5, 1964.
        Beach Party (William Asher).

December 14: Baldwin Hills dam bursts; 277 homes lost and five deaths.

1964   Christopher Isherwood, *A Single Man*.
Dorothy Chandler Pavilion opens as home of Los Angeles Philharmonic; first element of the Los Angeles Music Center.
Los Angeles becomes second most populous city in the United States.
Bracero Program ends.
Urban League survey ranks Los Angeles as the most desirable city for African Americans to live in.

1965   *Beach Blanket Bingo* (William Asher).
Los Angeles County Museum of Art opens.
Immigration Act of 1965 shifts sources of immigration to Asia and Latin America.
August 11. Watts Rebellion begins after California Highway Patrol stops Marquette Frye, an African American said to be driving erratically. As the officer questions Frye and his brother, a crowd gathers and a struggle ensues. Police arrest the Frye brothers and their mother, who is also present. The riots last for five more days.
September. Watts Writers' Workshop founded.

1966   Alison Lurie, *The Nowhere City*.
Thomas Pynchon, *The Crying of Lot 49*, and "A Journey into the Mind of Watts."
The Wild Angels (Roger Corman, 1966) initiates the biker movie genre.
John Martin founds Black Sparrow Press.
Kwanzaa created in Los Angeles by Maulana (Ron) Karenga.
May 7. LAPD stop Leonard Deadwyler, a black motorist, for speeding and running stoplights as he rushes his pregnant wife to the County hospital. Police say he acted erratically during the stop and is "killed accidentally" by Patrolman Jerold Bova.

1967   Budd Schulberg, ed., *From the Ashes: Voices of Watts*.
The Graduate (Mike Nichols).
The Advocate, oldest continuing gay publication in the United States, founded as *The Los Angeles Advocate*, a newsletter edited by Dick Michaels and Bill Rand.

Mark Taper Forum and Ahmanson Theater open at the Los Angeles Music Center.

1968 Joan Didion, *Slouching Towards Bethlehem.*
George Drury Smith begins publishing *Beyond Baroque*; Beyond Baroque's readings series begins the next year.
June 5. Robert Kennedy assassinated in the Ambassador Hotel.

1969 Manson Family murders.

1970 Joan Didion, *Play It As It Lays.*
August 29. Chicano Moratorium.
Population: City 2,816,061; County, 7,041,980.

1971 Charles Bukowski, *Post Office.*
Reyner Banham, *Los Angeles: The Architecture of Four Ecologies.*
Sweet Sweetback's Baadasssss Song (Melvin Van Peebles), initiates the "blaxploitation" genre.
Sylmar (San Fernando Valley) earthquake.

1972 Oscar Zeta Acosta, *The Autobiography of a Brown Buffalo.*
Philip K. Dick moves to Fullerton, in Orange County; moves to Santa Ana in 1976 and dies there March 2, 1982.

1973 Oscar Zeta Acosta, *The Revolt of the Cockroach People.*
Woman's Building opens (closes 1991).
Tom Bradley becomes Los Angeles' first African-American mayor.

1974 *Chinatown* (Roman Polanski).
J. Paul Getty Museum opens in Malibu, in a re-creation of the Villa of the Papyri at Herculaneum.

1975 With a grant from the National Endowment for the Arts, the NewComp Graphics Center at Beyond Baroque offers typesetting services for noncommercial literary publishing.

1977 X and Black Flag, early LA punk bands, form. Black Flag's Keith Morris forms the Circle Jerks in 1979.

1978 Luis Valdez, *Zoot Suit.*
Proposition 13 passed, limits property-tax revenue, will severely hinder public service.

1979   Joan Didion, *The White Album*.
        Wanda Coleman, *Mad Dog Black Lady*.
        Beyond Baroque moves into the old Venice City Hall.

1980   Crystal Cathedral, designed by Philip Johnson for televangelist
        Rev. Robert Schuller, opens in Garden Grove.
        Population: City 2,966,850; County, 7,477,421.

1982   *Blade Runner* (Ridley Scott).

1983   *El Norte* (Gregory Nava).

1984   Kim Stanley Robinson, *The Wild Shore*, first volume of the Three
        Californias Trilogy (*The Gold Coast*, 1988; *Pacific Edge*, 1990).
        Terminator (James Cameron).
        Repo Man (Alex Cox).
        Los Angeles hosts Summer Olympic Games.

1985   Bret Easton Ellis, *Less Than Zero*.

1986   Friends of the Los Angeles River, nonprofit environmental
        group, founded.

1987   Carolyn See, *Golden Days*.
        James Ellroy, *The Black Dahlia*, first volume of the L.A. Quartet
        (*The Big Nowhere*, 1988; *L.A. Confidential*, 1990; *White Jazz*,
        1992).

1988   N. W. A.'s *Straight Outta Compton* establishes West Coast rap.

1989   *Invocation L.A.: Urban Multicultural Poetry*, ed. Michelle
        T. Clinton, Sesshu Foster, and Naomi Quiñonez.

1990   Mike Davis, *City of Quartz: Excavating the Future in Los Angeles*.
        Walter Mosley, *Devil in a Blue Dress*, first "Easy" Rawlins
        mystery.
        Charles Harper Webb, ed., *Stand Up Poetry* (2nd edition 1994;
        3rd edition 2002).
        Population: City 3,485,398; County, 8,863,164.

1991   *Boyz N the Hood* (John Singleton).
        March 3. After a high-speed chase, LAPD beat Rodney King, a
        black motorist; the beating is captured on video by George
        Holliday and broadcast on local news.

1992   Neal Stephenson, *Snow Crash*.
        Cynthia Kadohata, *In the Heart of the Valley of Love*.

The Player (Robert Altman).
April 29. Riots erupt after four white policemen are found not guilty in beating of Rodney King.

1993   Octavia Butler, *Parable of the Sower*; *Parable of the Talents* follows in 1998.
Falling Down (Joel Schumacher).
CityWalk opens.

1994   Anna Deavere Smith, *Twilight: Los Angeles, 1992*.
Pulp Fiction (Quentin Tarantino).
Northridge earthquake.

1995   T. C. Boyle, *The Tortilla Curtain*.
O. J. Simpson murder trial.

1996   D. J. Waldie, *Holy Land: A Suburban Memoir*.
Wanda Coleman, *Native in a Strange Land*.

1998   Walter Mosley, *Always Outnumbered, Always Outgunned*, first of the Socrates Fortlow books.

2000   Population: City 3,694,820, of which 46.5 percent are Hispanic, 11.2 percent African American, 10 percent Asian American, 29.7 percent white, and 5.2 percent two or more races. LA County population 9,519,338, of which 44.6 percent are Hispanic, 9.5 percent African American, 10 percent Asian, 31.1 percent white, 4.9 percent two or more races.

2001   *Mulholland Drive* (David Lynch).

2002   San Fernando Valley residents narrowly vote to secede from Los Angeles, but citywide the measure fails two-to-one.

2003   Joan Didion, *Where I Was From*.
Walt Disney Concert Hall (Frank Gehry, architect) opens in the Los Angeles Music Center as new home of the LA Philharmonic.

2004   *Crash* (Paul Haggis).

2005   Antonio Villaraigosa becomes first Latino mayor of Los Angeles since 1872.

2006   October 26. President George W. Bush signs the Secure Fence Act of 2006 to provide funding for a border fence between the United States and Mexico.

KEVIN R. McNAMARA

Introduction: landmarks

A good deal about California does not, on its own preferred terms, add up.
Joan Didion, *Where I Was From* (2003)

Defining the geographic extent of Los Angeles is the first challenge for anyone who would study its literature. Concentration defines New York, where even Brooklynites refer to Manhattan as "the city." Los Angeles is defined by sprawl. Much of iconic Los Angeles, from the beaches of *Baywatch* to the streets of *Beverly Hills, 90210*, lies beyond the city limits. The larger Los Angeles County still fails to encompass Disneyland, Fontana (Mike Davis's "Junkyard of Dreams"), and Huntington Beach, whose pier is "one of the constituent monuments of the surfing life."[1] As a literary subject, however, Los Angeles is less a city, county, or "metropolitan statistical area" than a state of being (of grace, fear, emergency, or exception, depending on whom one reads) anchored in the area south of the Tehachapi Mountains, north of San Diego, west of the desert, and squarely in the collective imagination of utopia, dystopia, and, more recently, the urban future. A tour of some of mythic Los Angeles' landmark features will introduce our subject.

More than any other American city, Los Angeles is a city made of words. It "did not so much grow as sell itself into existence," William Alexander McClung observes. This marketing effort was not limited to the Chamber of Commerce and developers. The visual and verbal artistry of painters, photographers, and writers like the coterie around Charles Fletcher Lummis at the magazine *Land of Sunshine*, and even the logos on crates of produce shipped back east, helped to transform climate into a "palpable ... commodity that [could] be labeled, priced, and marketed."[2] The story of one possible Los Angeles begins with the boosters – the School of Sunshine we might call them – who celebrated Los Angeles as paradise found, and spun Arcadian myths from the world of the Californios, or early Spanish settlers. This myth quickly enough spawned its counter-myth. The School of Noir depicted the rot in Eden, from political corruption and financial chicanery to the ersatz culture and kitsch spewing from Hollywood. Mythic Los Angeles thus condensed into a generation the transit from "fresh, green breast of the new world" to land of "foul dust float[ing] in the wake of ... dreams" that F. Scott Fitzgerald charted for the United States over three centuries in *The Great Gatsby* (1925).[3]

It was also possible to imagine Los Angeles as an extension of the film industry soon after the studios were established early in the second decade of the twentieth century. The city's actual streets featured back-lot hodgepodges of "half-timbered English peasant cottages, French provincial and 'mission-bell' type adobes, Arabian minarets, [and] Georgian mansions on 50 by 120 foot lots with 'Mexican Ranchos' adjoining them."[4] Local gentry reenacted the Spanish past as Arcadian fantasy in Days of the Dons celebrations, *Ramona* pageants (which rewrote Helen Hunt Jackson's 1884 Indian-rights novel into a love story), and annual performances of John Steven McGroarty's *Mission Play* (1911), a three-hour panorama of California history from the founding of the missions through their 1834 disestablishment to the end of Mexican rule. Protestantism itself became theatrical, with twelve-part Christmas pageants performed by a cast of professionals and ordinary citizens in the Hollywood Hills, and later in the Hollywood Bowl, which also hosted Easter sunrise services. Evangelism's leading lady, Canadian-born Aimee Semple McPherson, started a radio station along with her Foursquare Gospel Church; she became tabloid fodder with rumors of a faked kidnapping and a seaside love nest.

The most idiosyncratic expression of this Los Angeles was confected by Missouri transplant Hubert Eaton, who made his fortune selling immortality at Forest Lawn Memorial Park (or cemetery). Banishing all reminders of death, including deciduous trees, and stocking the landscape with "immortal" works of art (in reproduction) and religious architecture (in scaled-down, scrubbed-up models) that provided the city a cultural inheritance, Eaton launched Forest Lawn as a destination not only for departed "loved ones," but also for schoolchildren, artists, and over 65,000 people who had married on the grounds by the mid-1990s. Evelyn Waugh made Forest Lawn a target in his 1948 LA satire, *The Loved One*, which finds no difference between Eaton's handiwork and Hollywood's. Both industries, the novel suggests, are dedicated to the production of illusion, the negation of culture and tradition, and the repression of the human fact of tragedy.

Hoping to discover what Los Angeles had become by the 1960s, another Briton, architectural historian Reyner Banham, took his cue from The Beach Boys and turned to the surfers. With none of the irony that marks Jean Baudrillard's later account of "the *only remaining primitive society*" in *America* (1988), Banham described an Angeleno innocence

[d]eeply imbued with standard myths of the Natural Man and the Noble Savage ... [that] flourishes as an assumed right in the Southern California sun, an ingenious and technically proficient cult of private and harmless gratifications that is symbolized by the surfer's secret smile of intense concentration and

the immensely sophisticated and highly decorated plastic surf-board he needs to conduct his private communion with the sea.[5]

Its open roads cruised in customized T-birds and deuce coupes, its standardized apartment blocks covered with facades that make "statement[s] about the culture of individualism," Los Angeles, west of the West, figures for Banham as the last stand of the American Romance. The Watts Towers – "tapering traceries of coloured pottery shards bedded in cement on frames of scrap steel and baling wire" erected over thirty-three years by Sabato ("Simon") Rodia, a self-taught, Italian-immigrant construction worker – are Angeleno culture's "perfected" emblem. The Watts Rebellion of 1965 does not figure in Banham's account beyond an epigraph, "Burn, Baby, burn!" under the heading, "Views of Los Angeles."[6]

Nor does Joan Didion, the quintessential LA essayist, discuss Watts, except to note that "the city burning is Los Angeles's deepest image of itself … and at the time of the 1965 Watts riots what struck the imagination most indelibly were the fires." At least as striking as the two authors' shared oversight is the fact that even as Banham was crafting his paean to sunny Southern Cal, Didion was creating a much darker profile of a city to which "the narrative on which many of us grew up no longer applies." Infidelities turn homicidal in Didion's Los Angeles, while Jaycees buffeted by events feel "not merely shocked but personally betrayed by recent history." Biker movies portray "the extent to which the toleration of small irritations is no longer a trait much admired in America, the extent to which a nonexistent frustration threshold is seen not as psychopathic but as a 'right'" by people "whose whole lives are an obscure grudge against a world they think they never made."[7]

It fell to Thomas Pynchon to begin connecting Los Angeles' "two very different cultures: one white and one black" in his 1966 diptych, *The Crying of Lot 49* and "A Journey into the Mind of Watts." Oedipa Maas, *Lot 49*'s Young Republican heroine, is an ingenue to Didion's ironist. Arriving in "San Narciso," a postwar defense-industry suburb developed by her deceased ex-lover, she finds herself in something "less an identifiable city than a grouping of concepts – census tracts, special purpose bond-issue districts, shopping nuclei" – outfitted with imported ruins (explicitly recalling Forest Lawn) and vaguely Mediterranean names.[8] The self-referential self-containment signaled by the town's name, its master-planned regularity, and the constant buzz of media throughout the novel, strongly imply that Southern Californian individualism is not the ideal that Banham took it for, but an illusion or simulacrum maintained by powerful institutions and interests. The shadowy mass of the discontented and disinherited (suggestive of what Michael Harrington called *The Other America* in his 1962 exposé of American poverty and stunted opportunity) flit at the edge of Oedipa's consciousness until the novel's end, when they emerge with visionary clarity as emissaries of an alternative American experience.

While Oedipa's quest for the meaning of the "revelation in progress all around her" does not lead her to Watts, Pynchon made the journey to this neighborhood, just off the Harbor Freeway yet "psychologically, uncounted miles further than most whites seem ... willing to travel," the year after the Watts Rebellion. When he described disinherited black Angelenos as experiencing during the rebellion "whatever it is that jazz musicians feel on certain nights: everybody knowing what to do and when to do it without needing a word or a signal," he invoked the scene in *Lot 49* where Jesús Arrabal defines an "anarchist miracle" as a moment "[w]here revolutions break out leaderless, and the soul's talent for consensus allows the masses to work together without effort, automatic as the body itself."[9] The Watts Rebellion of 1965, Pynchon suggested, was a utopian *moment* counterpoised to the endless monotony of white, suburban Los Angeles.

Watts and the rebellion are amply chronicled in the poetry and fiction of Wanda Coleman, Walter Mosley, the Watts Prophets, and other writers, as well as memoirs of the postwar jazz scene. But Watts soon faded from the consciousness of most white Angelenos. It was replaced by other anxieties both sensational (the Manson Family murders) and routine. Gasoline shortages, factory closings, and immigration from Asia and Latin America soon changed the County's racial and economic make-up; Anglos (the local term for whites, regardless of ethnicity) declined from 70 percent in 1970 to 40 percent in 1990, and undocumented immigrants supported a sweatshop economy that thrived in the shadow of the downtown high-rises. The "retrofitted" Bradbury Building in *Blade Runner* (1982) brilliantly figures Anglo Angelenos' contemporaneous anxieties about the future. Inspired by Edward Bellamy's description of a department store in his utopian tract, *Looking Backward: 2000–1887* (1888), as "a vast hall full of light, received not alone from the windows on all sides, but from the dome, the point of which was a hundred feet above," George H. Wyman's 1893 gem is remade in the film as the dank and decayed site of Rick Deckard's climactic pursuit of replicant leader Roy Baty.[10] Its delicate ironwork is a frail skeleton; the skylighted roof leaks rain.

The nine years between *Blade Runner* and the Justice (or Rodney King) Riots were marked in the popular imagination of Los Angeles by road rage, drive-by shootings, and "crack wars." The city had become "Third World"; a night out required "dodging bullets," said Tom Gilmore, and swarms of homeless people thrusting their "Will work for food" signs at passers-by, added Lawrence Spungin, when, two months before the Justice Riots, they announced CityWalk, a pedestrian mall lined with shops and restaurants ensconced on the 415-acre complex of Universal Studios.[11] Taking design cues from Venice Beach's surf aesthetic, Hollywood, Los Angeles' art-deco icons, and the trendy shops and restaurants along Melrose Boulevard, CityWalk's facades celebrate the "'screw you'" sentiments that Richard Orne, CityWalk's project director, says built the city.[12] Yet its adolescent insouciance is a calculated effect. The ensemble does for the 1960s what Disneyland does for the 1950s, and it is readable only against the backdrop of white Angeleno anxiety at a time when the region's newest migrant laborers were the predominantly Anglo tech workers who inspected semi-conductors and lived in motels, having been priced out of even the rental market.[13] It makes most sense as a monument to their own innocence built by Banham's surfers, who are older and fear that they will soon be numbered among the disinherited of a now majority–minority city.

Didion performed her own analysis of the state of the LA myth at this time. She focused on the "Spur Posse," a gang of high school boys devoted to competitive (and likely forcible) sex, who became a local and, later, a national scandal. Their activity was centered in Lakewood, a 1950s-vintage subdivision for blue-collar aerospace and shipyard workers that is also the setting of D. J. Waldie's *Holy Land: A Suburban Memoir* (1996). A lifetime resident and a city official, Waldie writes of Lakewood as a community of people clinging to the belief that they are middle class, "even though 1,100 square-foot tract houses on streets meeting at right angles are not middle class at all… In a suburb that is not exactly middle class," he observes, "the necessary illusion is predictability."[14] The predictability of the landscape, the path from high school to factory job and family, and the neighbors like oneself, all once upon a time added up to the illusion of having arrived in postwar Eden.

By 1993, when the region had lost "six to eight hundred thousand jobs" and losses of "four to five hundred thousand more jobs" statewide were forecast over the ensuing two years, Lakewood was an appropriate site at which to ponder what comes after the Southern California dream. As Didion put the question, "what happens when [an artificial ownership] class stops being useful?" Her answer in part confirms her earlier speculation that biker movies were "ideograms of the future."[15] As the story broke, the Posse turned from forcible sex to physical threats, beatings, guns, and even a pipe bomb, all the while pursuing their moment of disaffected fame on local news and national talk shows. Parents blamed the media for sensationalizing the story and the state for teaching sex education, or they blamed the girls.

Denial was not confined to the threatened enclave of Lakewood. Didion recalls being assured by realtors that layoffs in Lakewood would not affect life in "Bel Air, where the people lived who held the paper on the people who held the mortgages" in the affected cities. Instead, Didion recalls, as the local economy soured, "virtually everyone to whom [she] spoke" said

> how much the riot had "changed" the city... After the riot, I was told, it was impossible to sell a house in Los Angeles. The notion it might have been impossible to sell a house in Los Angeles that year for a simpler reason, the reason being that the money had gone away, was still in 1992 so against the grain of the place as to be largely rejected.

Nevertheless, Didion concludes, loss of faith in the future is "what people in Los Angeles were talking about when they talked about the 1992 riot," even if they could not acknowledge it because, on their terms – the terms of the LA myth – it did not add up.[16]

If the Justice Riots were neither the cause of the 1990s real-estate crunch nor the commencement of the apocalypse prophesied in paint by Tod Hackett in Nathanael West's *The Day of the Locust* (1939), neither were they the catalyst of "a new metropolitan idea" in which a city "famous as a collection of separate suburbs" finally recognized itself as an interdependent whole, as Richard Rodriguez speculated it might be.[17] It may be, however, that the riots hastened the end of Californian exceptionalism – except, perhaps, in "the contemporary white Southern imagination," which seems to need Los Angeles to be an illusory promise of "opportunity at its extreme, eroticized limit" whose superficiality redeems the burden of the American South's own myth-saturated history.[18]

The city once advertised as a haven from waves of immigrants flooding into the established cities of the United States is now a new Northeast: north from Latin America, east from Asia, and entwined with these histories and geographies. The protagonist of Héctor Tobar's novel, *The Tattooed Soldier* (1998), flees Guatemala after his wife and son are murdered by the army. He pursues his "electric idea" of Los Angeles only to find himself homeless in a city of Latino and Asian immigrants. Rodney King means nothing to him until he discovers the soldier who killed his family, now retired and pursuing his own dream of peace and order, and exacts retribution during the Justice Riots, which he imagines as "the municipal day of vendettas."[19]

This globalized Los Angeles is a prime site, Waldie notes, of "*mestizaje* – the promiscuous amalgamation of Hispanic, African, Asian and Native American peoples ... emerging from this landscape supposedly tamed by white, middle-class suburbanization," and perhaps of a post-European American culture.[20] Whether or not this forecast proves to be one more version of the exceptionalist myth is a question for future historians of Los Angeles. Our interest is not the region's history, but its mythology, which is a record of desires and anxieties about the American, the Western, or even the global future in which Los Angeles is by turns a hope and a symptom. Mythic Los Angeles is a construct that writers inevitably engage as they create their own versions of the city.

The first half of this *Companion* presents a broadly chronological examination of LA literature; the second half studies particular genres. We begin with the Californios. Too frequently overlooked, their writings are important both as part of the region's literature and as records of life in early Southern California, points that Rosaura Sánchez and Beatrice Pita have done much to establish. Moreover, they are important to this *Companion*'s subsequent chapters because we can fully understand the work of the makers of LA myth only if we are familiar with the history out of which they invented Arcadia.

William Alexander McClung addresses the creation of paradise in his study of the first seventy or so years of the region's English-language literary output. His chapter reveals how influential these early writers were to establishing the idea of Southern California country as a land with distinctive climate, topography, and cultural inheritance and marketing that idea to potential settlers from the eastern United States.

David Wyatt picks up the story with the boom years before World War II, when the city's population swelled from just over 300,000 in 1910 to more than 1.5 million in 1940. Wyatt finds a city defined in its literature less by place, history, and adopted or invented traditions than by motion, speed, and futurity: "the fantasy of having a plan." A frenzy of speculation that accelerates bodies and capital, and that extends the city ever farther outward, is coded into the very rhythms of many LA novels of the period. When the motion stops in the noir fictions of West, Horace McCoy, John Fante, and, after the war, Charles Bukowski and John Rechy, the various drifters, grifters, and idle dreamers awaken to an existential void. But just occasionally, Wyatt notes, an LA novel yields a story of hard work and some satisfactions, a "real world" within the fantasy of plans and planning.

Russell Berman considers the British and German writers who expatriated to find Hollywood work or sought refuge from Nazism and formed European cultural outposts on the Pacific. These writers produced not only splendid satire and often acute, frequently withering criticism of the Southland as an index of cultural decline, but even, on occasion, warm appreciations of Los Angeles. And the Jewish refugee Frederick Kohner created the iconic California surfer girl Gidget, whom he modeled on his LA-born daughter, Kathy.

Master-planned Eden is the most potent myth of Los Angeles, particularly the Cold War-era city of suburbs. Patrick O'Donnell's examination of five novels limns the social distinctions that structure paradise and the forms of disaffection that it induces. Didion's *Play It As It Lays* (1970) and Bret Easton

Ellis's *Less Than Zero* (1985) survey an LA wasteland through the eyes of affectless, alienated, but socially privileged narrators. T. C. Boyle's *The Tortilla Curtain* (1995) follows the disillusionment of a canyon-dwelling couple that imagine themselves eco-friendly and politically liberal but become increasingly resentful of "incursions" of actual nature and living Hispanics into their idyll. Accommodations are possible, however. Katherine Cattleman changes coasts with her husband, Paul; she discovers – or reinvents – herself in Los Angeles while Paul flees east in Alison Lurie's *Nowhere City* (1965), while optimistic survivors of an apocalypse reestablish the vision of the Golden Dreamers in Carolyn See's *Golden Days* (1987).

Charles Scruggs turns our attention to the "invisible" city, the centrifugal African-American community within "centripetal" Los Angeles that was centered in Watts for most of the twentieth century. His chapter focuses first on the efforts to carry westward a usable past and to build a sense of community in a place where the golden dream is always visible but ever beyond reach, particularly in the work of Arna Bontemps, Chester Himes, Walter Mosley, and Wanda Coleman. Scruggs then turns to recent writing that explores the opportunities and costs of integrating into the larger city in the post–Civil Rights era, notably Bebe Moore Campbell's *Brothers and Sisters* (1994) and Paul Beatty's *The White Boy Shuffle* (1996).

Both Asians and Latino/as are long established in Los Angeles, but their numbers have grown markedly over the past few decades. James Kyung-Jin Lee opens his comparative reading of Los Angeles' Latino/a and Asian literatures at the Pacific Fish Center before moving to the factory farms and the city's multicultural neighborhoods. Focusing on literary representations of labor and rights struggles, Lee shows us that the groups' histories do more than share significant parallels: they are marked by repeated instances of "horizontal assimilation" to each other and intergroup coalitions formed around common interests and objectives.

The historical section concludes, and the study of LA genres begins, with a chapter on the literature of urban uprisings. The threat of mass violence has been a constituent of dystopian LA visions at least since *Day of the Locust*. The 1943 Pachuco Riots, the 1965 Watts Rebellion, and the 1992 Justice Riots drew literary responses from without and particularly from within the affected communities that are Julian Murphet's subject in his chapter on a distinctive genre of LA writing.

The remaining chapters consider more widely recognized genres of LA writing. William Marling surveys the development of the LA detective story, which reached an early pinnacle in Raymond Chandler's Philip Marlowe novels. Chandler created a compelling social geography of LA communities distinguished by class, ethnicity, dates of arrival, and degrees of corruption. That geography – which often was determined by the Southland topography – has been expanded and updated by subsequent authors, notably Ross Macdonald, Joseph Wambaugh, and James Ellroy, and enriched with the new histories and new perspectives on old histories and conflicts offered by black and Chicano/a crime writers.

David Seed then surveys versions of the Southland's catastrophic fate in his chapter on Los Angeles' science fiction futures, a set of novels no doubt motivated in part by a desire to serve paradise its comeuppance by exploiting the tension between Arcadian myth and the facts of earthquakes, brush fires, mudslides, congestion, and pollution, as well as the region's economic reliance on the development and production of technologies of mass destruction.

Crime novels and science fiction have long, distinguished histories in Los Angeles, and both genres lend themselves to the transfer from page to screen. The movie colony also spawned its own genre of fiction. The Hollywood novel's depictions of the culture of the industry frequently serve as vehicles for writers' anxieties about a medium that threatens to supplant literary narrative (although Gen-X writers are considerably more at home with film and use it creatively). Chip Rhodes's analysis of the genre shows us how changes over time in the Hollywood novel track parallel shifts in the broader literary and popular culture, as well as the changing structure of film production.

Mark Shiel then turns to Hollywood itself, and given the ongoing cross-pollination between film and literature, this *Companion* would be incomplete without his chapter. The region's omnipresence on the silver screen for the past century and more has done much to shape the popular idea of Los Angeles, although it also frequently reflects popular perception back to audiences. Examining several of Los Angeles' starring and supporting roles in various film genres, Shiel shows us how the image of Los Angeles has changed in response to forces as diverse as audiences' genre preferences, historical events, and changes in the structure of film production.

Bill Mohr draws from his vast resources as a participant in, and more recently a historian of, Los Angeles' postwar poetry scene to fill the most conspicuous gap in the region's existing literary history. The Bay Area is virtually synonymous with West Coast poetry, he notes; however, his chapter establishes the distinctiveness of Los Angeles' poetry scene from the 1950s onward as it guides us through the region's coteries, movements, and venues for performance and publication.

Explaining the perceptions and roles of nature in a land portrayed by turns as Arcadian and poised on the edge of disaster – and increasingly as an unbroken slab of asphalt – is J. Scott Bryson's task in his examination of the natural world as fact and metaphor in the work of LA novelists, poets, and essayists. Bryson shows us how Southern California challenges ideas of nature imported from elsewhere in the United States, and he challenges us to rethink what we mean when we say "nature."

Finally Eric Avila turns our attention to four of Los Angeles' most prominent and comprehensive interpreters, Carey McWilliams, Reyner Banham, Joan Didion, and Mike Davis. His chapter is a fitting conclusion to a study of LA literature because it addresses principal versions of the LA myth through the writings of their most influential explicators: Carey McWilliams's "weirdly inflated village" in which the scribe enjoys "a ringside seat at the circus" of "the American people ... erupting like lava from a volcano"; Reyner Banham's new urban model that heralds a Golden Land of freedom and fulfillment; Joan Didion's bipolar city of placid beauty and random, senseless violence – Arcadia *and* the maelstrom; and Mike Davis's city that "only Darth Vader could love,"[21] its built environment the architectural expression of the American history of class war. None of them is Los Angeles either, but all contribute to the continuing American and global fascination with the Southland.

NOTES

The author wishes to thank William Boatman, literature librarian at UHCL, for his assistance with the preparation of this volume.

1. Mike Davis, *City of Quartz: Excavating the Future in Los Angeles* (New York: Verso, 1990), p. 373; Reyner Banham, *Los Angeles: The Architecture of Four Ecologies* (Harmondsworth, UK: Penguin, 1971), p. 53.

2. William A. McClung, *Landscapes of Desire: Anglo Mythologies of Los Angeles*, (Berkeley: University of California Press, 2002), p. 33; Carey McWilliams, *Southern California Country: An Island on the Land*, American Folkways (New York: Duell, Sloan & Pearce, 1946), p. 6.

3. F. Scott Fitzgerald, *The Great Gatsby* (New York, Scribner, 1995), pp. 189, 6.

4. Richard Neutra, quoted in McWilliams, *Southern California Country*, p. 344.

5. Jean Baudrillard, *America*, tr. Chris Turner (New York: Verso, 1988), p. 7; Banham, *Los Angeles*, p. 129.

6. Banham, *Los Angeles*, pp. 175, 129, 17, 16.

7. Joan Didion, "Los Angeles Notebook," in *Slouching Towards Bethlehem* (New York: Noonday Press, 1990), p. 220; Didion, "On the Morning after the Sixties," in *The White Album* (New York: Noonday Press, 1990), p. 205; Didion, "Good Citizens," in *White Album* p. 95; Didion, "Notes toward a Dreampolitik," in *White Album*, p. 101.

8. Thomas Pynchon, "A Journey into the Mind of Watts," *New York Times Magazine*, June 12, 1966, 35; Pynchon, *The Crying of Lot 49* (New York: Harper & Row, 1986), p. 24.

9. Pynchon, *Crying of Lot 49*, p. 44; Pynchon, "A Journey," pp. 78, 84; Pynchon, *Crying of Lot 49*, p. 120.

10. Edward Bellamy, *Looking Backward: 2000–1887* (New York: Signet, 2000), p. 66.

11. Tom Gilmore, CityWalk leasing director, and Lawrence Spungin, president of MCA-Universal, quoted in Amy Wallace, "Like It's So L.A.! Not Really," *Los Angeles Times*, Feb. 29, 1992, A1.
12. Richard Orne, quoted *ibid.*, A23.
13. Cited in Didion, *Where I Was From* (New York: Knopf, 2003), p. 100.
14. D. J. Waldie, *Holy Land: A Suburban Memoir* (New York: Norton, 2005), pp. 1–2.
15. Didion, *Where I Was From*, pp. 134, 113; Didion, "Notes Toward a Dreampolitik," p, 101.
16. Didion, *Where I Was From*, pp. 130, 131, 134.
17. Richard Rodriguez, "Slouching Towards Los Angeles," *Los Angeles Times*, April 11, 1993, M1. Rodriguez offers a subtle eulogy for Angeleno innocence in "Sand," in his *Days of Obligation: An Argument with My Mexican Father* (New York: Viking-Penguin, 1992), pp. 149–57.
18. Robert H. Brinkmeyer, Jr., and Debra Rae Cohen, "Forward into the Past: California in the Contemporary White Southern Imagination," in *Look Away!: The U.S. South in New World Studies*, ed. John Smith and Debra Cohn (Durham, N.C.: Duke University Press, 2004), pp. 251, 253.
19. Héctor Tobar, *The Tattooed Soldier* (New York: Penguin Books, 2000), pp. 41, 284.
20. Waldie, "Pornography of Despair," *Salon*, Sept. 21, 1998, www.salon.com/books/feature/1998/09/cov_21feature.html.
21. McWilliams, *Southern California Country*, pp. 375, 376; Carl Smith, "The Far Side of Paradise: California, Florida, and the Landscape of Catastrophe," *American Literary History* 13 (2001), 355.

I

ROSAURA SÁNCHEZ AND BEATRICE PITA

The literature of the Californios

The Pueblo of la Reina de Los Angeles was founded on what the Spanish named the Porciúncula, or Los Angeles River, by eleven families in September 1781, ten years after the establishment of the San Gabriel Mission.[1] A village composed of about forty-four individuals, mostly mulatto, mestizo, and Indian settlers from northwestern Mexico (Sonora and Sinaloa), Los Angeles was established in an area inhabited by several hundred Shoshana Indians, who after Spanish colonization were known as the Gabrielinos and Fernandinos, according to whether they served at the San Gabriel or San Fernando Mission.[2] The total population of the pueblo varied according to the comings and goings of *presidio* soldiers and their families, some of whom had come with the earlier colonists in 1769. By 1790 there were 140 Spanish-speaking settlers, the Californios, or *gente de razón* (rational people), as they called themselves, who, with this term, distinguished themselves from the local Indians.

The growth of the pueblo of Los Angeles, like that of Alta California, was limited during the second period of settlement under Mexican rule (1822–46); it attracted a few colonists from Mexico, and some foreigners, especially traders, sailors, and trappers. The US invasion of Alta California in 1846 brought hundreds of soldiers to the area, some of whom remained after the war's end. This third period, the US period, began with the 1848 signing of the Treaty of Guadalupe Hidalgo and was marked by political, racial, and cultural clashes in Los Angeles, whose population remained small even while the north grew exponentially during the Gold Rush. The following decades, however, would bring increased Anglo migration to Los Angeles and the definitive political and economic decline of the Californios. The last period, 1880 to 1929, was a period of global conflicts, technological changes, and the Mexican Revolution of 1910, a rebellion that displaced thousands of Mexicans, who were drawn again to resettle in the US Southwest, especially Los Angeles.

Clearly, Los Angeles was from the outset a heterogeneous area, multiracial and multiethnic as well as multilingual, marked from the beginning by social divisions that were determined by property, politics, and language. Californio writing in Los Angeles between 1781 and 1929 responded to social and political factors and functioned as a means to express the ideological positions and grievances of settlers, soldiers, officials, missionaries, and, later, the conquered and marginalized Californios. The various forms that Spanish-language cultural production took enabled individuals to chronicle noteworthy events, to describe local customs and traditions, and to mobilize the community to action.

Colonial period, 1781–1822: Los Angeles under Spanish rule

The arrival of the early colonists in Alta California from what was known as New Spain (Mexico) by ship and by land in 1769 and 1781 did not allow for the transportation of a printing press. None existed in California until 1833. Excepting the colonizing friars, the settlers were primarily workers, cogs in the colonizing project, many of them illiterate. The learned men of this period were, of course, the missionaries, who were multilingual and rapidly learned the local Indian languages in order to convert the Indians and force them to live and work at the missions. In the Spanish colony of Alta California, non-ecclesiastic books were hard to come by and often, once they were acquired from visiting frigates, were destroyed by the missionaries, who considered them heretical. Clashes between missionaries and military officials are regular topics of letters and reports.

The written texts of this early period are for the most part limited to the documents and correspondence of missionaries and government officials reporting back to the viceroyalty in Mexico. The early missionaries produced chronicles and diaries, like that of Fray Juan Crespi, who accompanied Junípero Serra to Alta California in 1769 and first described traversing the LA basin,[3] and letters, like those of Fray Francisco Palou,[4] who also wrote a biographical piece on Serra, the founder of the missions. Several of the friars also produced copies of sermons, and Fray Géronimo Boscano produced an ethnographic study of the customs of the Indians around San Juan Capistrano Mission.[5]

There are as well military reports of expeditions, like *The Diary of Captain Luis Antonio Argüello* (1821), which describes Argüello's reconnaissance in northern California to ascertain whether the British or the United States had established a presence there, and his contact with the Russian colony. José María Estudillo also wrote an account of his expedition in 1819 into the Tulares *rancherías* of gentile (non-Christian) Indians in search of neophytes (Christianized Indians) who had escaped from the missions.[6]

This early period is also recalled in the *testimonios* (oral interviews) of several Californios, including Eulalia Pérez, who in 1877 provided an account of her early life under Spanish rule.[7] Pérez, for many years the head house-keeper of the San Gabriel Mission, the wealthiest of all missions, provided detailed descriptions of the organization of Indian labor at the mission, including the punishments to which Indians were subjected. Her narrative, like other Californio *testimonios*, oscillates between praise for the mission-aries and insights into the exploitation of the mission Indians.

The distance between the mission outposts and the colonial centers of power in New Spain served to create a sense of California as a hinterland, especially after Spanish ships stopped bringing supplies and news, but this sense of abandonment was as well the impetus for the development of a new sense of identity as Californios and Angelenos.

Mexican period, 1822–1848: growth and land redistribution

The Los Angeles pueblo founders were part of a Spanish colonizing project. After Mexican independence in 1821, they became part of a Mexican state but continued their colonizing role in relation to the California Indians. Secularization of the missions in the 1830s under Governor José María Echeandía ostensibly meant that the Indians would be awarded mission lands that had been held in trust for them by the missionaries. Nothing of the kind happened, and it was the Californios, *gente de razón*, who came to claim and to control the mission lands and wealthy ranchos for themselves.

Far removed from the center of power, Californios first learned of Mexican independence in 1822. With this political change came increased trade with foreign ships and increased contact with foreigners (some of whom stayed in California, married Californio women, and were considered Californios). Independence also increased participation in local politics and underscored a new sense of territorial identity, to the point that there were soon calls for having a native son named as governor, or *jefe político*, as indeed happened in 1837 with the contested naming of Juan Bautista Alvarado as governor. There were as well regional differences within Alta California as Californios in San Diego and Los Angeles began resenting the prominence of the north in politics when two-thirds of the population resided in the south, especially in Los Angeles. In 1845, when Governor Manuel Micheltorena was over-thrown, an Angeleno, Pío Pico, became governor and moved the capital to Los Angeles. Los Angeles' standing as the territorial capital would, however, be short lived. These strained political relations are detailed in extant official documents of the period as well as in the numerous *testimonios* of eminent individuals, such as Alvarado, Pico, and Mariano Guadalupe Vallejo.[8]

Literature of the Mexican period includes a number of official pronounce-ments and reports, letters to the *diputación* (territorial assembly) and the

Mexican government, land requests and titles, treaties, and calls to action, generally against the Alta California governors. After the acquisition of a printing press in 1833, the administration, then located in Monterey, had a few official documents printed. Also in print from Mexico is the address by Carlos Antonio Carrillo, the Californio delegate, before the Mexican Congress in 1831. In 1846, at the onset of the US invasion, his brother, José Antonio Carrillo, also an Angeleno, published a report of the Californio battle against US invaders at San Pedro in the Mexican newspaper, *El Sonorense*. Also in 1846, a "*Pronunciamiento Contra los Norte Americanos*" exhorted Angelenos to organize against the US invaders.[9] Most texts from this period, however, exist in manuscript form and are available only in archives like the Bancroft Library, although some have subsequently been published.

The best Angeleno narratives about this period are the *testimonios* recorded for the late-nineteenth-century Bancroft historical project, like those of Eulalia Pérez, Antonio Coronel, Narciso Botello,[10] and Pico. Especially noteworthy is the extensive *testimonio* of Coronel, *Cosas de California (Things about California)*,[11] in which, with a clear eye for cultural history and seeing the need for another version of events, he describes in detail life in the mission, the customs of Californio men and women, trade with the Indians, the US invasion, his hiding from Colonel (later Governor) Stephen Kearney's troops, conflicts between Californios and the Anglos during and after the Gold Rush, his harrowing visit to Sonoma, his experiences in the mines, the lynching of Latino miners, and the massacre of the placer Indians. Coronel's fascinating manuscript also includes a significant collection of songs and poetry of the period, as well as descriptions of various dances.

This period also saw the beginning of writing about the region by European and US settlers, like Hugo Reid, who first came to California in 1832, married a Gabrielino woman in 1837, and took it upon himself to collect Indian tales, including "The Race between the Coyote and the Water."[12] Reid's letters to Abel Stearns and his short essays on the Indians, published as letters to the bilingual *Los Angeles Star/La Estrella* newspaper in 1852, constitute part of Los Angeles' literature of the Mexican period.[13] Also among the texts written during this period commenting on inhabitants of Los Angeles is the work of Alfred Robinson, who visited Alta California in 1829 as a trader, married a daughter of the wealthy Guerra y Noriega family from Santa Barbara, and in 1846 published his *Life in California*.

The archive of the victors is, of course, always more extensive, including documents written by US invaders that will not be discussed here. Non-Californio literary texts that also tapped this and subsequent periods include the work of Helen Hunt Jackson, whose *Ramona* (1884) is based in part on information supplied by Coronel and uses Reid's marriage to an Indian woman as a prototype.

The US invasion of Alta and Baja California and Mexico in 1846 radically transformed Alta California politically and economically, although cultural and demographic changes for Los Angeles would only come later.

First US period, 1848–1880: the neutralization of the Californios

Culturally, Los Angeles and Southern California continued to be character-ized by what Antonio Ríos-Bustamante calls "Northern Mexican culture" at the level of language, religion, foods, customs, occupations, traditions, culin-ary arts, music, dances and popular songs, card games, horse races, and other amusements.[14] But politically, Southern California was occupied territory with a majority Mexican-origin population living under the rule of an increas-ingly dominant Anglo minority. The first decades after invasion would bring land dispossession, lynchings of Mexicans, raids of bandit camps, battles against Indian raiders, and racial antagonisms between Californios and Anglo invaders, all issues that were addressed in the local press, especially in the *Star/Estrella* and later in *El Clamor Público*. What did soon become quite marked was the class division within the Californio community, with the wealthy Californios identifying and allying themselves with the ascendant class of Anglo merchants, landowners, and politicians.

The defining issue for landed Californios after 1848 was their dispossession through legal and illegal means. In response to the Land Act of 1851, north-ern Californios joined together to send Congress a letter expressing their grievances and asking for redress in view of promises made to them in the Treaty of Guadalupe Hidalgo.[15] There are no Angelenos, however, among the forty-nine Californios who signed the letter with Antonio María Pico. In time, most of the Californio titles were validated, but ultimately the Californios lost their lands to taxes or to lenders who underwrote the costs of their appeals using the land as collateral. Court documents, depositions, and case files provide compelling narratives of the process of land acquisition and loss among the Californios in the early US period and can be viewed as textual record of this population's history.

Southern California, unlike San Francisco, remained relatively unchanged demographically until after the Gold Rush, when displaced and disillusioned miners began to drift south. The arrival of gamblers, criminals, and those living outside the law brought a number of problems (vagrancy, thievery, banditry, and murder), with vigilantism and lynching adopted as expedient measures taken to ensure "law and order."

The decade of the 1850s was a period not only of generalized lawlessness and vigilantism, but of ethnic conflict and the decline of the Californios. It was a time of "racial profiling," with Californios subjected to arrests and lynchings when robberies were attributed to Californio bandits. Differential sentencing, too, was manifest as Californios were more apt to be hanged than Anglos for the same offenses. These issues would split Californios into two factions, those voicing support for the accused and those joining the vigilantes to capture the bandits.[16] In 1856–7 some fifty-two culprits were lynched in Los Angeles and surroundings, most after the killing of Sheriff James Barton and three deputies by the local Flores gang. These lynchings and the hostile climate created by this vigilantism would be opposed in print by Francisco Ramírez in his newspaper, *El Clamor Público*.[17]

LA Spanish-language newspapers, like the *Star/Estrella* and *El Clamor Público*, would serve as primary vehicles for the wider distribution of Californio political expression after regime change. Pablo de la Guerra's speech, "Los Californios," pronounced in 1860 before the state legislature, was published in *El Clamor Público*; here he attacked the Public Land Commission of 1851 and the Supreme Court for the dispossession of Californios. In the 1850s, editor Ramírez argued in an editorial that it was time for the *mexicanos* to stop calling themselves "Californios" because of the negative associations made between Californios and violence. Nomenclature aside, clearly socioeconomic and political conditions and increased immigration solidified the *mexicano* identity. In view of the racial tensions, the *Star/Estrella* even organized a return migration to the state of Sonora. Repatriation was likewise encouraged in the pages of *El Clamor Público*, but clearly the vast majority of Californios did not return to Mexico, although Ramírez did for a short period of time.

While in San Francisco literary production flourished in the 1850s and 1860s, in Southern California newspapers offered space for the publication of both Californio and Anglo poetry, narratives, cartoons, and essays. Richard Griswold del Castillo lists sixteen Spanish language or bilingual newspapers that operated in Los Angeles between 1850 and 1900.[18] The *Star/Estrella*'s Spanish language pages and *El Clamor Público* would be among the more prominent of the newspapers, with Francisco Ramírez sometimes working as editor, sometimes as journalist. Newspapers like *El Clamor Público*, the *Star/Estrella*, and *El Californio Meridional* were also vehicles for the publishing of Spanish and Latin-American poetry,[19] as well as humorous and satirical essays (like those of the seventeenth-century Spanish poet Quevedo, for example).[20] Though remote, Californio newspapers were part of a Spanish-language periodical network that enabled local newspapers to borrow items, like poetry and short narratives, used as filler, but sometimes poetry made its way into letters to the editor, as for example in one case in the *Star/Estrella* in which a pro-Democrat reader lambasted presidential candidate John C. Frémont with a satirical verse.[21]

By the end of the 1860s, Anglos dominated the city demographically, politically, and economically. Los Angeles was by then a highly segregated city, with the now minority *mexicano* population concentrated in an area north of the Main Plaza and west of Main Street, and in the southern section, with only a few families east of the LA River. The *barrio* as a minority Latino/a enclave had been born. This demographic concentration, although marked by poverty, enabled the maintenance of language and culture. Then, as now, the more affluent lived outside the barrio and tended more toward assimilation with the Anglos. By 1928 the barrio around the Plaza was run down; restoration of the Plaza and Olvera Street began during that decade, creating what is today El Pueblo de Los Angeles State Historic Park.[22]

Migration to California from the eastern United States increased after the establishment of the transcontinental railroad in 1869. By 1880 the population of the city itself was over 11,000 and there were in the county more than 33,000 people. For this period, especially important is the publication of *An Historical Sketch of Los Angeles County* (1876) by Col. J. J. Warner, Judge Benjamin Hayes, and Dr. J. P. Widney, three pioneers who look back from the perspective of the victors.

In the 1880s the Californios and subsequent Mexican immigrants continued to be a subordinate minority. Events in Los Angeles during this early US period are chronicled in the *testimonios* of Pico, Coronel, Botello, and Pérez as well as other Californios. Although not an Angeleno, María Amparo Ruiz de Burton is probably the best known Californio writer, with two novels, *Who Would Have Thought It?* (1872) and *The Squatter and the Don* (1885). The first novel focuses primarily on events in New York and Washington, D.C., during the Civil War, but *The Squatter and the Don*, a historical romance, recaptures the condition of dispossession, disempowerment, and proletarianization of Californios throughout the state. In her novel, Ruiz de Burton takes aim at issues already underscored in *El Clamor Público*, like the unfairness of federal and state legislation that allowed squatters to make claims on disputed Californio lands, and likewise the usurious and fraudulent practices of Anglo lawyers that led to the dispossession of Californios, as well as the corrupt and unethical practices of the railroad monopoly that trampled the rights of California citizens. Like the Spanish-language newspapers, *The Squatter and the Don* seeks to redress and defend the rights of the Californios, but now in English before a broader audience. In so doing, the novel also stresses the importance of a historical and cultural perspective in the formation of a strong Californio identity.

Second US period, 1880–1929: Latino demographic shift
under Anglo hegemony

The 1880–1929 period brought demographic shifts to Los Angeles that would increase the population by the thousands, beginning with the real-estate boom of the 1880s, the discovery of oil in 1892, and the construction of highways. This period also brought mass migration from Mexico during the Díaz dictatorship and the revolution of 1910. Among the Mexican exiles are journalists like Jorge Ulica (Julio G. Arce) and Adolfo Carrillo; both resided and wrote in San Francisco but Carrillo would write *Cuentos californianos*, a volume of short stories in Gothic style, that deal with events, historical or imagined, in Southern California.

The late nineteenth century also brought the domination of the California economy by the Big Four, the railroad monopoly that controlled transportation in the state. Ruiz de Burton takes up the critique of the railroad monopoly in *The Squatter and the Don*, as do two other notable authors, Josiah Royce and Frank Norris, who, in *The Feud of Oakfield Creek* (1887) and *The Octopus* (1901) respectively, reconfigure the Southern Pacific Railroad's role in the Mussel Slough Massacre of 1880 in Tulare County.

At another level, the growing labor movement that affected workers and stimulated strikes and protests, like those against the *Los Angeles Times* in 1910, increasingly affected all Californians. Given the proletarianization of the Californios and other Mexicans, renewed recognition of ethnic identity emerged along with a need to address and to protest the exploitation of working-class Chicanos, as is evident in Daniel Venegas's novel *Las aventuras de don Chipote o Cuando los pericos mamen* (*The Adventures of Don Chipote, or, When Parrots Suckle*), a picaresque novel published by a Los Angeles newspaper, *El Heraldo de México*, in 1928. Here, for the first time, we find the term *chicano* in print to refer to working-class *mexicanos* in the United States. In his novel, Venegas takes a naive Don Chipote from Mexico to El Paso to work on the rail lines and then to Los Angeles, where he discovers La Placita, and a Mexican community in the vicinity of today's Olvera Street. Descriptions in the novel of the community, the labor sector, the theater on Main Street, and other cultural activities connect the Los Angeles of yesterday with today's Latinized metropolis. Venegas, a playwright and editor of *El Malcriado*, a humorous weekly published in Los Angeles that included poetry, editorials, short narratives, and cartoons, is yet another instance of writers within a tradition of critical literature of resistance, first found in the proclamations and speeches of the Californios, in their *testimonios*, in Ruiz de Burton's novels, and much later in Chicano/a literature of the 1970s.

NOTES

1. The pueblo was also known as "El Pueblo de Nuestra Señora la Reina de Los Angeles de Porciúncula" and "El Pueblo de Nuestra Señora la Reina de Los Angeles." The Mission of San Gabriel was first founded in 1771 and relocated in 1774 to the site where it now stands. See Antonio Ríos-Bustamante, *Los Angeles, pueblo y región, 1781–1850* (Mexico: Instituto Nacional de Antropología e Historia, 1991), pp. 99–100.

2. Ríos-Bustamante, *Los Angeles*, p. 89.

3. John and Laree Caughey, *California Heritage* (Los Angeles: Ward Ritchie Press, 1962), p. 66.

4. Francisco Palou, *Historical Memoirs of New California*, ed. Herbert Eugene Bolton (New York: Russell & Russell, 1966).

5. Boscano's study is published as part of Alfred Robinson's *Life in California* (1846; New York: Da Capo Press, 1969).

6. José María Estudillo, *Expedición 1819 a los Tulares por cimarrones* (1819; Bancroft Manuscript, Bancroft Library, University of California, Berkeley, C-D 72).

7. Eulalia Pérez, *Una vieja y sus recuerdos* (Bancroft Manuscript C-D 139).

8. Alvarado, *Historia de California* (1876; Bancroft Manuscript C-D 1, 2, 3, 4, 5); Pico, *Narración histórica* (1877; Bancroft Microfilm X31-534); Vallejo, *Recuerdos históricos y personales tocantes a la Alta California 1874* (Bancroft Manuscript C-D 17, 18, 19, 20, 21).

9. Carillo, manuscript in Bancroft Library; see Ríos-Bustamante, *Los Angeles*, p. 263; "*Pronunciamiento*," translated in H. H. Bancroft, *History of California*, v. 5 (San Francisco: History Company Publishers, 1885–6).

10. Narciso Botello, *Anales del sur de la California, 1833–1844* (1878; Bancroft Manuscript C-D 49).

11. Antonio Francisco Coronel, *Cosas de California* (1877; Bancroft Manuscript C-D 61).

12. The tale was first published in the *Los Angeles Star* in 1851; see Caughey, *California Heritage*, pp. 9–10.

13. See Reid letters in Susana Bryant Dakin, *A Scotch Paisano* (Berkeley: University of California Press, 1939), pp. 215–86.

14. Ríos-Bustamante, *Los Angeles*, p. 247.

15. See "Petition of the California Landowners," in Robert Glass Cleland, *The Cattle on a Thousand Hills: Southern California: 1850–1870* (San Marino, Calif.: Huntington Library, 1941), pp. 280–5.

16. Richard Griswold del Castillo, *The Los Angeles Barrio, 1850–1890: A Social History* (Berkeley: University of California Press, 1979), p. 109.

17. Cleland appends a collection of *Star* newspaper articles on the killing of Sheriff Barton by the Flores-Daniel band and the subsequent raising and arming of a vigilante group to chase down and lynch the bandits; see *The Cattle on a Thousand Hills*, pp. 286–305.

18. Griswold del Castillo, *The Los Angeles Barrio*, p. 126.

19. See *Hispanic Poetry in Los Angeles 1850–1900: La poesía angelina*, ed. Reynaldo Ruiz (Lewiston, N.Y.: Edwin Mellen Press, 2000). See also Catherine Davies, Review of *Hispanic Poetry in Los Angeles*, by Reynaldo Ruiz, *Modern Language Review* 97 (2002), 213–14.

20. Francisco de Quevedo, "Letrados" and "La verdad y la justicia," reprinted in *El Californio Meridional*, June 20, 1855.

21. "*Así remato los males / Haciendo papel moneda; / California esto te queda / Para hacer sus funerales*," *Los Angeles Star/Estrella*, October 18, 1856.

22. W. W. Robinson, *Los Angeles, from the Days of the Pueblo* (Los Angeles: California Historical Society, 1981), pp. 95–109.

2

WILLIAM ALEXANDER McCLUNG

The Anglo invention of Los Angeles

From California's entrance into the Union in 1850 until the end of World War I, speakers of English – "Anglos" in California usage, regardless of ethnic ancestry – generated a large, though now mostly forgotten, popular literature in and around Los Angeles. What is of interest in the literary history of this otherwise ignored era is not the few works that rise above mediocrity, but the fact that almost all of these fictions merge imperceptibly with travel writing to constitute a literature of place, obsessed with analyzing, publicizing, and critiquing both the found and the constructed landscape. "Place" is the thesis of LA literature in the era that saw Anglos move from frontiersmen to bourgeoisie; the fictions they wrote and read are largely a pretext for appropriating Los Angeles to their own historical imperatives and cultural needs.

A definition of "Los Angeles": at the beginning of the period, it is synonymous with all of Southern California, or at least the region comprising today's counties of Ventura, Los Angeles, San Bernardino, Orange, and Riverside. Furthermore, the Mojave Desert presses upon Los Angeles' literary consciousness. Paradoxically, the dimensions of "Los Angeles" contract as the old pueblo itself becomes sufficiently populated to merit attention. At certain points other communities claim their own share of attention and become venues for subsets of the literary production of the period, especially the independent health-and-pleasure resort towns like Pasadena. Or they are conjured from the empty landscape, eventually becoming new zones that displace the center of gravity from the pueblo, now merely "downtown." By the end of our period, the amalgamation of at least Los Angeles County into a single conceptual region is within sight; the process has come almost full circle.

A new kind of "West"

Los Angeles, incorporated and made the county seat in 1850, was a wild place for the next several decades, yet even the most lurid accounts of the shootings, posses, and lynchings bear witness to two shaping phenomena of subsequent literary culture: the climate and the Californios, that is, the Mexican population, especially its upper crust of landowners and cattle ranchers. William Henry Brewer, describing "Los Angeles and Environs" of 1860, constructs the dialogue that would shape writing about the place for over a century: "all that is wanted to make it a paradise is *water*, more *water* ... no winter, but a perpetual spring and summer. Such is Los Angeles, where 'every prospect pleases and only man is vile.'"[1] LA writing would perpetuate his three topics: delight in an Arcadian paradise, frustration that a potential utopia is stalled for lack of water, and a critical eye cast on the citizenry.

Brewer acknowledges the lawlessness of the period, "fifty to sixty murders per year ... in Los Angeles."[2] Stephen Powers also describes degradation and poverty in the late 1860s. Powers walked from North Carolina to Southern California, preceding and outdoing Charles Fletcher Lummis, who walked to California from Ohio in 1884, except in the gift of self-promotion. With an irony that foreshadows the stance and tone later writers would take about mercantile and consumerist Los Angeles, Powers sketches a frontier town of mingled pretense, squalor, and real-estate opportunism:

> All the people are such nice people, so frank, so free, so generous, and all the while riding up and down in gorgeous buggies, bowing and smiling. You can buy lots on every street corner for nothing, and sell them for never so much money and get rich in an hour, or – the other thing. Everybody is so glad to see you, and jumps over the counter to shake hands, and wants to sell you some lots.

Powers also evokes an alienating landscape in the "glaring white monotony"[3] of all the land between the pueblo and the ocean, anticipating Robinson Jeffers's meditation on Pacific anomie, "At Playa Hermosa": "Here is not despair nor hope: / Only gray waves rise and drop. / Here against the level tides / Strange and ominous peace abides," an anxiety echoed in his "Noon": "the high sun is perfect dread, / And perfect terror the flat sea."[4] Ambivalence about the monotony of the weather will persist into and through the following century.

To the earliest Anglo period belongs John Rollin Ridge's *The Life and Adventures of Joaquín Murieta, the Celebrated California Bandit* (1854), a highly fictionalized account of the exploits described in the title. They are not confined to one part of the state and the work cannot be more than incidentally associated with Los Angeles. As a tale of derring-do across the landscape of Mexican California, however, it describes more a territory of the imagination than a real place and reads like a plausible screenplay for an early Hollywood Western, being all mountains, valleys, horses, pistols, and splendid Mexican outfits. The occasional mission or adobe fills out the set.

Horatio Bell's *Reminiscences of a Ranger* also testifies to the region in the period, although, as Franklin Walker remarks in his authoritative *Literary History of Southern California*, Bell seemed to know little about Murieta, whom Walker terms "putative" and "near-mythical." Bell was the dominating literary figure of these early "Wild West" decades. *Reminiscences*, "the first clothbound book to be printed, bound, and published in the city of Los Angeles,"[5] is a lively, journalistic overview of the rough-and-ready culture. Full of anecdote and narrative, it provides an extended backward glance at an adolescent Anglo culture fumbling and groping its way toward a distant maturity. Bell is sardonic about both the mission fathers and the Americans who exploit first the Indians and subsequently the Mexicans themselves, and he uses an elaborately metaphorical and euphemistic style to express the lewd, violent, and disorderly events. Nostalgic for the romanticized Hispanic culture that the Anglo ascendancy was displacing, he concludes with a "thirty years after" retrospective that shrewdly foresees the utter transformation of the region over the next half century, while embalming the past, together with his youth, in memory and testimonial.

The pioneer spirit's mutation into cultural imperialism was anticipated by the lyric quoted by Brewer about pleasing prospects and vile man. It comes from a popular missionary hymn that contrasts the beauty of exotic climes with the spiritual darkness of their benighted denizens, who "call us to deliver / Their land from error's chain."[6] It informs the first serious handbook for travelers and potential settlers, by Charles Nordhoff, who sees California as "the other" that has now become "ours": that is, it is the first

> tropical land which our race has thoroughly mastered and made itself at home in ... There, and there only, on this planet, the traveler and resident may enjoy the delights of the tropics, without their penalties; a mild climate, not enervating, but healthful and health-restoring; a wonderfully and variously productive soil, without tropical malaria; the grandest scenery, with ... strange customs, but neither lawlessness nor semi-barbarism.[7]

Sarah Bixby Smith's *Adobe Days* is a useful reminiscence of the 1870s. Her dry, witty style is keen on the shifting perceptions of the size of the place, which in the 1870s seemed substantially larger than when her father arrived in early 1854, but which appears a "frontier town" compared with 1925. She evocatively describes the landscape at Long Beach:

> The southern houses were each placed on the brow of a mesa, with a view across a characteristic California river which might be a dangerous torrent or a strip of dry sand, according to the season of the year. The eyes could follow across flat lands, treeless except for a few low-growing willows, to far blue mysterious

mountains. It was a very empty land, empty of people and towns, of trees and cultivated fields.[8]

The picture is unlike the romanticized Southwest promoted by Lummis.

To the close of this frontier era belongs Bret Harte's poem "Jack of the Tules (Southern California)," in which a priest parries the inquiries of a vigilante searching for the eponymous robber, Jack. The "priest" turns out to be Jack in disguise, and he tricks the vigilante, tying him up and escaping. Harte's authorship suggests that the region's colorful past had, by the 1880s, a literary audience. The taste for popular romance remained strong into the next century, producing Will R. Halpin's *Juan Pico* (1899) and Edward Carpenter's *Captain Courtesy* (1906). The latter title characterizes the eponymous Pimpernel-like bandit, product of an American father and a Spanish mother, who, as a couple, both enjoyed and exemplified the supposed cultural harmony of the pre-Mexican era. The Mexican regime is the villain of the piece, having ruined the supposedly benevolent mission system and then moved without justification to expel Americans. The American conquest of California is presented as a defensive necessity and act of liberation consequent upon the alleged Mexican campaign of extermination. This thesis aligns California with Texas in popular American thought about the justification for the Mexican War.

Selling the land

In 1876 the railroad arrived and with it the beginning of the most characteristic period of Anglo ascendancy, based on the exploitation of the land for real estate and profit. Two kinds of writing characterize this phenomenon: the promotion of Los Angeles, and the critique of that promotion. An increasingly elaborate narrative took shape to give historical and cultural depth to the empty acres awaiting development.

Writers of the boom era were "visitors, promoters, adventurers, and health seekers."[9] The most thorough and committed promoter was Lummis, who grasped the significance of the decayed missions as the key to an evolving mythology of the region. Lummis was the key "commodifier," who understood that the "epic story" could be deployed "to lure tourists and settlers." David Fine calls his strategy a "necessary fiction that would link the region to a past evoking Old World grace and charm, moral earnestness, and heroism." Lummis "focused on the two principal booster themes, Los Angeles as … the happy destination of the future-oriented Anglo settler and the legatee of the 'sun, silence, and adobe' culture of the Hispanic Southwest."[10]

Lummis was most influential as the editor of the periodical *Land of Sunshine*, which he eventually renamed *Out West* and which published its last independent issue in 1917. This journal publicized, promoted, and recorded Southern California, giving it an identity as both a climatic and archaeological resource of the first order and a civilization in the process of becoming. A typical volume might include a poem on the San Gabriel Mission, a physician's article on Southern California for invalids, a promotion of Los Angeles as a developing metropolis, a drawing of a mountain cabin, Mexican recipes, and a scholarly piece on fog. Lummis founded the Southwest Museum in 1914 and gathered the "Arroyo Circle" in his self-built house, El Alisal. The circle included Yosemite naturalist John Muir, cowboy novelist Eugene Manlove Rhodes, the expatriate Polish actress Modjeska, and the wits and actors Will Rogers, Douglas Fairbanks, and even Sarah Bernhardt. The most important figure was Mary Austin, who, although she had a poor opinion of Lummis,[11] was associated with him after 1889 and lived briefly around Los Angeles.

Known even today for her encomium of the desert, *The Land of Little Rain* (1903), Austin, together with John Van Dyke (*The Desert*, 1901), reconfigured the harsh backcountry of the early Anglo settlers into an austere Arcadia of natural ecological relationships. Austin's work is evocative of Los Angeles at one remove, as it evokes the desert that literally defines Los Angeles, even though her literary venues are in the deep interior. The settings of her fiction and drama, including *The Basket Woman* (1904), *Isidro* (1905), *Lost Borders* (1909), *The Arrowmaker* (1911), and *Fire* (1914), are also remote. Her contribution to LA literature is primarily the evocation of beauty and sublimity in the default terrain of the region, often ignored or invisible, but arguably prepared to reclaim its authority. Furthermore, *The Ford* (1907), about the Owens Valley water scandal, could be said to be the most significant work of California fiction between Helen Hunt Jackson's *Ramona* (1884) and the 1920s, although its action is displaced to Northern California. It confirmed her as a moralist who pioneered, without satire, the critique of Los Angeles as despoiler. Her 1932 autobiography evokes a Los Angeles of 1888 still noticeably "Spanish" in appearance, but subsequently affirms

> the deep resentment I feel toward the totality of Southern California. It can't possibly be as inchoate and shallow as on its own showing it appears, all the uses of natural beauty slavered over with the impudicity of a material culture. Other times, away from it, I wake in the night convinced that there are still uncorrupted corners from which the Spirit of the Arroyos calls me, wistful with long refusals, and I resolve that next year, or *next* at farthest ... and I am never able to manage it.[12]

In the Preface to *Millionaires of a Day*, his shrewdly analytic novel of the land rush of the 1880s, Theodore Strong Van Dyke (John Van Dyke's brother) observes that "this boom ... lasted nearly two years, embraced a vast area of both town and country, and involved an amount of money and players almost incredible to even those who were in it." As is characteristic of much of the writing of this period, *Millionaires* is only quasi-fictional, more interested in exposing facts than telling a tale. Citing the climate as an inducement for settlers, despite setbacks, to remain, he terms the LA area "a grand play-country." Eventually he sees it transformed by irrigation into a semi-tropical paradise so attractive that even financial failure does not drive settlers back east. Lyrical over the natural and the improved landscapes, the narrator remains caustic about the boom's ethics and observant of what would become a characteristic motif of twentieth-century LA fiction, the self-promoter who shifts his calling and his clothing with equal ease. At a lavish "free lunch" picnic at the development site "Excelsior Heights," "the auctioneer, arrayed in costly garb, was an ex-minister of the Gospel who had been lured from the path of duty by the superior attractions of the rising real-estate market."[13]

Other novels similarly tease slender fictions out of the development of Greater Los Angeles. The eponymous hero of Frank Lewis Nason's *Vision of Elijah Berl* "almost singlehanded, tries to set up an entire irrigation system in order to get rich quick on an orange-ranch development scheme."[14] A phrase from the novel, "struggle in the land of golden promise," could have been the subtitle. Berl is driven by a "vision" of "when these great, barren red hillsides are all covered with orchards; with beautiful houses and thousands of happy, prosperous people; when the snows and rains of the San Bernardinos, instead of running to waste, will flow through tunnels and canals and make the desert blossom as the rose."[15] But the debunking theme is also present: cold, clammy mists that belie the promise of eternal warmth and sunshine, property speculation, sharp practice, and runs on the bank.

Other fiction also narrates the Anglo experience of coming to grips with the strangeness and difficulties of a paradoxically bounteous and desolate region. Margaret Collier Graham's *Stories of the Foot-Hills* (1895) consists of tales largely in dialect. She carves out a primitive Yankee or Appalachian territory in the Cucamonga area ("Sawpit Canyon"), with occasional references to Los Angeles ("Loss Anglus," "Los Anjelus"), often pausing for the descriptive local color that in this period usually signals the fascination with the climate. Frequently enhancing the novels, for example, Stephen K. Szymanowski's *The Searchers* (1908), are plates showing actual persons, places, and curiosities of Greater Los Angeles, suggesting that the fiction is merely a device for narrating the city itself.

For a wealthy audience, Charles Dudley Warner's expensively produced *Our Italy* promoted a favorite analogy by means of a detailed apologia for the equability of the climate, emphasizing that Easterners typically misconceived it as "tropical" when in fact it was nearly uniformly temperate. Warner characterizes such ill-informed visitors as prepared to denounce the climate as "a fraud, all this visible display of summer, and of an almost tropical summer at that; it is really a cold country."[16] This is an important early defensive gambit in the sunlight/noir dichotomy: the disjunction between the visual and the experiential would be fodder for LA writers for another century and beyond.

Appropriating the past

The Anglo "invention" of Los Angeles required a narrative of paradise lost as well as found. Eventually the former would be defined by a half-imagined Spanish past that could be prefixed to the Anglo ascendancy. One work succeeded for many years in defining Los Angeles and its environs to the exclusion of any competing mythology: *Ramona*. Helen Hunt Jackson's romance spawned four Hollywood productions and a vast tourist industry by revising the Anglos' acquisition of a territory with their acquisition of its history. The *Ramona* tourist industry reconfigured the landscape as an accessible past to be not only passively appreciated but also actively improved, so that its vanished glories would be resurrected in a new, more vigorous form. As Dydia DeLyser observes, "the 'real California' had become complexly intertwined with the fictional."[17]

Jackson did not simply invent romantic Old California; she developed it from a background of similar, if less fluently expressed, sentiments. Samuel Cozzens in *Crossing the Quicksands*, a quasi-fictional boys' adventure narrative of camping and hunting, narrates a set piece of a Californio rancho and its hospitality as well as observations on the decay of Indian culture and, interestingly, an expression of regret by one character that he cannot speak Spanish. An elegy for a vanishing civilization of hierarchy, self-sufficiency, and generosity is delivered by a Californio whose account of "the old Californians" shows them to have been "almost identical with that of the Spanish hidalgos living at the present time in Mexico." The account is remarkable in the depth and breadth of the condemnation, which sums up its narrative of Anglo fraud and violence with the accusation that "you Americans ... have ruined our country by forcing upon us what you are pleased to term 'your civilization.'" The indictment is even more remarkable because the narrator accepts it without demur as "simple, honest."[18] He does not, however, feel obliged to seek a remedy or even to apologize: Anglo innocence is impervious to the very historical crimes that it acknowledges.

Ramona remains too well known to require much explanation. The tale of the half-European, half-Indian girl who gains and loses an Indian husband with the oddly Italian name Alessandro, perpetuated itself in a vast tourist industry that sought with considerable success to transmute the narrative into a rhetoric of place, discovering rival claimants to the "real" Home of Ramona and to other venues in her odyssey. DeLyser asserts that the novel was a mechanism for making sense of Southern California;[19] Karen Ramirez similarly argues that it was important in redefining Southern California as a civilized and replete culture, full of history and ritual, rather than part of some "primitive, empty, and wild" West.[20] The novel's power to foster Anglo nostalgia for a displaced civilization lies, however, in its evocation of Southern California, in a moment of mythical time, the final stage of a supposed Arcadia summed up in the description of the Moreno estate as a place of perpetual fruit and flower, an earthly paradise.[21] Immediately and immensely praised, *Ramona* sold over 74,000 copies by 1900. *The Dial* observed that "[t]he contrast between the refined Spanish civilization of southern California and the insolent vulgarity of the American type which crushed it is drawn in such a way as to make that questionable chapter of our history seem even more difficult than ever for patriotism to defend."[22] Mary Austin, however, thought *Ramona* factitious and second rate.[23]

Numerous volumes, enhanced with photographs, followed in *Ramona*'s wake, striving to identify the locales and even survivors that Jackson might have used as models. These include A. C. Vroman and T. F. Barnes's *The Genesis of the Story of* Ramona (1899), David Hufford's *The Real Ramona* (1900), George Wharton James's *Through Ramona's Country* (1909), and Edwin Clough's pamphlet "Ramona's Marriage Place" (1910). Sometimes, as in the case of the album *Ramona*, publishers simply appended the magic title to pictures of sites offered without any text. Decades after publication, *Ramona* was still so important that a large, lavishly printed, and extensively illustrated book, Carlyle Davis and William Alderson's *The True Story of "Ramona,"* was still disputing the originals of the characters and the venues. The fulsome dedication, "To the memory of Helen Hunt Jackson, the most brilliant, impetuous, and thoroughly individual woman of American literature,"[24] indicates how far her reputation has sunk in a century.

The term *Ramona myth* dates only from 1910,[25] but the romanticization of the displaced Hispanic culture informs earlier works, such as Constance Goddard Du Bois, *A Soul in Bronze* (1900), a sentimental and implausible interracial Indian/Anglo tragedy, and Marah Ellis Ryan, *For the Soul of Rafael* (1906), a melodrama of dispossessed Californios. Amanda Mathews's *The Hieroglyphics of Love* offers "tales dealing with the

Mexican *peonada* ... written that you may love, as I love, a dark and lowly people who are yet rich with the riches of the poor, and wise with the wisdom of the simple."²⁶ Jackson's social consciousness finds expression in Nancy K. Foster's *Not of Her Race*, an intercultural romance against the backdrop of the Anglo dispossession of the Californios:

> When one realizes that barely fifty years ago this entire country belonged to the Mexicans or Californians, as they preferred to be called; that they dwelt here on their vast ranches in patriarchal style, owning leagues of land and thousands of horses and cattle, entertaining stranger and friend alike with a lavish hospitality unexampled; and that now these people are practically exterminated, it is one of the most pathetic race-tragedies in history.²⁷

Jackson's influence persists to the very end of the period, in works such as Rose Ellerbe's *Tales of California Yesterdays* (1916), and Charles Franklin Carter's *Stories of the Old Missions of California* (1917). Ellerbe's sentimental magazine fiction evokes an imaginary moment in which Anglos participate in the earlier system without displacing it. That system is, anachronistically, the California both of the Spanish missions and of the Mexican ranchos, whose heyday in fact coincided with the decay of the mission system. Carter evokes the Mission culture of Indians and padres and prophesies the end of Indian civilization in California. He blurs the distinction between fiction and travel literature, claiming that all but one of his six short stories are based on fact, and that all are intended "to give a faithful picture of life among the Indians and Spaniards in Nueva California during the early days of the past century."²⁸

Anglo nostalgia, safely insulated from any possibility of reversing the past, informs Percival Cooney's long-forgotten *Dons of the Old Pueblo*: "in the hearts of those who love the smiling vales and azure skies of the Golden State there will ever be a throb of kindly sympathy for the gentle, chivalrous race that once lived a life of Arcadian simplicity amid these scenes now tumultuous with the myriad activities of modern civilization."²⁹ More enduringly, however, Jackson provided the ideological basis for John Steven McGroarty's immensely successful *Mission Play* (1911), a pageant of local history that even the otherwise clear-sighted Mary Austin admired.³⁰ Opening on the grounds of the San Gabriel Mission in 1912, with a cast of over one hundred, the pageant was a huge and immediate success. The *Los Angeles Times* observed that the script "has been taken almost literally from the history of California," yet "before long, that qualifying 'almost' would be excised from public perceptions of the play ... and regional culture would canonize the play as Southern California history itself, come back to life exactly where all assumed it had begun, under the stars at the San Gabriel Mission."³¹

Productions continued well beyond the end of this period, perpetuating the sentiments and mythologies of the late nineteenth century deep into the twentieth.

NOTES

The author is grateful to the Henry E. Huntington Library for a Fletcher Jones Foundation fellowship.

1. William Henry Brewer, *Up and Down California in 1860–1864: The Journal of William H. Brewer*, ed. Francis P. Farquhar (New Haven: Yale University Press, 1930), p. 13.
2. *Ibid.*, p. 14.
3. Steven Powers, *Afoot and Alone; A Walk from Sea to Sea* (Hartford: Columbian Book Co., 1872), pp. 272, 277.
4. John Robinson Jeffers, *Flagons and Apples* (Los Angeles: Grafton Publishing Company, 1912), pp. 274, 275.
5. Franklin Walker, *A Literary History of Southern California* (Berkeley: University of California Press, 1950), pp. 53, 54.
6. Cited in Brewer, *Up and down California*, p. 13.
7. Charles Nordhoff, *California: For Health, Pleasure, and Residence. A Book for Travellers and Settlers* (New York: Harper & Bros., 1872), p. 11.
8. Cited in Walker, *Literary History*, p. 182.
9. *Ibid.*, p. 106.
10. David Fine, *Imagining Los Angeles: A City in Fiction* (Albuquerque: University of New Mexico Press, 2000), pp. 29, 35.
11. *Ibid.*, p. 39.
12. Mary Austin, *Earth Horizon: An Autobiography* (Albuquerque: University of New Mexico Press, 1991), pp. 188–9.
13. Theodore S. Van Dyke, *Millionaires of a Day: An Inside Story of the Great Southern California "Boom"* (New York: Fords, Howard & Hulbert, 1890), pp. 19, 20, 59.
14. Walker, *Literary History*, p. 213.
15. Frank Lewis Nason, *The Vision of Elijah Berl* (Boston: Little, Brown, 1905), pp. 10, 19.
16. Charles Dudley Warner, *Our Italy* (New York: Harper & Brothers, 1891), p. 49.
17. Dydia DeLyser, *Ramona Memories: Tourism and the Shaping of Southern California* (Minneapolis: University of Minnesota Press, 2005), p. 61.
18. Samuel Woodworth Cozzens, *Crossing the Quicksands; Or, the Veritable Adventures of Hal and Ned upon the Pacific Slope* (Boston: Lee & Shepard, 1877), pp. 303, 305.
19. DeLyser, *Ramona Memories*, p. xii.
20. Karen E. Ramirez, *Reading Helen Hunt Jackson's* Ramona (Boise, Idaho: Boise State University Press, 2006), p. 23.
21. Helen Hunt Jackson, *Ramona* (New York: Modern Library, 2005), p. 17.
22. Cited in Edgar Joseph Hinkel and William E. McCann, eds., *Criticism of California Literature: Fiction, Poetry, Drama: A Digest and Bibliography*, 3 vols. (Oakland: Alameda County Library, 1940), vol. II, p. 422.

23. Fine, *Imagining Los Angeles*, p. 44.
24. Carlyle Channing Davis and William A. Alderson, *The True Story of "Ramona": Its Facts and Fictions, Inspiration and Purpose* (New York: Dodge Publishing Co., 1914), n.p.
25. DeLyser, *Ramona Memories*, p. xvii.
26. Amanda Mathews, *The Hieroglyphics of Love: Stories of Sonoratown and Old Mexico* (Los Angeles: Artemisia Bindery, 1906), p. 19.
27. Nancy K. Foster, *Not of Her Race* (Boston: R. G. Badger, 1911), p. 119.
28. Charles Franklin Carter, *Stories of the Old Missions of California* (San Francisco: Paul Elder, 1917), p. vii.
29. Percival J. Cooney, *The Dons of the Old Pueblo* (Chicago & New York: Rand McNally, 1914), n.p.
30. William Deverell, *Whitewashed Adobe: The Rise of Los Angeles and the Remaking of Its Mexican Past* (Berkeley: University of California Press, 2004), p. 218.
31. *Ibid.*, pp. 208, 209.

3

DAVID WYATT

LA fiction through mid-century

Upton Sinclair's *Oil!* (1927) begins as a dream of speed. Sinclair calls his opening chapter "The Ride" and bases it on a trip he and his wife Craig took with a big oilman who wanted to buy two lots they owned on Signal Hill, near Long Beach. He "asked us to come and look at a ranch he offered in exchange," Craig writes in *Southern Belle* (1957). "So we let him drive us in a big fast car, breaking all the speed laws." [1] The property they saw that day would become the Watkins Ranch in San Elido, the site of Dad's big strike in *Oil!* and a place that would stimulate in Sinclair a prescient depiction of the soon-to-be-developed oil field near Bakersfield at Kettleman Hills.

"The road ran, smooth and flawless, " *Oil!* begins,

> precisely fourteen feet wide, the edges trimmed as if by shears, a ribbon of grey concrete, rolled out over the valley by a giant hand. The ground went in long waves, a slow ascent and then a sudden dip; you climbed, and went swiftly over – but you had no fear, for you knew the magic ribbon would be there, clear of obstructions, unmarred by bump or scar, waiting the passage of inflated rubber wheels revolving seven times a second.

Thrown into "a storm of motion," Sinclair's reader can only come along for the ride. Like Dad, his "business is with the things that lie before" him, "and the past is past." As impatient a driver as he is deliberate a businessman, Dad wants "a speed law turned inside out," and dreams of a California where it will one day be illegal, on such roads, to drive less than forty miles an hour. "You were racing with the other people, who were always threatening to get your oil." [2]

Sinclair chooses to make his protagonist a "kind" capitalist who keeps coming up with "a happy solution" to his son Bunny's "ethical problems." He thus directs his critique onto forces rather than men, a recurrent theme in the procession of big California novels that runs from Frank Norris's *The Octopus* (1901) to John Steinbeck's *The Grapes of Wrath* (1939), novels which depict the state as uniquely hospitable to concentrations of power. Each writer imagines a conglomerate – railroads, oil, agribusiness – acquiring a momentum of its own, "a huge machine in which every cog had its place" – and devoted to mystifying its own workings.[3] It demands a fictional response of answerable scale. The challenge becomes to keep the resulting loose baggy monster moving. As Norris maintains, "No one who sets a thing in motion but keeps an eye and a hand upon its speed." Like an engineer guiding a train, an author must keep his mind upon the "releasing of the brake." Norris, Sinclair, and Steinbeck each set out to write a story that will keep readers moving toward an anticipated "pivotal event."[4] Yet to write toward such an end is also to identify with the momentum of the very thing being resisted, with the machine itself. And so these writers find themselves attracted toward digressive form. In a fictional field where relations stop nowhere, the call is less toward the pivotal event than it is to stop and think.

Sinclair's *Oil!* chronicles the birth of the world that Philip Marlowe will later be hired to investigate. Marlowe's clients in *The Big Sleep* (1939) are made of oil money, and the body he is asked to find lies buried in the nearby sump. The Sternwoods can still "look out of their front windows and see what had made them rich," the oil fields down below.[5] By the late 1930s, Los Angeles has become mired in the ironies of adjacency. Horse-head pumps nod away in so many urban backyards; the activity of extraction defaces a Southern California Eden even as it finances it.

In *The Boosters* (1923), Mark Lee Luther discerned this pattern early on. Arriving in Los Angeles by train, Boston-trained architect George Hammond falls into a sprawl of parking lots and orange juice stands and outsized mansions. "The faults of structure were surpassed only by the sins of decoration."[6] Pitted against the relentless booster of the title, developer Spencer Ward, Hammond eventually makes a separate peace with Los Angeles by withdrawing to the Hollywood Hills, where he designs houses expressive of California's pre-conquest built forms and in harmony with the climate he has come to appreciate.

In *Oil!*, Dad bribes politicians to achieve the "promptness and efficiency that business men had to have, and that couldn't be got under our American system."[7] In the Los Angeles of the 1920s and 1930s, the word that best covers the ongoing greasing of the system is *development*. "Perhaps more than any other modern city," Roger Lotchin maintains, "Los Angeles was the product of a development conspiracy by its leadership."[8] Real estate would lie always at the center. And development occurred even when there was no market to develop. In *Millionaires of a Day* (1890), Theodore Van Dyke chronicled the boom and bust of the 1880s, where "all that was necessary was a sufficient acreage chopped up fine enough."[9] Before the first big boom collapsed, the LA basin had been chopped up into over one hundred new towns, a third of which promptly disappeared in the planning stage, and into enough lots to accommodate some two million new immigrants. "Towns located in swamp lands," Carey McWilliams writes, were "laid out as 'harbor cities.'"[10] A century later, Mike Davis's urban histories would read the built form of Los Angeles as a steady darkening into noir, as out-of-control growth produces a city of dreadful night.

The most romantic conspiracy of development involved William Mulholland's bringing of water to Los Angeles in 1913, a theft from the Owens Valley that made possible the growth of the modern city. The big oil strikes of the 1920s made possible the next big advance, along with the Julian Oil Swindle, an investment scheme in which 40,000 shareholders lost $150 million after buying into a company promising dividends far beyond its actual earnings. Twentieth-century Los Angeles would see its most dramatic population growth in the decade of the 1920s, the city rising from 576,000 to 1.2 million in those ten years; the county grew even faster, from 936,000 to over 2.2 million. McWilliams called this shift of population from the middle of the country to Southern California "the largest internal migration in the history of the American people."[11] In the brilliant *Chinatown* (1974) and its bathetic sequel, *The Two Jakes* (1990), Robert Towne would script two movies dealing, in turn, with bringing the water and finding the oil. For Noah Cross, Towne's planning monster, development has less to do with buying up space than with the attempt to master time. Asked what it is that he still wants to buy, Cross answers, "The future ... the future!"

As Bunny and Dad approach Angel City in *Oil!*, they encounter "one or more 'subdivisions,' as they were called; 'acreage' was being laid out into lots, and decorated with a row of red and yellow flags fluttering merrily in the breeze."[12] Sinclair may have backdated the action of his novel to 1912, but he is writing about the real-estate boom of the 1920s. In 1923 alone, some 11,000 acres were subdivided and 25,000 one- and two-family dwellings were erected. By the next year, Los Angeles had 43,000 real estate agents. Like the boom of the 1880s, this one also collapsed in an excess of speculation, in 1925, but not before the incorporation of cities that would survive, like Bell, Lynwood, Torrance, and South Gate. Seven years after Sinclair imagined Dad and Bunny arriving in Los Angeles, Frank and Cora drive out of the city in James M. Cain's *The Postman Always Rings Twice* (1934), passing on their way "a house that was being built, and all the way out we talked about how not many of them have gone up lately, but the whole section is going to be built up as soon as things get better."[13] Even in 1933, in the depths of the Great Depression, there was a sense that Los Angeles was only going to continue to grow. *Acceleration* has become the theme of the story, one that will culminate in the Arroyo Seco in 1940, when the region opened its first "freeway."

The felt sense of momentum was one that could reach down even into a writer's style. When Sartre called Horace McCoy's *They Shoot Horses,*

Don't They? (1935) the first important existential novel, he meant to invoke its sense of human thrownness. But McCoy's depiction of life as "continuous motion" has as much to do with a specific set of local conditions, the dance marathons and taxi dances offered up in Los Angeles to those with too little money and too much time. Gloria and Robert have come to California to make it in the movies, and, failing that, decide to enter a marathon dance down at the beach. Robert estimates it will take 2,000 hours to win. Even before she enters the contest, Gloria admits that all she wants to do is "die." As her shoes wear out and her misery deepens, she pressures Robert to end it for her. Finally she produces a pistol. Robert then remembers his grandfather shooting a horse with a broken leg. "*It was the only way to get her out of her misery,*" the grandfather explained.[14] So Robert takes the pistol from Gloria and shoots her in the head, offering up the title of the book as his reason for doing so.

Perhaps McCoy's novel does deserve to be called existential, at least insofar as it deals with being in time. Unlike Sinclair's *Oil!*, there is nothing in *They Shoot Horses* to explain the feelings and actions of the characters, no attention to material conditions or to the political and economic practices native to Los Angeles. It is a novel of speed. The novel of speed takes as given a background that must be inferred. It tends to be short, and to be marked by striking economies of style. It leaves little room for the direct expression of emotion, preferring fascinating surfaces to mere depth. It can also question these efficiencies, and come to know that there has to be a better, more life-affirming way. And it is a kind of novel that seems to arise from, and to be especially suited to, the place called Los Angeles.

"They threw me off the hay truck about noon." The opening sentence of *The Postman Always Rings Twice* (1934) is justly famous as a sudden setup. Frank blows into the Twin Oaks Tavern "in a hurry" and within fifteen pages is talking murder. Three pages after that, Cora attempts it. "We played it just like we would tell it," Frank says, but he would be wrong. The murder he stages in his head – "I was to take the water up to my room" – gradually slips into the conditional tense.[15] Then all of Frank's "would's" give way to what actually happens, the state cop showing up, the cat shorting out the lights. So much for playing it like you would tell it.

Postman and *Double Indemnity* (1936) both deal with the fantasy of having a plan. Plans reach into the future; they try to shape ends. The problem is, other forces are at work. At the end of *Postman*, Frank is convicted of carrying out a plan he has never made – of killing Cora. "To hell with the subconscious," he says, in response to a cellmate who suggests he might have meant to do it, after all.[16] To look into the subconscious would take too much time and would cut against the extreme hurry to which Frank and Cora are dedicated, an activity of self-outrunning reflective of, and produced by, the inescapable momentum generated by the place in which they live.

Cain is dealing with characters who do not make time for themselves. Frank's rejection of depth is a way to renounce thinking, and what comes with it. "With thinking," Thoreau argues in "Solitude," "we may be beside ourselves in a sane sense." In thinking, "I come to know myself as a human entity; the scene, so to speak, of thoughts and affections; and am sensible of a certain doubleness by which I stand as remote from myself as from another."[17] Or, as Frank's cellmate says, "you got two selves, one that you know about and the other that you don't know about."[18] In the novel of speed, hasty planning usurps reflective thought. Yet Cain's and his characters' careening plots have the paradoxical effect of arousing an awareness of the need to slow down in order to get to know parts of the self about which one may be unaware.

Raymond Chandler did not take to Cain's sensibility, but he did admire the dialogue:

> "I'm no good, but I love you."
> "Yes, and I love you."
> "'Stall him. Just this one night."
> "All right, Frank. Just this one night."[19]

Chandler saw it as all about speed. "These unevenly shaped chunks of quick-moving speech hit the eye with a sort of explosive effect. You read the stuff in batches, not in individual speech and counterspeech."[20] It was dialogue like this, as well as the sheer velocity of the plot, that made *Postman* "unlaydownable."[21]

The novel of speed locates much of its force in sentence sound. "All in one day, his wife had left him, Colossal Pictures had renewed his contract, his mistress had returned unexpectedly from location, his lawyer had informed him that a charge of driving while intoxicated had been 'fixed', and his tests – both film and Wasserman – had turned out favorably."[22] This is the third sentence of Carroll and Garrett Graham's 1930 novel, *Queer People*. Paul Cain's *Fast One* (1933) "scrapes away conjunctions," Irvin Faust writes, as in the sentence: "He swore softly, continuously, obscenely." Protagonist Gerry Kells finds himself "mixed up" in five shootings in thirty-six hours. "The pace takes over," Faust continues, "is itself a major character, perhaps *the* major character, and it controls the book."[23] A "fast one" turns out to be not simply a tall tale or a tailing police car, but the shape and rhythm of a sentence or a story itself.

The great sadness in James M. Cain's early novels lies in the unrequited wish "to start out with her again clean." In *Postman*, Frank wants this with Cora, just as Walter knows it will never be accomplished with Phyllis. Frank and

Cora go out swimming, after being married at City Hall, further out than they have ever been before. Cora is pregnant, and strains herself. "I hurried," Frank tells us, and "when you hurry in the water you're sunk." He also hurries in the car, on the drive to the hospital, there is a crash, and Cora "was dead." The real wish here is for the age-old revenge against "time and its 'it was,'" as Nietzsche puts it. Behind the hurtling quality of Cain's plot and style lies not a love of speed but the impossible, Gatsby-like counter-motion and hope of having all the "no-account stuff ... pressed out and washed off," the regressive American desire to undo history and to get back "to a certain starting place," a moment before it all went wrong, before we became ourselves.[24]

John Fante writes with a barrio awareness of the "others" left out of the LA novel of speed. His four-novel Arturo Bandini cycle presents a challenge to historical criticism, however, since only two of the novels, *Wait until Spring, Bandini* (1938) and *Ask the Dust* (1939), were published in the 1930s. After a mention by Charles Bukowski revived his reputation in the 1970s, Fante, who died in 1983, would not live to see the publication of *The Road to Los Angeles* (1985), a book he had completed in 1933, or the final novel in the sequence, *Dreams from Bunker Hill* (1985), dictated by a dying Fante to his wife from his hospital bed.

Fante slows things down. Arturo Bandini, a down-and-out poet living in a hotel room on Bunker Hill, is going nowhere fast. He has "nothing to do." So he begins ambling, down the hill on Olive, past the Philharmonic, over to the Biltmore. "Then a great deal of time" passes as he stands in front of a pipe shop and imagines himself "as a great author." Bandini is Los Angeles' first flaneur, a walker in the city, a wannabe who lives in a perpetual state of yearning, in a "time of dream and reverie."[25]

Bandini's reveries are less interesting than the milieu he inhabits. His wanderings remind us that while Los Angeles might have appeared to be "a predominantly white city" in the middle 1920s, it had also long been home to a mélange of immigrant groups.[26] The Mexican Revolution of 1910 and the rising demand for cheap agricultural labor lifted the Mexican-born population of the city to 368,000 by 1930. When the Depression hit, this population had become so large, and the tax base had fallen so low, that federal officials began a plan of "repatriation," shipping out boxcars of Mexicans on a one-way ticket south. They just disappeared, like Camilla Lopez.

Camilla is Fante's most compelling creation. "Oh for a Mexican girl!" Arturo exclaims to himself, but when he meets Camilla in the saloon, and takes in her "Mayan" nose and her "dark but not black" skin, he imagines her to be laughing at him, and so sneers preemptively back. Not liking his coffee, he insults Camilla's shoes. "I hate you," she replies. He puts five cents on the table, spills the coffee over it, and walks out.[27]

Thus begins one of the strangest love affairs in American fiction. Camilla and Arturo do little but insult each other. They make a date, and then he calls her "a filthy little Greaser." He will claim to love her, but never sleep with her. "Where was the desire and the passion?" he will ask himself, as he fails to connect. Camilla can only be possessed by way of a surrogate, the strange woman who turns up out of nowhere and who offers Arturo "all of California" by way of her body, a replaying of the primal conquest in which she plays "Princess Camilla" and he plays Cortez.[28]

"I'm like Cortez," Arturo agrees, "only I'm an Italian." Camilla's unreality for Arturo has to do with the anxiety he experiences as an Italian American positioned between the white and the brown worlds. Why does Arturo take special umbrage at being mistaken for a Mexican by the hotel clerk? Because of the abjection to which Mexicans were made to submit, an ongoing humiliation they live out in their original homeland of California and a condition which Arturo chooses to inflict rather than to suffer. "Camilla's people had had their chance. They had failed. We Americans had turned the trick."[29] "We Americans," Arturo says, but he does not really believe himself to be a part of the "we."

Arturo's romantic confusion over Camilla, his mingled feelings of longing and contempt, express the arbitrariness of racism, especially when inflected by the narcissism of small differences. He knows himself to be a part of Los Angeles' rich and complex nonwhite otherworld, yet he longs, also, to be an "American." He wants to be one of "the new Californians," one of the old folks from Kansas or Des Moines in their bright polo shirts and sunglasses. "But down on Main Street," he knows, is where he belongs, down with "the tens of thousands of others" who cannot afford sunglasses. The racial "hurt" "drove me to books," he admits, and the rage at being forever associated with those who have "dust" on their shoes makes his books bitter.[30] He thus proceeds to act out the continual acts of exclusion by way of which California attempted to purge itself and to remain, as Lynwood liked to be called, a "friendly Caucasian city."

Camilla simply disappears, diffuses back into the dust the way Toni Morrison's Beloved vanishes back into air and water. She leaves "no sign."[31] But the lost brown or black or yellow Californian survives as an ineradicable trace, turning up in such unlikely scenes as in the opening drive in Aldous Huxley's *After Many a Summer Dies the Swan* (1939), where "the first thing to present itself was a slum of Africans and Filipinos, Japanese and Mexicans."[32] Angelenos of color even surface in the novel of speed. In Richard Hallas's *You Play the Black and the Red Comes Up* (1938), Dick Dempsey blows into town the way Frank does into Nick and Cora's tavern; sick of moving and yet wedded to motion, he has "nothing to do but move on somewhere." Hallas's novel has all the noir trappings: the knowing drifter, the promise of westering, the casual greed, the friendly film director, the misplaced guilt, and the inchoate, unfulfillable desire. But it also stays in touch with the non-starring characters who do the work of the place.[33]

All was not commercial exploitation or desperate yearning. Many Angelenos did live in houses and neighborhoods about which they cared, and in which they found some version of happiness. "Somewhere near the heart of the LA ethos," Jan Morris wrote in the 1970s, "there lies, unexpectedly, a layer of solid, old-fashioned, plain hard work. This is a city of hard workers."[34] It became so by the 1930s. The original economy had been founded on tourism, retirement, real estate – and agriculture. Well into the 1950s, Los Angeles County would remain the most productive agricultural county in the nation. Oil had been a significant industry in the Southland since the early 1890s. Douglas Aircraft was incorporated in Santa Monica in 1920; by the middle of the next decade it was pumping out hundreds of DC-3s. San Pedro grew into the busiest port on the West coast by 1930. In the years before World War II, Los Angeles became home to the largest stockyards in the eleven Western states, the nation's number one oil refinery complex, and its second largest tire factory. Movies remained a central industry, and one that for most of the people involved required some physical work.

Yet who works in Los Angeles fiction? "Around quitting time," *The Day of the Locust* begins, and most of the salient writing about life in the city takes place after work is finished.[35] The detective novel proves an exception. "I'm selling what I have to sell to make a living," Marlowe tells a police captain, and what he sells is himself, and his time. In the middle of kissing Vivien Sternwood, he breaks off to question her about Eddie Mars. When she protests, he replies that he is a detective. "I work at it, lady, I don't play at it."[36] In refusing to allow himself to be distracted from work by play – especially by love – Marlowe is somehow never *not* working, and so stands in for all those hard workers in the city whose lives escape representation.

After the 1987 movie *Barfly*, Charles Bukowski may be thought of by many as Los Angeles' most distinguished bum. But his self-character, Henry Chinaski, actually works very hard at two things: drinking and writing. "What mattered was drinking and sitting at the machine." Bukowski's career wrestles with the ever-present danger of being drawn into a "productive" and a mundane job, like the one he himself held at the Post Office from 1958 to 1969. What most people call "work," Bukowski judges to be a "ritual of misdirected energy."[37] So he leaves in order to write his first novel, *Post Office* (1971), which he finished in three weeks. The book becomes the cry of its occasion, dramatizing Chinaski's struggle to replace killing labor with expressive work, and ends not with the act of quitting the Post Office but with a further resolve: "Maybe I'll write a novel, I thought. And then I did."[38]

From this point on, Bukowski's industry never faltered. He produced five more novels, four collections of short stories, a score of essays, and so many poems in small magazines and with his great supporter, Black Sparrow Press, that their number is difficult even to count. Bukowski's career thus testifies to his will to "make it through creation" and to one man's dedication to the privilege of making art.[39]

The narrator of *City of Night* (1963) works as hard at hustling as Henry Chinaski does at drinking. If Bukowski sings the praises of martinis at Musso and Frank, John Rechy is the poet of "Los gay Angeles" as it swirls around Pershing Square. Fueled by a "one-way desire," his half-Mexican narrator flees El Paso and undertakes his "rebellion against an innocence which nothing in the world justified." And so he descends into an almost anthropological trawling through the homosexual cultures of the night in New York, New Orleans, and, above all, Los Angeles. Southern California offers him a cornucopia of options – "coffin," "sanatorium," "last stop." "The invitation to rot obliviously, to die without feeling it, to grow old looking young, is everywhere in this glorious, sunny, many-colored city." Like Fitzgerald, Rechy extends considerable empathy toward the dreamers of the golden dream, and, both men know that every rise is followed by a fall: "Immediately, you're disappointed," Rechy writes. This is the fruit of seeking to be "envied and desired," a task Rechy's hustler judges to be not only "narcissistic" but circular, which is why the pages about his time in Southern California end with his clipping the same man he encounters on his "first afternoon in Los Angeles."[40]

Nathanael West's Midwesterners "come to California to die," become bored, and turn to violence. They come for the "sunshine and oranges" and discover that they have "been tricked."[41] *The Day of the Locust* (1939) is a story of anger at false promises. As McWilliams points out, "the utopian mentality, so vividly described by West, is a national, not a local phenomenon." West's disillusioned sunseekers mark the end of the line for the Gatsby myth of self-making, a myth at once generated and undermined by a culture of advertising. Los Angeles has been thoroughly "sold" to them: the city's response to the collapse of the 1880s boom was to launch its Chamber of Commerce, an entity that had within ten years made Los Angeles "the best advertised city in America."[42] Near the end of *The Great Gatsby* (1925), George Wilson looks out his window at the billboard of Dr. T. J. Eckleburg and says, "God sees everything." "That's an advertisement," a friend responds. But Wilson would be right. Wilson and West's migrants no longer live under God's gaze but the billboard's – by the late 1930s advertising has come to see "everything" and to determine the content of human wants. West's characters prove as a result largely "mechanical" in their behavior, having ceded agency to the desire- and dream-producing machines of Madison Avenue and Hollywood.[43]

As for West's rage over the deceptiveness of surfaces in Los Angeles, all that imagination tied up in reproductions of "Mexican ranch houses, Samoan huts, Mediterranean villas, Egyptian and Japanese temples," he has again identified a tendency as national as it is local, the love of false fronts Joan Didion locates in the mansions of Newport and Fitzgerald in those of Long Island.[44] The quest for instant identity and the wish to pass as something one is not was surely an American instinct before it was a Californian one. And West's take on the movie industry is anticipated in *Queer People*, where the Grahams, too, imagine a world in which people meet and fall into careers "in an awful hurry." Whitney White actually goes to work in the movies, and gets caught up in the major industrial trauma of the period, the switch from silent to sound pictures in the late 1920s. People "suddenly found themselves" in or out, caught in a shift of "centrifugal force." The problem became one of synchronization, not only of sound with image but of one's talent with the emerging paradigm. "One could no more control the future than one could control the winds that whistle through Cahuenga Pass." The movie business chews up people and blows them away; Hollywood, too, is dominated by forces, not men. *Queer People* even anticipates *The Day of the Locust* by staging its final scene in front of Grauman's Chinese Theater.[45]

West is perhaps Los Angeles' most distinguished debunker, but a taste for debunking depends upon one's feel for locality. New to Los Angeles, James M. Cain wrote an essay for *The American Mercury* called "Paradise." Southern California boasted many good things, he admitted: friendly and courteous people, excellent spoken English, a reading public, superb roads, the country's best schools. Yet he could not get past a sense that "life takes on a dreadful vacuity here." Angelenos needed to get beyond their "piddling occupations"; what was needed was some "great, slashing industries."[46] A year later, he proposed an "aesthetic history of America" that would convey "a much more vivid appreciation of what we do well and what we do badly."[47] *Mildred Pierce* (1941) provides such a history and an adequate image of the hard-working place he had come to call home and the people who manage to live well there. In fully realizing a way of life lived in its locality, it also becomes a classic of American literature.

What we do well, it turns out, is entrepreneurship and home ownership. The two poles of Mildred's experience are the workplace and the self-owned house. In locating the action in these two locales, Cain responds to the fact of Los Angeles as a cityscape comprised largely of freestanding, single-family, and sometimes owner-built homes, as well as an economy in which the invitation to dream encourages a venture as chancy as Mildred's Chicken and Waffle restaurant.

Cain locates his story in Glendale, an upscale independent city seven miles north of downtown Los Angeles that in 1925 proclaimed itself the "Fastest-Growing City in America." Herbert Pierce is a contractor who "built this very home that he now occupied."[48] But the self-built house was even more typical of working-class suburbs and of a population that experienced homes as "sites of production." Lots in South Gate and in the adjoining community of Watts were often large enough to accommodate a vegetable garden, poultry coops, or fruit trees. "Rural and urban rhythms blurred" in such places; visiting my grandmother in Compton, in the early 1960s, I remember nearby fields where we picked sweet corn. Factories were also part of the landscape; people in South Los Angeles found good jobs with General Motors, Firestone, and Purex. South Gate became the "Detroit of the Coast," producing an ethic of "self-reliance, independence, Americanism, familism, and racial separation."[49] There is no LA novel about the lives of such people; the book that comes closest to them is *Mildred Pierce*. And there is nothing dishonest in Cain's restricting his vision to a world that is middle-class, aspiring, and white, since this is the context in which many people, during these years in Los Angeles, actually lived.

In *Mildred Pierce*, Cain also slows things down. His heroine is not "fast"; she is deliberate. Gifted at self-survey, Mildred responds to loss by being tactical: "She must take stock," she thinks to herself after divorcing Bert, "see what she had to offer against what lay ahead." She takes a systemic view and refrains from reducing her story to a matter of individual self-fashioning. Challenged by her mother-in-law to explain the breakup of her marriage, Mildred makes a careful answer. "I don't say it was *anybody's* fault, unless it was the Depression's fault." Refusing reductive "interpretations of life," she remains warily positioned between the awareness of being determined and the hope of being free.[50]

Mildred clings to her gentility and at first resists becoming a waitress, but she needs "some work she could get." She goes on to learn the restaurant business, and she decides to start her own. Cain's achievement in these pages is to make us feel the excitement of entrepreneurship and to appreciate the attentiveness required to succeed at it. Late in the novel, on the night her daughter Veda sings at the Hollywood Bowl, Cain will write of "the climax of Mildred's life." But the true climax comes earlier, on the day Mildred opens her restaurant and settles down "to what she really liked, which was cooking."[51] Cain proceeds to reveal the sublimity of the ordinary, the sheer pride and satisfaction that can be taken in the proper cutting up of a chicken.

Not many California novels imagine the possibility of living well; the imagination of the region is often haunted by standards long set elsewhere. Mildred learns to live well because she declines the extremes of either a utopian or a dystopian view. For her, Los Angeles is neither the Emerald City nor the Great Wrong Place, but a house and a job and even sometimes a husband – in Glendale.

NOTES

1. Mary Craig Sinclair, *Southern Belle* (Phoenix: Sinclair Press, 1957), p. 302.
2. Upton Sinclair, *Oil!* (New York: Penguin, 2008), pp. 1, 82.
3. *Ibid.*, pp. 276, 134, 302.
4. Frank Norris, "The Mechanics of Fiction" (1901), in *Norris: Novels and Essays* (New York: Library of America, 1986), pp. 1161, 1163.
5. Raymond Chandler, *The Big Sleep*, in *Stories and Early Novels* (New York: Library of America, 1995), p. 603.
6. Mark Lee Luther, *The Boosters* (Indianapolis: Bobbs-Merrill, 1923), p. 21.
7. Sinclair, *Oil!*, p. 143.
8. Roger W. Lotchin, *Fortress California, 1910–1961: From Warfare to Welfare* (New York: Oxford University Press, 1992), pp. 68–9.
9. Theodore S. Van Dyke, *Millionaires of a Day: An Inside Story of the Great Southern California "Boom"* (New York: Fords, Howard & Hulbert, 1890), p. 97.
10. Carey McWilliams, *Southern California Country: An Island on the Land*, American Folkways (New York: Duell, Sloan & Pearce, 1946), p. 121.
11. *Ibid.*, p. 135.
12. Sinclair, *Oil!*, p. 21.
13. James M. Cain, *The Postman Always Rings Twice*, in *Crime Novels: American Noir of the 1930s and 40s*, ed. Robert Polito (New York: Library of America, 1997), p. 68.
14. Horace McCoy, *They Shoot Horses, Don't They?*, in *Crime Novels*, ed. Polito, pp. 118, 113, 210.
15. James M. Cain, *Postman*, pp. 3, 14.
16. *Ibid.*, p. 23.
17. Henry David Thoreau, *Walden; or, Life in the Woods*, in *Thoreau: A Week, Walden, Maine Woods, Cape Cod* (New York: Library of America, 1985), p. 429.
18. James M. Cain, *Postman*, p. 94.
19. *Ibid*, p. 31.
20. Frank MacShane, *The Letters of Raymond Chandler* (New York: Columbia University Press, 1981), p. 28.
21. Roy Hoopes, *Cain* (New York: Holt, Rinehart & Winston, 1982), p. 245.
22. Carroll and Garrett Graham, *Queer People* (Carbondale: Southern Illinois University Press, 1976), p. 9.
23. Paul Cain, *Fast One* (Carbondale: Southern Illinois University Press, 1978), pp. 308, 119–20, 311.
24. James M. Cain, *Postman*, pp. 119, 120, 121, 91.
25. John Fante, *Ask the Dust* (New York: HarperCollins, 2006), pp. 11, 13, 15.

26. Kevin Starr, *Material Dreams: Southern California through the 1920s* (New York: Oxford University Press, 1990), p. 120.
27. Fante, *Ask the Dust*, pp. 15, 34–5, 37.
28. *Ibid.*, pp. 44, 124, 94.
29. *Ibid.*, pp. 94, 44.
30. *Ibid.*, pp. 45, 46, 40.
31. *Ibid.*, p. 162.
32. Aldous Huxley, *After Many a Summer Dies the Swan* (Chicago: Ivan R. Dee, 1993), p. 5.
33. Richard Hallas, *You Play the Black and the Red Comes Up* (Pittsburgh: Carnegie-Mellon University Press, 1986), p. 18.
34. Jan Morris, "Los Angeles: The Know-How City" (1976), in *Writing Los Angeles: A Literary Anthology*, ed. David L. Ulin (New York: Library of America, 2002), p. 601.
35. Nathanael West, *The Day of the Locust*, in *West: Novels and Other Writings* (New York: Library of America, 1997), p. 241.
36. Chandler, *The Big Sleep*, pp. 674, 703.
37. Charles Bukowski, *Run with the Hunted: A Charles Bukowski Reader*, ed. John Martin (New York: Ecco, 2003), pp. 432, 323.
38. Bukowski, *Post Office* (Los Angeles: Black Sparrow Press, 1971), p. 196.
39. Bukowski, *Run with the Hunted*, p. 323.
40. John Rechy, *City of Night* (New York: Grove Press, 1963), pp. 95, 54, 55, 87, 60, 178.
41. West, *Day of the Locust*, pp. 242, 380.
42. McWilliams, *Southern California Country*, pp. 310, 129.
43. F. Scott Fitzgerald *The Great Gatsby* (New York: Scribner, 1995), p. 167; West, *Day of the Locust*, p. 92.
44. West, *Day of the Locust*, p. 243.
45. Graham, *Queer People*, pp. 46, 194, 214, 194–5.
46. James M. Cain, "Paradise" (1933), in *Writing Los Angeles*, ed. Ulin, pp. 117, 122, 124.
47. Hoopes, *Cain*, p. 262.
48. James M. Cain, *Mildred Pierce* (New York: Random House, 1989), p. 9.
49. Becky M. Nicolaides, *My Blue Heaven: Life and Politics in the Working-Class Suburbs of Los Angeles, 1920–1965* (Chicago: University of Chicago Press, 2002), pp. 3, 38, 5.
50. James M. Cain, *Mildred Pierce*, pp. 28, 29, 18, 37.
51. *Ibid.*, pp. 39, 278, 137.

4

RUSSELL A. BERMAN

British expatriates and German exiles in 1930s–1940s Los Angeles

The growth of Hollywood attracted writers from around the world, soon joined by the wave of refugees fleeing Hitler. The cosmopolitan colonies of British expatriates and German (and Austrian) exiles made noteworthy contributions to the literary representation of Los Angeles, often placing the urban space of their new home in relation to the memory of their cultures of origin.

Prominent British novelist Aldous Huxley's first impression of Los Angeles in 1926 was negative: "thought is barred in this City of Dreadful Joy and conversation is unknown."[1] Yet returning in 1937 on a speaking tour with the historian and philosopher Gerald Heard, he responded well enough to settle in Hollywood, before moving to Llano in 1940. The anxieties set out earlier in his famous dystopia, *Brave New World* (1932), evolved in his later writing, combining biology and science with Indian spirituality, meditation, and drug use. In Los Angeles, European culture found Asian religion: Huxley met proponents of expanded spiritual consciousness such as Jiddu Krishnamurti (who had moved to Ojai in 1922) as well as Swami Prabhavananda, founder of the Vedanta Society of Southern California (1930).

After Many a Summer Dies the Swan (1939), the first of Huxley's five novels from his LA years, opens with an abrupt encounter between Europe and America, as Jeremy Pordage, an Englishman carrying a volume of Wordsworth, arrives to be greeted by "a coloured chauffeur in a grey uniform with a carnation in his button-hole." British literature faces Los Angeles with bemused irony tempered by condescension. "Anxiously he began to wonder whether, in this democratic Far West of theirs, one shook hands with the chauffeur – particularly if he happened to be a blackamoor, just to demonstrate that one wasn't a pukka sahib even if one's country did happen to be bearing the White Man's burden." Huxley has Pordage survey a Californian landscape of crass commercialism and bizarre spirituality, before meeting his new employer, the plutocrat Jo Stoyte, whose enormous mansion invokes

William Randolph Hearst's San Simeon, here transported to the San Fernando Valley. Stoyte collects great works of art to furnish this grotesque residence – a Vermeer hangs in the elevator – and embodies, for Pordage, the commercial barbarism of the United States. In a letter to his mother in England, Pordage reports how Stoyte intentionally singles him out for disrespect "because I happen to have read more books than the rest and am therefore more of a symbol of Culture. And Culture, of course, is a thing for which he has positively a Tartar's hatred. Only, unlike the Tartars, he doesn't want to burn the monuments of Culture, he wants to buy them up."[2]

While most of the novel takes place at Stoyte's castle, Huxley's Los Angeles includes, in addition to the cameo appearances of the black chauffeur and the Chinese cook, a gripping treatment of the poverty of migrant agricultural workers whom Stoyte is eager to abuse. Stoyte's neighbor and long-time adversary, Mr. Propter, serves as Huxley's philosophical mouthpiece for various agendas: social reform (especially care for the migrants), utopian technologies (including solar power), and mystic spirituality. Dr. Mulge, president of the local Tarzana College (modeled on Occidental College), benefits from Stoyte's philanthropy, as does Dr. Obispo, Stoyte's personal physician, whose research involves that most Californian of themes, the search for eternal youth. Obispo's assistant, Pete Boone, is the wholesome young American, an idealist veteran of the Spanish Civil War, and hopelessly in love with Stoyte's mistress, who has eyes and affection only for Dr. Obispo. Deriding her erotic aura sarcastically as "exquisitely spiritual and Pre-Raphaelitish," Pordage characteristically deploys a rhetoric of contrast between high European norms and the putative insufficiency of American popular culture: "A Pre-Raphaelitish expression demands Pre-Raphaelite clothes... When you see [her], as I did today, in combination with white shorts, a bandana and a cowboy hat, you're disturbed, you're all put out."[3]

Yet Huxley undermines the credibility of Pordage's judgments. Stoyte has brought Pordage to Los Angeles to edit the records of an impoverished aristocratic British family. The archive, which seems at first to be one of the baubles hoarded by American wealth, includes the memoir of an ancestor's search for biological immortality, presented as an artifact of eighteenth-century Enlightenment mentalities. Stoyte's own obsessive pursuit of youth, which Pordage incorporates into his condemnation of the American West, turns out to draw on a tradition – so we learn from the documents – that leads back to England, and this unsettles Pordage's too comfortable contrast between Old World and New: California youth culture draws on very Old-World traditions. Far from endorsing the denunciation of Los Angeles as barbarian, Huxley – not unlike the German exile philosophers Max

Horkheimer and Theodor Adorno – uncovers a dialectic in the Enlightenment which finds its starkest expression in his new home.

Evelyn Waugh served in the British army during World War II. His *Put Out More Flags* (1942) attacked Christopher Isherwood and W. H. Auden for emigrating to the United States during wartime. The success of *Brideshead Revisited* (1945) brought Waugh to Hollywood in 1947 to explore a film version; those negotiations failed, but the visit led to his satirical short novel, *The Loved One: An Anglo-American Tragedy*. When an aging British writer and expatriate finds his contract with a film studio terminated, he commits suicide, and the novel explores the grotesque extremes of funeral culture, particularly at "Whispering Glades," modeled on the Forest Lawn Memorial Park in Glendale.[4] Waugh interweaves three major themes. As a visitor but not a resident of Los Angeles, he treats the British colony with derision. The central figure, Dennis Barlow, is an unsuccessful and unproductive British poet who fraudulently woos an American naive by plagiarizing the best of English verse; a failure and a fraud, he embodies Waugh's harsh judgment on the émigrés. In addition, Waugh conveys contempt for the crassness he imputes to American culture, the combination of cost and cosmetics in the funeral practices; in this, he comes close to Huxley's description of Forest Lawn in *After Many a Summer Dies the Swan*. Yet while Huxley subverts Pordage's derision of American culture through a transatlantic parallel, Waugh treats the United States as caustically as he does the misguided British who have chosen to settle here. Finally Waugh, a convert to Catholicism who took religious topics very seriously, is suspicious of American spirituality: "Liturgy in Hollywood is the concern of the Stage not the Clergy." Waugh displays discomfort with American secularism as well as with the religious diversity of Los Angeles: he parodies the fascination for Indian mysticism by naming the local advice for the lovelorn column "The Wisdom of the Guru Brahmin," and his designating a Hollywood business meeting as "the Grand Sanhedrin of the Corporation" adds an anti-Semitic element to the already pejorative account of the film industry.[5]

Isherwood arrived in Los Angeles in the late thirties, just as his novel *Goodbye to Berlin* (1939) appeared; it built on his years in Germany and later became the basis of the musical and film *Cabaret*. His first American novel, *Prater Violet* (1945) recounts his collaboration in London in the 1930s with the Viennese director Berthold Viertel. Viertel had already settled in Los Angeles in 1928 with his wife Salka, and their home later served as a center of the German and Austrian exile community during the thirties and forties. (One of their sons, Peter Viertel, authored the novel *White Hunter Black Heart*, a fictionalized account of the filming of *The African Queen*; in 1960 he married the British actress Deborah Kerr.) With his own background in Berlin of the 1920s, Isherwood exemplifies the international environment in which British expatriates and German exiles mingled in and around Hollywood.

Isherwood's next novel, *The World in the Evening* (1954), opens in a dystopic LA setting at a party in 1941:

> high up on the slopes of the Hollywood hills, in a ranch-style home complete with Early American maple, nautical brasswork and muslin curtains: just too cute for words. It looked as if it had been delivered, already equipped, from a store; and you could imagine how, if the payments weren't kept up, some men might arrive one day and take the whole place back there on a truck.[6]

The description presents a familiar European Los Angeles: bad taste, inauthenticity, and economic insecurity amidst fantastic opulence. The event is a social gathering for the film industry, against the backdrop of "the enormous cheap-gaudy nightscape of Los Angeles which sparkled away out to the horizon like a million cut-rate engagements rings." The landscape is a metaphor for the culture. The first-person narrator continues the negativism of his diatribe: "God curse this antiseptic, heartless, hateful neon mirage of a city! May its swimming pools be dried up. May all its lights go out for ever. I drew a deep dizzying breath in which the perfume of star jasmine was mixed with chlorine."[7]

Yet Isherwood – unlike Waugh – made Los Angeles his home, and his judgment matured. During the 1950s and early 1960s, he taught courses in creative writing at Los Angeles State College (now California State University, Los Angeles), and in 1964 he collaborated on the screenplay for *The Loved One*. Also in 1964 *A Single Man* appeared, a novelistic account of a day in the life of the main figure, George, a fifty-eight-year-old expatriate professor of English, whose gay American lover has recently died in a car accident. The narrative carefully integrates complex ideas into a subdued existentialist rhetoric: the phenomenology of the body, consciousness and subjectivity, homoerotic desire, death and mourning, and the expatriate experience. Between morning and night, George's itinerary leads through the urban space of Los Angeles, through distinct neighborhoods and archeological layers in the history of the city, often in terms of a nostalgia for a lost past, as the narrative of personal mourning colors the account of the journey.

George resides in a small house in a community not far from the Pacific, once a haven for bohemian outsiders, "pioneer escapists from dingy downtown Los Angeles and stuffy-snobbish Pasadena" who "saw themselves as rear-guard individualists, making a last-ditch stand against the twentieth century." However these hardy nonconformists gave way in the late 1940s to the masses of veterans and their new brides "in search of new and better breeding grounds in the sunny Southland ... So, one by one, the cottages which used to reek of bathtub gin and reverberate with the poetry of Hart Crane have fallen to the occupying army of Coke-drinking television watchers." Just as he identifies the original scene of the baby boom and the cultural conformism of the 1950s, Isherwood also takes us to the setting where, within a few years, the wave of student protests would erupt: the anonymous alienation of the mass university system, where George teaches: "A clean modern factory, brick and glass and big windows, already three-quarters built, is being finished in a hysterical hurry... When the factory is fully operational, it will be able to process twenty thousand graduates. But, in less than ten years, it will have to cope with forty or fifty thousand."[8] Despite the cultural conformism, George has a loyal following of intellectual and artistic students; on this day, he delivers a lecture on Huxley's *After Many a Summer*, an indication of the tight intellectual and intertextual network within the expatriate group.

Between the beach and the campus, we also catch a glimpse of minority Los Angeles, "the tacky sleepy slowpoke Los Angeles of the thirties, still convalescent from the depression, with no money to spare for fresh coats of paint ... Mexicans live here, so there are lots of flowers. Negroes live here, so it is cheerful." For Isherwood this romantic poverty provides an alternative to the antiseptic modernization that he sees devastating the city. Meanwhile the Japanese-American experience generates an additional outsider perspective and enhanced cultural criticism: because of her wartime internment, one of George's female students refuses to consider marrying a Caucasian and, as her white boyfriend reports, "'She says she can't take people in this country seriously. She doesn't feel anything we do here *means* anything. She wants to go back to Japan and teach... She says the Negroes were the only ones who acted decently to them [during the internment]. And a few pacifists.'" While Huxley interrogated the credibility of Pordage's British condescension toward American culture, Isherwood uncovers a critical standpoint within the United States of minorities and dissidents, who face the threats of a mass society that persecutes difference through "annihilation by blandness." Yet his judgment remains complex: for all his criticism of Los Angeles as the epitome of conformism, he denounces the elitism of European denigration of the United States. Similarly, while he complains about smog, "the sick yellow fumes which arise from the metropolitan mass below" the campus, he also conveys an enthusiasm for automobile culture: "George feels a kind of patriotism for the freeways."[9] Despite critical perspectives, *A Single Man* displays an underlying affection for Los Angeles, in the multiplicity of its spaces, which Isherwood eagerly defends against a process of impoverishing homogenization.

Like the British writers, the German exile authors evaluated Los Angeles in relationship to their memories of Europe. Yet while Huxley and Isherwood had chosen freely to come to California – and they faced harsh denunciations in England for having abandoned their homeland as it faced the violence of the Luftwaffe – the Germans who arrived after 1933 had been forced to flee Hitler, whether because they were Jewish or because of their political beliefs. Nearly all of the prominent intellectuals and writers in the colony were refugees, so the political questions of Nazism and the future of Germany constantly drew their attention back across the Atlantic, which explains why their works dwell much more on German topics than on accounts of life in the Southland. (One should not forget, however, that some Germans had immigrated to Hollywood during the twenties, long before the Nazi threat became clear; nor should one overlook the presence of pro-Nazi sympathies in other parts of the German-American community in Southern California and elsewhere.)[10]

The public face of the German exiles was the novelist Thomas Mann, 1929 Nobel laureate, who first arrived in the United States in 1939 and taught at Princeton before moving to Pacific Palisades in 1942. Although he became a citizen in 1944, American topics, let alone California, are absent from his fiction. His major work in this period was *Doctor Faustus* (1947), an allegory of German culture and modern art, although it does build in part on material borrowed from a fellow LA exile, the composer Arnold Schoenberg, and a fictional German-American musician, albeit from Pennsylvania, figures prominently in a crucial episode. Still, in response to a plea to return to postwar Germany, Mann affirmed an implicitly Californian allegiance:

> I am now an American citizen… My children, including two sons who are now serving in the American army, are rooted here, and English-speaking grandchildren are growing up around me… I have built my house on this magnificent coast, full of the future, and I want to finish my life's work in its protection – taking part in its power, reason, prosperity and peace.[11]

He appreciated the democratic culture, praising as progressive what other Europeans demeaned as conformism: "The whole world smokes the same cigarettes, eats the same ice cream, sees the same movies, hears the same music on the radio; even the difference in clothing is disappearing more and more, and the college student who earns his way through college, which would have been very much beneath his class dignity in Europe, is here a commonplace."[12]

For the passages dealing with music theory in *Doctor Faustus*, Mann relied on the advice of another member of the exile group, the philosopher and sociologist Theodor Adorno, who, collaborating with Max Horkheimer, co-authored *The Dialectic of Enlightenment* (1944), the central text in the tradition of social criticism that came to be known as the Frankfurt School.

Others in the group, like Leo Lowenthal and Herbert Marcuse, would pursue academic careers in the United States, while Horkheimer and Adorno would return to Frankfurt after the war. None of their writing is, strictly speaking, literary, except for Adorno's cultivation of the essay as form with his distinctively stylized prose. He devotes considerable attention to the commercialization or, in his Marxist terminology, commodification of culture, especially in popular forms, such as film. He and Horkheimer approached the "culture industry," as they labeled it, with skepticism and developed an argument which, in its strongest form, suggested a parallel between the conformism purveyed by Hollywood and the techniques of domination in Nazi Germany. Their predisposition as exile writers to compare the homeland and the host country combines with the constant anxiety of the period: Can it happen here? Are there tendencies in the United States that might lead to an outcome similar to Nazi Germany? *Dialectic of Enlightenment* implies an ominous answer; in his collection of philosophical aphorisms, *Minima Moralia: Reflections on a Damaged Life* (1951) Adorno's perspective is similarly pessimistic but focused more on a gradual evisceration of experience, comparable to Isherwood's diagnosis in *A Single Man*, rather than a prediction of imminent political catastrophes. In his later years, his reminiscences of the United States often included positive aspects of democratic culture, such as inclinations toward fairness and equality, which he emphasized as a retort to the cultural anti-Americanism current in intellectual circles in Europe during the sixties.

Among the German exiles, Bertolt Brecht provided the most literary – and negative – accounts of Los Angeles. The acclaimed playwright arrived on July 1, 1941, by ship from Vladivostok to San Pedro. Settling in Santa Monica, he spent productive years working on screenplays – including Fritz Lang's anti-Nazi film, *Hangmen Also Die* (1943) – completing one of his most important plays, *The Good Person of Szechwan* (1943) and an adaption of *Galileo* in collaboration with Charles Laughton (1945), while also producing a large corpus of poetry. Although most of the poems involve reflections on the war and developments in Germany, a significant group addresses Los Angeles directly, as do his *Journals* from the period. The entry of August 1, 1941, a month after his arrival, joins a critique of aesthetic appearance with a complaint about the tough conditions of American capitalism: "almost nowhere has my life ever been harder than here in this mausoleum of *easy going*. the house is too pretty, and here my profession is gold-digging, the lucky ones pan big nuggets the size of your fists out of the mud and people talk about them for a while." Brecht transports the ur-Californian gold rush imagery into the metropolis of business. His status as refugee becomes the basis for a cultural criticism of Southern California, even its landscape, as in the entry of August 9:

i feel as if i had been exiled from our era, this is tahiti in the form of a big city ... they have nature here, indeed, since everything is so artificial, they even have an exaggerated feeling for nature, which becomes alienated. from [Wilhelm] diet- erle's house you can see the san fernando valley; an incessant, brilliantly illumi- nated stream of cars thunders through nature; but they tell you that all the greenery is wrested from the desert by irrigation systems. scratch the surface a little and the desert shows through.[13]

While the *Journals* also include Brecht's reports on the Japanese internments, the focus is never primarily on Los Angeles or California; instead he reports on the internal life of the German community, his own work, and the war news from Europe.

In his poetry, Brecht presents Los Angeles as a melancholy landscape; its inadequacies evoke sad reflections rather than the emphatic derision of Waugh. "Landscape of Exile" records the first impression:

> The oil derricks and the thirsty gardens of Los Angeles
> And the ravines of California at evening and the fruit market
> Did not leave the messenger of misfortune unmoved.[14]

The dialectic of industry (oil derricks) and nature (gardens), or of emptied nature (ravines) and the surfeit of the market, provide the scaffolding for Brecht's thinking, which comes to a head especially in "On Thinking about Hell." Recalling that his "brother Shelley" imagined Hell to be a lot like London, Brecht insists that "it must be / Still more like Los Angeles." Los Angeles is a venue of broken promises (like the films of the culture industry for Horkheimer and Adorno), "with great heaps of fruit," which nonetheless have neither "smell nor taste," and "houses, built for happy people, therefore standing empty / Even when lived in."[15] Brecht develops these themes in the "Hollywood Elegies," some of which Hans Eisler set to music in the *Hollywood Songbook*.

However, the Southland was not hellish for everyone. One of the most affirmative and most widely circulated representations of life in Los Angeles involved beaches and surfers. Its key literary source was Frederick Kohner's *Gidget* (1957). A Hitler-era refugee, Kohner captured the experiences of his fifteen-year-old daughter in the summer of 1956 when she learned to surf on the beach at Malibu. He juxtaposes the constraints a teenage girl felt in middle-class family life with the tempting freedom of the surfers against the backdrop of the beauty of the Pacific. Beneath the teen romance narrative, there is a touch of emancipation when Gidget recognizes that it was in the end her mastering the sport and her ability to "shoot the curl" that mattered more than the boys: "maybe I was just a woman in love with a surfboard."[16]

Yet beneath this optimism, *Gidget* conveys a worrisome note, the hallmark of exile writing, the return of the repressed past. Her parents, we learn, are immigrants (a feature fully erased from the 1959 film with Sandra Dee). References abound to Central Europe, but all light-hearted – vacations in the Alps and Austrian pastries. No reference is made to the circumstances under which the parents emigrated. Yet when the surfers celebrate one evening and sparks from their torches set the dry Southern Californian hillside on fire, the naive narrator refers to it twice as a "holocaust," a term incongruous in her teenager vocabulary but which has a long history as a designation of massacres of Jews.[17] The word choice surpasses Gidget's own consciousness and reveals the genocide as the otherwise unspoken subtext. The radiance of surfer culture, at least as generated by *Gidget*, bears mute testimony to the conflagrations from which the exile authors had escaped.

NOTES

I wish to thank Eric Messinger for his help researching this chapter.
1. Nicholas Murray, *Aldous Huxley: An English Intellectual* (London: Little, Brown, 2002), p. 182.
2. Aldous Huxley, *After Many a Summer Dies the Swan* (Chicago: Ivan R. Dee, 1993), pp. 3, 215.
3. *Ibid.*, pp. 214, 215.
4. Waugh's essay, "Death in Hollywood" (*Life*, Sept. 29, 1947, 73ff.), provides the germ of his critique.
5. Evelyn Waugh, *The Loved One: An Anglo-American Tragedy* (Boston: Little, Brown, 1950), pp. 62, 100, 26.
6. Christopher Isherwood, *The World in the Evening* (New York: Random House, 1954), p. 3.
7. *Ibid.*, p. 9.
8. Isherwood, *A Single Man* (New York: Simon and Schuster, 1964), pp. 17–18, 18, 42.
9. *Ibid.*, pp. 41, 168, 27, 47, 33.
10. See Erhard Bahr, *Weimar on the Pacific: German Exile Culture in Los Angeles and the Crisis of Modernism* (Berkeley: University of California Press, 2007), p. 5.
11. Thomas Mann, "Warum ich nicht nach Deutschland zurückgehe," in *Essays*, ed. Kermann Kurzke and Stephan Stachorski, 6 vols. (Frankfurt: S. Fischer, 1997), vol. VI, p. 36.
12. Mann, "The War and the Future," in *Thomas Mann's Addresses Delivered at the Library of Congress* (Rockville, Md.: Wildside Press, 2008), p. 40.
13. Bertolt Brecht, *Journals*, tr. Hugh Rorrison, ed. John Willet (London: Methuen, 1993), pp. 137, 139.
14. Brecht, "Landscape of Exile," in *Poems 1913–1956*, ed. John Willett and Ralph Manheim (New York: Routledge Books, 1987), p. 364.
15. Brecht, "On Thinking about Hell," in *Poems 1913–1956*, p. 367.
16. Frederick Kohner, *Gidget* (New York: Berkley Books, 2001), p. 154.
17. *Ibid.*, pp. 129, 131.

5

PATRICK O'DONNELL

Postwar Los Angeles: suburban Eden and the fall into history

I'd be safe and warm
If I was in L.A.

The Mamas and the Papas, "California Dreamin'"
(1965)

Driving over a hill into San Narciso, the LA suburb where she will begin her quest to execute the will of Pierce Inverarity, Oedipa Maas, the heroine of Thomas Pynchon's *The Crying of Lot 49* (1966), views the scene spread out before her:

> she looked down a slope ... onto a vast sprawl of houses which had grown up all together, like a well tended crop, from the dull brown earth; and she thought of the time she'd opened a transistor radio to replace a battery and seen her first printed circuit. The ordered swirl of houses and streets, from this high angle, sprang at her now with the same unexpected, astonishing clarity as the circuit card had. Though she knew even less about radios than about Southern Californians, there were to both outward patterns a hieroglyphic sense of concealed meaning, of an intent to communicate.[1]

The "circuit" of the suburban sprawl that Oedipa observes is remarkably similar to the "grids" of D. J. Waldie's *Holy Land: A Suburban Memoir* (1996), the seemingly endless proliferation of tract home developments in Southern California laid out in mathematically precise matrices that contain "an indefinite number of beginnings and endings" and are built "outward without limits ... the antithesis of a ghetto."[2] San Narciso's punning name is indicative of the voyeuristic narcissism to be found in the Southland's suburbs: mapped onto the real Southern California, Oedipa is conceivably coming over the Newhall Pass into the San Fernando Valley, home to Los Angeles' major television and movie studios and, since the 1970s, center of the US porn industry. "[L]ess an identifiable city than a grouping of concepts – census tracts, special purpose bond-issue districts, shopping nuclei, all overlaid with access roads to its own freeway,"[3] San Narciso is a place where, beneath the veneer of domestic order, lies a chaos of cross-hatched intentions, dreams gone wrong, and the concealed vestiges of power's machinations.

Such is the suburban Los Angeles described in Mike Davis's classic study, *City of Quartz* (1990), where LA suburbs with "scented brand-names like Fox Run, Mardi Gras, Bravo, Cambridge, Sunburst, New Horizon, and so on," represent the "repackage[d]" myth of the good life in "sites stripped bare of nature and history, masterplanned only for privatized family consumption." Pynchon envisioned San Narciso in the Cold War 1950s and 1960s, when sprawl in the San Fernando, San Gabriel, and San Bernardino valleys was commencing in earnest; Davis is commenting on the spread of the suburbs eastward to the high desert, northward to Santa Barbara and over the mountains toward Bakersfield, and southward through Orange and Riverside counties to San Diego in the 1990s. As Davis informs us, at the time he wrote *City of Quartz*, the LA region, "with a built-up surface area nearly the size of Ireland and a GNP bigger than India's" was "the fastest growing metropolis in the advanced industrialized world."[4] A patchwork of plans and populations, zoning and uncontrolled growth, the Los Angeles suburbs, for which San Narciso serves as a prescient fictional example, are a product of legislation such as the Serviceman's Readjustment Act of 1944, which allowed returning World War II veterans to obtain college degrees and buy homes inexpensively, and a military–industrial build-up commencing in the war-time 1940s that exploded with the implementation of Cold War MAD ("mutually assured destruction") policies that brought thousands of aerospace and defense industry jobs to Southern California. The fiction of the Los Angeles suburbs reflects the contradictions and fractures inherent in the suburban fantasies that flowered in the wake of war: secure domesticity built upon an economy fueled by the death-drive of the Cold War; here, racy mobility and the availability of anything, anywhere, anytime; there, grid-locked freeways and the class and racial prisons of Watts, Compton, Boyle Heights; both the New Eden and the site of final and complete expulsion of nature from culture; the "California" where, as Joan Didion viewed the San Bernardino Valley in 1966, "it is possible to live and die without ever eating an artichoke, without ever meeting a Catholic or a Jew ... the California where it is easy to Dial-A-Devotion, but hard to buy a book."[5] Much has changed on the surface since 1966, yet as the suburbs continue to proliferate in the California Southland, so does the foundational fantasy associated with establishing a home in paradise. In this chapter, I will explore the ways that California dreaming, as exemplified in the suburbs, has been portrayed in LA fiction of the last four decades. But first, an Arcadian interlude.

I grew up in the suburbs of Los Angeles during the 1950s and 1960s, and was something of a rare item in 1950s California: a full second-generation Angeleno (both of my parents were born and raised in Los Angeles). My father worked for the electrical sign industry, then booming as the need for signs advertising fast-food franchises and gas stations grew astronomically. My first suburban memories are associated with Baldwin Park, at that time primarily an enclave of white, lower-middle-class families, though there were Mexican-American families here and there (a childhood friend, Frankie Cisneros, was the son of a Mexican-born father and a mother from Liverpool). Located next to a series of ravines and gravel pits and bordered on the south by industrial parks, Baldwin Park is named after Elias Jackson "Lucky" Baldwin (1828–1909), who once owned 63,000 acres of prime real estate in Southern California now completely taken up by suburban housing communities.

One of these, Arcadia, was the next stop in my suburban journey. When I was ten, my upwardly mobile family moved to the (even) whiter, more arboreal, and more affluent realm named after the Peloponnesian district made famous in Virgil's *Eclogues* as a pastoral paradise. My adolescence was spent in this California setting where the higher one ascended into the San Gabriel foothills, the larger and more exclusive the houses became, a topographical gradation reflected in the social clans and hierarchies of the local high school. Arcadia is also where one comes upon, near city center and situated side by side, the Santa Anita Park racetrack that horse-racing fanatic Lucky Baldwin founded in the 1890s, and the Los Angeles County Arboretum, a 127-acre remnant of the Baldwin estate so convincingly exoticized with South American and African foliage that it has served as the location for dozens of "jungle" films from the original *Tarzan*s to the *Jurassic Park*s. My family home was located on the southwest border of the city, just a mile or so drive south through Azusa to El Monte, at that time a "mixed" lower-middle-class white and Latino suburb: as James Ellroy describes it in 1958, when the body of his murdered mother was found in a road running next to El Monte's Arroyo High School, "a shitkicker town and a good place to have fun. Recent settlers called it 'the City of Divorced Women' ... a honky-tonk place with a more-than-distinct western atmosphere" located in the southern San Gabriel Valley, "the rat's ass of Los Angeles County – a 30-mile stretch of contiguous hick towns due east of L.A. proper."[6]

Thus perched between the grasping vision of rising affluence in the suburbs and its opposite as one went south to the crowded towns of cheap housing, "white trash" anomie, increasing racial conflict, gang activity, and the fractured dream of mobility visible in cars on blocks and gargantuan RVs crowning the housetops, one gained a sense of the striations and disparities of the California dream. What I did not see, or foresee, was the rapidity with which the landscape could change while the dream remained the same. When I returned to Sandra Avenue in Arcadia in 1988, fifteen years after my family moved to yet a third LA suburb, Glendora, I found a world transformed, the street names double-signed in English and Vietnamese, the neighborhoods populated with multi-generational households of Cambodian and Vietnamese immigrants living in new, large, multi-story houses built alongside the aging, single-story ranch homes of the older white population. It was a Monday, and as I drove Las Tunas Boulevard through Temple City, San Gabriel, and Alhambra going west toward downtown Los Angeles, I was surprised at the contrast between the streets filled with a multiracial cast of people shopping, talking, strolling, and what I would have witnessed of sleepy suburbs and sparsely populated strip malls on a weekday in the 1960s. Paradise become multicultural? Hardly. Well into the twenty-first century, the affluent white suburbs continue to be built to the east, south, and north; many of the newer developments – especially those that could get one close to the beach or up into the foothills of the nearest transverse mountain range – simply reflect white flight from increased numbers of Asians, blacks, and Latinos in the older suburbs. But what can be surmised from the voracious spread of the suburbs in Los Angeles with their rapidly shifting populations is that they represent both a dream of mobility and the mobility of the dream of paradisiacal domesticity that covers over the continued racial and class divisions and sequestrations upon which the dream appears to be founded. An observation, from the midst of it, that will inform my discussion of a succession of LA novels by Joan Didion, Brett Easton Ellis, Carolyn See, Alison Lurie, and T. C. Boyle, whose imaginative portraits of life in the suburbs of Southern California after World War II unfailingly reflect the trouble in paradise.

Being lost amidst the tangle of freeways and roadways that constitute the greater LA transportation system is, David Fine notes, the symptomatic condition of the protagonist in an LA novel, but "[n]o character in Los Angeles fiction … has lost her bearings the way Maria Wyeth has in Didion's *Play It As It Lays*."[7] Published in the wake of *Slouching Towards Bethlehem* (1968), Didion's startling collection of essays on the California scene in the 1960s where the subjects include homicide in the suburbs, runaways in San Francisco, the psychological effect of the Santa Ana winds, and Howard Hughes's "communication center" in a seedy part of Hollywood, *Play It As It Lays* (1970) depicts the spiral toward nihilism and self-destruction of an unsuccessful film actress in the era of free love, plentiful drugs, and existential dread. In many respects, *Play It As It Lays* is a Hollywood novel that depicts the dark side of "glittertown." Didion's Hollywood dystopia, however, is more accurately viewed as a series of snapshots of Southern California in the 1960s and the drift of desire across a landscape where the dream of success for an aspiring celebrity is no different from that of an upwardly mobile suburbanite: a place in the sun, free and immediate access to all that material paradise has to offer ("everything, all the time," as the quintessential Southern California rock band, The Eagles, puts it in "Life in the Fast Lane"), security and visibility, wealth and pleasure.

The moving figure in the novel's multiple scenarios is Maria, who is suffering mentally from the aftermath of a failed marriage, a stalled acting career, and a string of broken or troubled relationships with friends and colleagues in the film industry. Maria attempts to escape her problems through drugs, parties, and casual sex, but her preferred method of flight is to drive the LA freeways for hours at a time in her Corvette:

> She drove the San Diego to the Harbor, the Harbor up to Hollywood, the Hollywood to the Golden State, the Santa Monica, the Santa Ana, the Pasadena, the Ventura. She drove as a riverman runs a river, every day more attuned to its currents, its deceptions, and just as the riverman feels the pull of the rapids in the lull between sleeping and waking, so Maria lay at night in the still of Beverly Hills and saw the great signs soar overhead at seventy miles an hour, *Normandie ¼ Vermont ¾ Harbor Fwy 1*. Again and again she returned to an intricate stretch just south of the interchange where successful passage from the Hollywood onto the Harbor required a diagonal move across four lanes of traffic.[8]

Like Oedipa descending into the LA basin, Maria navigates the labyrinth of the freeway system in search of a secret or solution to the puzzle of the identity she has lost along with her dreams of success and happiness. For Maria, the freeway system of the LA metroplex represents a realm where she is in complete control of her own direction and velocity.

Maria's view of the freeway system as a self-determined escape route is easily countered in such film representations of the Southern California "grid" as we find in Joel Schumacher's dystopian *Falling Down* (1993), a film about a man whose descent into madness and death is instigated by rage that comes from being trapped in a freeway traffic jam, or Paul Haggis's *Crash* (2004), a somewhat less pessimistic approach to the freeways as the site of multiple accidents that interconnect the lives of dispersed Angelenos. In reality, there appears to be little that is "free" or systematic about a roadway system that is gridlocked more often than not, and whose development over time has been more dependent upon the fluctuations of speculation, land grabs, and political deals than any form of rational regional planning.[9] Maria's sense of the freeway system as a vehicle for temporary liberation is oddly reflected in the work of Reyner Banham, a British architectural critic who claims that Los Angeles' "polymorphous landscapes and architectures were given a 'comprehensible unity' by the freeway grid in a metropolis that spoke 'the language of movement, not monument.'"[10] Davis is sharply critical of this view, but it represents one of the reigning myths of a road system that was built to facilitate movement outward toward the suburbs, indeed, to be the arterial lifeline *of* the suburbs. In this respect, the freeway system represents the dream of mobility and access that is fundamental to the suburban consumerist fantasy writ large. For Maria the freeway is a kind of "id-way" where she can escape a life gone bust and where she can still feel, as she drives past the endless signs naming access roads and gas stations while negotiating the geometry of cloverleaf and bypass, that she is going somewhere, and that there is something more she hasn't yet seen, bought, or desired. Adrift in California, she is a symptomatic representation of the LA subject searching through the vast reaches of the Southland for a center that will not hold in the architecture of Eden.

Maria exists as a kind of nihilist survivor, but her nihilism – that there is nothing beyond the circularity of "escape" on the freeway – pales in comparison to that of the protagonist of Bret Easton Ellis's novel *Less Than Zero* (1985). Set in the early years of the Reagan era, *Less Than Zero* is a nightmarish, satirical version of 1980s suburban youth gone haywire. The novel's narrator and protagonist is white and privileged, come home to stay with his family in their luxurious, gated Mulholland Drive house overlooking the San Fernando Valley while on winter break from a private college in the East. During the few weeks of his sojourn in Los Angeles, Clay (last names are not used in the novel) indulges in numerous orgies involving sex, drugs, and stomach-churning violence interspersed with scenes of parodic boredom and inanity as he converses with friends and strangers while touring the restaurants, malls, and clubs where the hip and the wealthy hang out. Clay is a comic-book nihilist (he says at one point, "I realize that money doesn't matter. That all that does is that I want to see the worst") adrift in the world where materialistic novelty, the objectification of the body, and the pursuit of desire have resulted in death-driven culture. The novel is replete with scenes of death: a dying coyote struck by a car in the Hollywood Hills; the dead body of an overdosed teenager in an alley; the tortured bodies of two teenagers in a putative snuff film. At one point, a loathsome ethos is enunciated by Rip, a drug dealer who is about to engage in the gang rape of a twelve-year-old girl, "'What's right? If you want something, you have the right to take it. If you want to do something, you have the right to do it.'" This maxim rings out as the founding assumption underlying the will to power which serves as the engine for the LA consumerist culture visible everywhere in the brand names, logos, and fashionable locales that appear on every page of *Less Than Zero*. As his own name indicates, Clay is base matter shaped by cultural forces; his deadpan tone, which never wavers as he registers everything from the utterly inane to the horrific, is that of youth already dead, possessing and experiencing everything, yet becoming in the end "less than zero." As Clay puts it, "'I like nothing,'" with the emphasis on the second word of the phrase.[11]

The condition that Ellis illustrates in this over-the-top portrait of young suburban zombies in the era of trickle-down economics might be viewed as one manifested at the furthest edges of "the Me generation," "Generation X," or "the thirteenth generation," as it is variously and loosely called: the media-saturated children of the postwar baby boomers, always already jaded with material excess, apolitical, hedonistic, narcissistic. This is a stereotype, to be sure, and in Ellis's hands the stereotype is transformed into caricature of youth culture in a novel that is conceivably as self-indulgent and superficial as its subjects. Clay's nihilism is merely the obverse of SoCal sunniness and the promise of a secure paradise in the tracts and material well-being in the malls, and just as insubstantial. In the dull, repetitive prose that is characteristic of the novel, Ellis localizes the anomie infecting Clay and his crowd as an LA phenomenon and a sign of the 1980s when he describes Clay, like Maria on the freeways, aimlessly driving along the boulevards of West Los Angeles into the San Fernando Valley until he lands at an all-night restaurant:

> I drive down Wilshire and then onto Santa Monica and then I drive onto Sunset and take Beverly Glen to Mulholland, and then Mulholland to Sepulveda and then Sepulveda to Ventura and then I drive through Sherman Oaks to Encino and then onto Tarzana and then Woodland Hills. I stop at a Sambo's [a restaurant franchise now bankrupt, in no small part due to the racist associations of its name] ... and sit alone in a large empty booth and the [Santa Ana] winds have started and they're blowing so hard that the windows are shaking and the sounds of them trembling, about to break, fill the coffee shop. There are these two young guys next in the booth next to mine, both wearing black suits and sunglasses and the one with a Billy Idol button pinned to his lapel keeps hitting his hand against the table, like he's trying to keep the beat.[12]

A parody of Hemingway's "A Clean, Well-Lighted Place," this scene suggests that the "everything" of California is, indeed, nothing, and that Los Angeles is the last place where one might go to be "safe and warm." Ellis's dystopic vision of Los Angeles and youth in the suburbs is narrow and hyperbolic, focused entirely on the grotesque excesses of a group of 1980s Valley twenty-somethings who are white, affluent, and, for the most part, male, but we can regard *Less Than Zero* as starkly etching the dark contours of the broader fantasy of paradise in Los Angeles, and its discontents.

Alison Lurie is well known as a novelist who meticulously documents the complexities of domestic life in the United States. In *The Nowhere City* (1965), she employs the devices of domestic comedy to provide a satirical view of Southern California mores and lifestyles among the upwardly mobile suburban set. Taking place at the transition point between the beatnik and hippie eras, *The Nowhere City* might be considered a proto-yuppie novel. Twenty-somethings Paul and Katherine Cattleman move from the East Coast to an apartment in Mar Vista, a coastal LA suburb undergoing rapid change as a new freeway is constructed in its midst, he to take on a position with the Nutting Research and Development Corporation (a prime exemplar of what President Eisenhower had termed the "military–industrial complex"), she coming along for the ride to paradise. Katherine immediately takes a thorough dislike to the LA scene. Suffering from frequent migraines attributable to her sinuses, or the smog, or to the anguish of displacement she experiences in her new home, she views the environs as fake and surrealistic: "Vista Gardens: a long row of two-story plaster apartment buildings backing onto the San Diego Freeway. There was no vista, of course, and no gardens, Katherine thought. This whole city was plastered with lies: lies erected in letters five feet tall on roofs; lies pasted to the walls, or burning all night in neon." Contrarily, Paul, a historian recruited to write a chronological profile of Nutting R&D for public relations purposes, regards Los Angeles as "the last American frontier," a place that "suggested a kind of relaxed energy, the sense of infinite possibilities":

> Since his arrival, he had sometimes entertained himself by imagining that he saw parallels between Los Angeles and his "own" period of English history, the late sixteenth century. Here was the same tremendous expansion of trade, building, and manufacture; the flowering of new art forms; the discovery of new worlds. And still the city remained a city of walled gardens like the imaginary gardens in late medieval romances, full of allegorical blooms – fruit and flowers ripe at the same time. Perhaps here, too, he might find other paraphernalia of courtly love: the impenetrable castles, the opening-night pageants and tournaments, the elaborate ceremonies of public praise, the worship from afar of the beloved movie starlet.

Predictably, Paul first has an affair with an artist/waitress living in beatnik Venice, and then with an aging movie star in the "castles" of the Pacific Palisades, while Katherine becomes increasingly disenchanted until she is "turned" to Los Angeles by a dominating psychoanalyst with whom she has her own affair. In the end, Paul and Katherine have changed places, she, newly empowered and independent, becoming "a pretty girl in tight yellow pants, with a smooth California tan and ash-blonde hair piled onto her head like a mound of whipped cream; an obvious Los Angeles type," he returning alone to an academic job in New England in full flight from a place for which he turns out to be much too "square."[13]

The comic symmetry of the Cattlemans' trading places is but one of the many ironies that stud Lurie's mildly dystopian view of 1960s Los Angeles, where one can see, as Paul does, a "dozen architectural styles" on any suburban block: "little Spanish haciendas with red tiled roofs; English country cottages, all beams and mullioned windows; a pink Swiss chalet; and even a tiny French château, the pointed towers of which seemed to be made of pistachio ice-cream." This is the Los Angeles about which Katherine, before her transformation, exclaims, "'I hate the oranges here as big as grapefruits and the grapefruits as big as ... advertisements for grapefruit. Everything's advertisements here ... it's always a lie, like an advertisement. For instance, this is Mar Vista, which is supposed to be Spanish for "view of the sea." That's because it has no view of the sea; it's all flat, it has no view of anything.'" In Los Angeles, according to the pre-change Katherine, there is no time, no seasons: "'It's so confusing ... there's not really any day or night here either. You go to a restaurant for dinner and you see people sitting at the next table eating breakfast. Everything's all mixed up and *wrong*.'" Revealingly, the moment that marks Katherine's change from alien to "Hollywood type" is her reversed vision of herself wearing a new "LA outfit" when she is encouraged to "dig" her new self in a mirror. For Paul, the architectural hybridity of the LA suburbs at first signifies a landscape of endless opportunity and infinite combination, but as time goes on and his optimistic view of Los Angeles dims, the simulacrum of the city leads to a growing sense of disproportion and dislocation: "It was a beautiful landscape ... but inhuman, like some artist's vision of the future for the cover of *Galaxy Science Fiction*. People looked out of place here: they seemed much too small for the roads and the buildings, and by contrast rather scrappily constructed, all awkward limbs and shreds of cloth." In a place where everything is "built in a different style"[14] and where time seems to have stalled in a present of self-mirroring and the simulated difference of "everything, all the time," Lurie suggests that what has been lost is history *per se* – not the academic history of Paul Cattleman which leads him to the absurd comparison of California in the 1960s to Elizabethan England, but the sense of a visible past evident in the architecture and landscape of place, where quick-change transformations and nightless days are indicative of "nowhere." Recalling *Erewhon* (1872), Samuel Butler's satirization of Victorian England's "advanced civilization," Lurie's *Nowhere City*, while far from offering the dystopic nightmare of Los Angeles found in *Less Than Zero*, reveals "the last American frontier" to be a hybrid garden of surfaces and images where transformation can be found, but only in the illusory depths of the mirror.

Kyra Mossbacher, real estate broker and wife of "Delaney Mossbacher, of 32 Piñon Drive, Arroyo Blanco Estates, a liberal humanist with an

unblemished driving record and a freshly waxed Japanese car with persona-
lized plates," reflects on the flood of immigrants into greater Los Angeles from
Mexico in T. C. Boyle's *The Tortilla Curtain* (1995):

> In an ironic way, the invasion from the South had been good for business to this
> point because it had driven the white middle class out of Los Angeles proper and
> into the areas she specialized in: Calabasas, Topanga, Arroyo Blanco. She still
> sold houses in Woodland Hills – that's where the offices were, after all, and it
> was still considered a very desirable upper-middle-class neighborhood – but all
> the smart buyers had already retreated beyond the city limits. Schools, that was
> what it was all about. They didn't bus in the country, only in the city.[15]

In Boyle's compelling social novel bearing the derisive name for the border
separating Mexico from the United States, the Mossbachers are an affluent
white couple who live in a suburb perched in the steep terrain of Topanga
Canyon, an area in the Santa Monica mountains which for decades was a
funky haven for artists, movie stars, and California kooks of every stripe. As
Kyra Mossbacher's commentary indicates, however, in the 1990s, Topanga
and other largely undeveloped areas of the mountains and canyons ringing
Los Angeles became sanctuaries for white flight from the "classic" suburbs of
the San Fernando and San Gabriel Valleys for those fleeing the "invasion" of
immigrants from Mexico, Central America, and Southeast Asia. Living in the
still-primitive area at the bottom of the canyon is another couple in Boyle's
novel, Candido Rincon and his pregnant wife América, illegal immigrants
from Mexico who have come to Los Angeles to pursue the dream but can
barely eke out an existence living off the land and take what little work is
given them while bearing the burden of resentment at their presence as
illegals, "wetbacks," aliens. The lives of these couples intersect as the vertical
gap between them is closed, not through any fantasy of social mobility or
cultural assimilation and acceptance, but because they literally collide in the
brutalities of the natural order and historical process. *Tortilla Curtain* thus
orchestrates an allegory of inevitability in Los Angeles on the verge of the
twenty-first century – one in which the false dream of security and well-being
in the suburbs is shattered by cultural contact, and shown up for its depen-
dence on the suffering and alienation of others.

There are fences and borders of many kinds in *The Tortilla Curtain*. There
is the 1,950-mile border between the United States and Mexico itself, 700
miles of it to be fenced pursuant to federal legislation passed in 2006. Between
the Mossbachers' property and the open land of the canyon existing outside
the confines of the Arroyo Blanco development there is a chain-link fence that
fails to keep out the coyotes that kill two of the Mossbachers' dogs. Delaney, a
nature writer and journalist who pens a nauseatingly New Agey series entitled

"Pilgrim at Topanga Creek" (clearly, a riff on Annie Dillard's *Pilgrim at Tinker Creek*, an insistently post-anthropomorphic reflection on the beauties, oddities, and dangers of the natural world), is contradictorily fascinated by the wild coyotes in the abstract, yet furious about the attack on domesticity they represent. When a group of Arroyo Blanco householders proposes that a block wall be built around the entire development to keep out not just coyotes but also illegal immigrants and other "undesirables," Delaney, the "humanistic liberal," at first resists and, later, capitulates as class and race xenophobia builds in the community and in his personal life. The walls and fences are there to keep out both human and natural "others," but as *Tortilla Curtain* unfolds, events reveal the permeability of borders real and symbolic: the novel opens with Delaney accidentally running over Candido with his Japanese import, and giving the slightly injured man $20 as "compensation." Candido is hired on a temporary work crew that builds the wall around Arroyo Blanco; attempting to cook a free Thanksgiving turkey that has been patronizingly given to him by white customers at a convenience store, Candido accidently starts a fire that burns to the edge of the development. Subsequently, seeking a new refuge, Candido and América, who has borne her child at the height of the blaze while escaping it, construct a temporary home in the canyon just below the Mossbachers' house. During the torrential rains that fall shortly after the blaze, Candido, América, their child, and Delaney (out hunting for the intruders who have invaded his territory) are swept by a mudslide into swollen Topanga Creek, and the novel concludes with Candido attempting to save the individual attached to a white hand and "the white face [that] surge up out of the black swirl of the current" – possibly Delaney Mossbacher, the "liberal humanist" who has sought to evict him from the neighborhood and the nation. *Tortilla Curtain* may be transparently orchestrated, but the import of Boyle's novel – much like that of John Steinbeck's *The Grapes of Wrath* (1939), cited in its epigraph – is that "they" are "us," and that the borders and walls that separate "them" from "us," erected out of racial fear, a mania for security, a desire to keep the wealth to ourselves, or the paranoiac need for a suburban citadel to keep us safe and warm even in paradise, are bound to fail. In the end, the LA suburbs as portrayed by Boyle represent paradise for some, and hell for others in a naturalistic world where the parceling out of the human into lots threatens all.

The Tortilla Curtain ends with a series of human-induced natural cataclysms: a raging brush fire that threatens expensive domiciles which should never have been built along dry, steep canyon-sides in earthquake country; a landslide that occurs in the aftermath of the fire when heavy rains turn the scorched earth into mud. The novel's apocalyptic concluding scenes are thus in keeping with a long line of LA novels that view the city eschatologically, at the far end of time and history, the last possible holdout of westward expansion and the realization of a new Eden in America, or the site of the dream's collapse under the weight of its own excess.

Perhaps no novel imagines "LA apocalypse" more starkly, or iconoclastically, than Carolyn See's *Golden Days* (1987). Born in Pasadena and a lifelong resident of Greater Los Angeles, See has chronicled the fictional and real lives of Southern Californians in seven novels and three works of nonfiction on subjects from the writing life in Los Angeles to the porn industry. In *Golden Days*, See portrays the life of a woman who, fleeing two failed marriages, has come to Los Angeles with her two young daughters and finds a home in the same Topanga Canyon that the couples of *The Tortilla Curtain* inhabit; unlike the Mossbachers, however, Edith Langley lives in one of the aging bungalows of "classic" Topanga. For Edith, the "real" Los Angeles lies downtown and in the hidden suburban culverts like Topanga or Sierra Madre, throwbacks in time where artists gather and truly alternative lifestyles are explored:

> They say L.A. is large, but they lie. It's true there are a zillion places no one in his right mind would like: Lakewood, Torrance, Brea, Compton, Carson, no one *real* lived there… "Real" L.A. had its thick, coiled root downtown, and on the east, little underground rootlets… Then a thin stem, the Santa Monica Freeway, heading due west and putting out greenery, places in this western desert where you'd love to live – if things went right.

Things do go right for Edith as she discovers her own independence, raises her daughters to become unconventional, freethinking young women, amasses wealth as a successful businesswoman, reconnects with a lifelong friend, Lorna, and commences a platonic relationship with an older man, Skip, who serves as a surrogate father for her daughters and a mentoring life companion for Edith. The embodiment of self-construction and adaptability, California-style ("I, who was thirty-eight years old … ended up doing something, it seems to me now, everyone in Los Angeles did then: I made myself up half hour by hour"), Edith appears to fulfill "our dream in the West – sun and fun, love and family affection."[16]

But something goes terribly wrong as history encroaches on the dream. The warning signs of apocalypse are scattered throughout the novel: set in the mid-1980s in the final years of the Cold War, there appears to be serious trouble at home and abroad:

> The draft in America had started up again. But this time our poor, our wretched, our blacks and browns were not quite so compliant as they once had been. After a dozen wars in the past decade, and a dozen more in the twenty years before

that, the underclasses had finally learned that there would be no reward for going away to murder women and children even poorer and sadder than they.

Instead, after completing basic training, the draftees desert in droves, taking their weapons with them. Nature, too, appears to be in revolt: "Volcanic eruptions on the other side of the world had given us weeks of spectacular sunsets."[17]

Then the apocalypse occurs as a series of "minor" nuclear skirmishes in Mexico lead to the feared worst outcome of the Cold War: nuclear holocaust. A survivor to the core, and armed with the seemingly superficial "positive thinking" philosophy that she learned from Lion Boyce, a motivational speaker who encourages total surrender to the "flow" of life, Edith and a small band of fellow survivors who have not been killed by the explosions or subsequent radiation, including Skip and one of her daughters, manage to adapt to the world of post-holocaust Los Angeles. At the extremities of existence and on the edge of history and the American continent, Edith proclaims that "'Some people say these are bad times, but *I* say they are *good* times. We have bravery! We have love! We have the future! We have the Beginning!'" Edith believes that, both symbolically and literally,

> the ones who decided to come *west* instead of heading east, were by and large the ones who made it. And the wackos, the ones who used their belief systems were the ones who got control over the radiation. Control is a silly word. It was surrender, really. The ones who *relinquished* control, who took it as it came, who seem – out here, at least – to have lived.

Contrary to most of the horrific portrayals of nuclear holocaust, and in spite of the burned bodies, decay, and wreckage that Edith describes as she and her band travel through the former suburbs of Southern California, the novel appears to conclude on a triumphant, prophetic note as Edith recounts the survival of "a race of hardy laughers, mystics, crazies, who knew their real homes, or who had been drawn to this gold coast for years, and they lived through the destroying light, and on, into Light ages."[18]

One hardly knows what to make of such a conclusion: Eden reborn, after utter destruction? The dream intact and reshaped for a new age and a new race of equals led by a feminist hero, despite the betrayal of the dream by its very components, signifying its durability? Or an absurdist response to the absurdity of the dream of wealth, security, and love promised by life in the suburbs – a promise derailed in all of the Arcadian fictions considered here? See's novel is unique in that it satirizes all of the aspects of the suburban California dream within the context of Cold War politics and New Age eccentricity, and yet simultaneously posits that dreamers were not wrong to go west in the first place in search of paradise, just misguided, that the dream was there all along and can be realized once the world is stripped bare of its materiality. But therein, of course, lies the rub: for it is the material of the dream that constitutes its substance, and as these fictional chroniclers of paradise and hell in the LA suburbs suggest, the material is gross, and the dream itself founded upon greed, narcissism, out-of-control capitalism, racism, alienations of self and other. Or perhaps *Golden Days* attempts to strike a balance between polarized representations of the suburbs by suggesting that they do somehow embody a common vision that rises above its base material. As D. J. Waldie posits with quiet irony in *Holy Land*, as a lifelong inhabitant of Lakewood (one of those south LA suburbs that Edith opines is one of those "zillion places no one in his right mind would like"), he has "found a place that permits restless people to be still," where "houses are close enough so that you might hear, if you listened, a neighbor's baby cry, a father arguing with a teenage son, or a television playing early on a summer night. Most things here are close enough for comfort."[19] Yet such small comfort, Waldie makes clear, is purchased at a cost: the stripping bare of the land, the exhaustion of natural resources, the confinement of life to the material constraints of the dream. The fictions of the LA suburbs apprise us of the cost, as well as the durability of the dream of Eden, in both its seeming necessity and its inevitable vanishing.

NOTES

1. Thomas Pynchon, *The Crying of Lot 49* (New York: Harper & Row, 1986), p. 24.
2. D. J. Waldie, *Holy Land: A Suburban Memoir* (New York: Norton, 2005), pp. 116, 118.
3. Pynchon, *Crying of Lot 49*, p. 24.
4. Mike Davis, *City of Quartz: Excavating the Future in Los Angeles* (New York: Verso, 1990), p. 6.
5. Joan Didion, "Some Dreamers of the Golden Dream," in *Slouching Towards Bethlehem* (New York: Noonday Press, 1990), p. 4.
6. James Ellroy, *My Dark Places* (New York: Vintage, 1997), pp. 25, 22.
7. David Fine, *Imagining Los Angeles: A City in Fiction* (Albuquerque: University of New Mexico Press, 2000), p. 247.
8. Joan Didion, *Play It As It Lays* (New York: Noonday Press, 1990), pp. 15–16.
9. See Davis, *City of Quartz*, p. 122.
10. Cited in Davis, *City of Quartz*, p. 73.
11. Bret Easton Ellis, *Less Than Zero* (New York: Vintage, 1998), pp. 172, 189, 205.
12. *Ibid.*, p. 61.
13. Alison Lurie, *The Nowhere City* (New York: Henry Holt, 1997), pp. 36, 6, 9–10, 341.
14. *Ibid.*, pp. 6, 47, 181, 287, 288.

15. T. C. Boyle, *The Tortilla Curtain* (New York: Penguin, 1996), pp. 3, 158–9.
16. Carolyn See, *Golden Days* (Berkeley: University of California Press, 1996), pp. 6, 12, 117.
17. *Ibid.*, pp. 86, 91.
18. *Ibid.*, pp. 190, 193, 196.
19. Waldie, *Holy Land*, pp. vii, 134.

6

CHARLES SCRUGGS

Los Angeles and the African-American literary imagination

> The function of the imagination is not to make strange things settled,
> so much as to make settled things strange.
> G. K. Chesterton, *The Defendant* (1901)

No generalization about the African-American writers of Los Angeles can do justice to the rich variety of their perspectives upon their city, but they do tend to focus on two interrelated themes: its utopian promise of beauty, ease, riches, even fame, and the possibility of racial violence whose eruption is as unpredictable as the region's earthquakes. Los Angeles is "full of surprises," as Bebe Moore Campbell said.[1]

The racial past that ruptures without warning the delicate world of "settled things" is a recurrent theme. The African-American aphorism *"quiet as it's kept,"* used by detective fiction writer Paula Woods in *Stormy Weather* (2001), implies that a secret not kept is no longer quiet.[2] The promise of safety is carried in images of community like Gary Phillips's "three B's" – "beauty shops, barber shops, and barbecues" – or it is claimed as the fundamental rights to liberty and justice in a city that for most of its history has given blacks little of either.[3] The struggle to turn urban space into livable places produces a condition diagnosed by Wanda Coleman in the title of her 1996 collection of essays; the black Angeleno is a *Native in a Strange Land*.

The most dramatic example of this condition may occur in Octavia Butler's science fiction novel *Kindred* (1979). Butler's protagonist, Dana, is repeatedly thrust from the present into the historical past of 1815–30 Maryland and back, so that the familiar becomes strange, the strange familiar. The LA house that she shares with her white lover, Kevin, is no longer familiar; the slave past becomes "a sharper, stronger reality." As she struggles to ensure her own birth by keeping her despicable ancestor Rufus alive long enough to father another generation, Dana finds this past more plausible than her life in Los Angeles. The novel thus questions the nature of reality, the cost of survival, and the claims of kinship (Rufus) versus kind-ship (Kevin). Dana returns permanently to Los Angeles after Rufus dies, leaving behind one arm and part of her soul. Yet her life has gained meaning; what makes her "sane" is knowing that her existence in Los Angeles is connected to a vital past else-where, no matter how horrible it was.[4]

To Watts ...

Dana's time travel is perhaps the most extreme form of Los Angeles' legend-ary mobility, but the theme is present in the earliest black Angeleno novels. Set in the last quarter of the nineteenth century and the first decade of the twentieth, Arna Bontemps's *God Sends Sunday* (1930) is a picaresque novel about Little Augie, a black jockey. The novel documents his success in the days when "all the painted brown girls were partial to jockeys, for the horse-racing game ... was one of the most lucrative fields open to ambitious young blacks. The fantastic renown won by jockeys was comparable to that of prize-fighters."[5] Bontemps charts his fall as racism in the age of Jim Crow drives him from the saddle.

In old age, Augie joins his sister in "Mudtown, the Negro neighborhood on the edge" of Watts, which for years had been a railroad town. With the advent of the transcontinental railroad, many black Pullman porters settled in Watts, as did other African Americans who arrived by train. Watts was the symbol of modernity, infused with the rhythms and styles of the South Central jazz clubs, but "Mudtown was like a tiny section of the deep south literally transplanted," the trace of a usable past. Augie learns as much when he goes to a dance in Watts wearing out-of-date clothes and sees the young people trying "a new dance that they had picked up in the city, on Central Avenue, in some of the less respectable places." Bontemps notes that "the denizens of Mudtown were seeing the shimmy for the first time in a public place."[6] Before long, they themselves would be shimmying, as would Jazz Age white Americans.

The presence of a folk community in the modern city has often provided a support system for new immigrants, but "even supposing a whole community migrates in a body, the communal life cannot go on," Carey McWilliams observes, "because it was based upon the other locality. Emigrants turn into detached individuals, like so many grains of sand."[7] Chester Himes's *If He Hollers Let Him Go* (1945) illustrates the point. Set in 1944, when "nearly two hundred thousand black Americans were employed in the nation's ship-yards, some two-thirds of them on the Pacific Coast,"[8] *If He Hollers* tells a surreal tale about Bob Jones, a "leaderman" for a gang of black workers in the Atlas Shipyard, who makes his 1942 Buick Roadmaster a substitute for a missing community. The car gives Bob the illusion of freedom and equality as he challenges even white drivers to race him on Los Angeles' streets, all the while knowing that even someone living in Beverly Hills cannot buy a

Roadmaster during the war. Yet instead of a badge of freedom, the Buick brands Bob as an arrogant, uppity Negro as it heightens his aggression, already at fever pitch because of racial hostility at the shipyard. The car becomes his weapon in a fantasy not of escape but revenge: "the snowcapped mountains in the background, like picture postcards, didn't mean a thing to me. I didn't even see them; all I wanted in the world was to push my Buick Roadmaster over some peckerwood's face."[9]

Like Dana's in *Kindred*, Bob's world is torn open by the conflict between the horizontal surface of Los Angeles' modern highway system and the vertical nightmare of the past erupting into the present. His actual dreams, which reflect his sense of living "like some sort of machine being run by white people pushing buttons," merge with his waking experience in dreamlike Los Angeles. He finds himself less a driver than someone driven by a will not his own into a closed room with Madge Perkins, an aging blonde from Texas who works in the shipyard. She pretends to be terrified of him, and he wants nothing to do with her, but as in a nightmare he lives out Freud's repetition–compulsion cycle. The more he tries to escape her presence, the more he becomes entangled in it. The whole thing, Bob reflects, "didn't make sense,"[10] as though Madge herself has become for him a grotesque symbol of the mazelike city. When she cries rape as he is desperately trying to run out the door (a scene that mirrors one of his dreams), Bob is caught, beaten, and jailed. His ultimate "freedom" is conscription as he and two Mexican youths are inducted into the Navy to fight for American liberty.

Ezekiel "Easy" Rawlins's story begins just after Bob Jones's ends, marking both continuity and change in Los Angeles. Where Bob lost a shipyard job in 1944, Easy has just lost his job at Champion Aircraft in 1948 when we first meet him in Walter Mosley's *Devil in a Blue Dress* (1990). Writing from the perspective of the end of the twentieth century, Mosley knows that black Los Angeles has extended itself beyond Central Avenue and Watts. Mosley also understands not only how Los Angeles' horizontal, centrifugal energy compromises the centripetal nature of the neighborhood, but also that the centripetal nature of the black community provides refuge from the seeming spatial disorder of postwar Los Angeles and the "vertical" intrusions of a Gothic racial past into the present. Reversing the opening of Raymond Chandler's *Farewell, My Lovely* (1940), in which a white man looking for a particular woman wreaks havoc upon a black bar, *Devil* begins with a white man entering a black bar to make Easy an offer that is hard to refuse: Find a white girl named Daphne Monet, Albright says, and you will have enough money to pay the mortgage on your house. Albright thus gives Easy a new vocation, but Easy is not a knight living in a fallen world, like Chandler's Marlowe. Easy *is* the fallen world, but he longs for a house enmeshed in a world of communal values, while Marlowe lives in a sparsely furnished efficiency apartment.

If Bob Jones is in love with his Buick, Easy's house is the passion that drives him along the LA streets. "Maybe it was that I was raised on a sharecropper's farm or that I never owned anything until I bought that house, but I loved my little home," Easy muses.[11] This tension between the detective's mobility and the desire for home gives the opening scene of *Devil in a Blue Dress* its special resonance. Easy associates the idea of home (space made place) with the intangible values of community, neighborhood, and friendship. However, home ownership also incites his capitalist passion to acquire more property, following the lead of the speculators and developers who built Los Angeles. As he says in *White Butterfly*, "I dreamed about being one of the few black millionaires in America."[12] The distinction between home as part of a neighborhood and home as real estate defines two worlds that place different values on self and community and pull Easy in different directions:

> Looking out the window is different in Los Angeles than it is [back] in Houston. No matter where you live in a southern city (even a wild and violent place like Fifth Ward, Houston) you see almost everybody you know by just looking out your window. Every day is a parade of relatives and old friends and lovers you once had, and maybe you'd be lovers again ... [I]n L.A. people don't have time to stop; anywhere they have to go they go there in a car. The poorest man has a car in Los Angeles; he might not have a roof over his head but he has a car. And he knows where he's going too. In Houston and Galveston, and way down in Louisiana, life was a little more aimless. People worked a little job but couldn't make any real money no matter what they did. But in Los Angeles you could make a hundred dollars in a week if you pushed. The promise of getting rich pushed people to work two jobs in the week and do a little plumbing on the weekend. There's no time to walk down the street or make a bar-b-q when somebody's going to pay you real money to haul refrigerators.[13]

Nostalgic for a communal past that he left behind, Easy also wants the promise of riches as reward for hard work.

Still, the dream can turn him into a seeming slave catcher as he pursues a mixed-race woman who stole $30,000 from her white lover, mayoral candidate Todd Carter, and betrays the unwritten code of the community by turning a black man over to the police. *White Butterfly* (1992) is more Gothic. Four black women have been murdered, but only after a young white woman, Robin Garnett, is killed does the LAPD insist that Easy find the killer. What he finds is a horrific past that has resurfaced in 1950s Beverly Hills. Robin's own father murdered her because she had a black child. Fleeing her oppressive home, Robin lived a double life as a UCLA student and a stripper, the "White Butterfly." The father, too, lives a double life; he is a respectable businessman, but he also is a racist so virulent that he murders several times to keep his daughter's "shame" a secret.

One of the best novels of the series, *Black Betty* (1994), involves Easy's reencounter with a beautiful woman he had worshipped as a boy in Houston and, through her, with echoes and visions of the slave past in the present. As Easy drives beyond the city limits to find Betty at the farm of Cain, a rich white man for whom she works as a maid, he travels "out of California, back through the south, and all the way into hell." At first the farm looks "like Heaven," but on closer inspection Mexican-American and African-American adults and children work the land like slaves.[14] The woman to whom he makes the observation is Cain's wife's maid; neither of those women know that she is also Cain and Betty's illegitimate daughter, a secret that recalls the nonconsensual sexual unions between slaveholder and slave.

Mosley's use of the Bible underscores the Gothic dimension to Cain's farm. The biblical Cain founded the first city, whose aim, St. Augustine tells us, is domination. The prophet Ezekiel, Easy's namesake, had a vision of the restored Jerusalem, a figura of Revelation's holy city. While Easy seeks that redeemed city in Los Angeles, he must struggle to make it through the hellish earthly city of racial domination whose initials, some black residents suggest, really stand for Lower Alabama. Easy eventually solves the novel's crime. But he cannot keep his property from being stolen by white venture capitalists who want to build a plaza on it. Easy signs on to the plaza project as a common laborer, puts too much sand in the cement, and the buildings begin to crumble after a year. The potential black millionaire has become a trickster, making sure that Los Angeles' "bad luck" is truly democratic.

Over the course of this series of novels that chronicle different periods in Los Angeles' history and the protagonist's life, Easy begins to accept himself as he is, a janitor at an elementary school and a surrogate father to his own children and the students. The past continues to erupt into the present – the Cain–Abel murders in *A Little Yellow Dog* (1996) and the grotesque mother–son relationship in *Little Scarlet* (2004) – but Easy becomes more and more like Chandler's Marlowe: an honorable man. In the later novels, Easy creates his own niche in Los Angeles, finding a woman he loves (and forgiving her betrayal) and a family and a black community he cares for. As a detective, he still has the potential to trouble the waters; a character in *Bad Boy Brawly Brown* (2002) calls him a "good friend" and then adds, "But if I had my druthers, I'd never have to call on you again."[15] Nevertheless, he has traveled a long way from the tainted slave catcher of *Devil in a Blue Dress*, the betrayer of both friends and community in *A Red Death* (1991), and the morally ambiguous prowler of mean streets in *White Butterfly*.

Another Mosley protagonist, Socrates Fortlow, appears in three collections of stories to date, *Always Outnumbered, Always Outgunned* (1998), *Walkin' the Dog* (1999), and *The Right Mistake* (2008). A man with a horrific past, Socrates murdered a man, raped that man's woman, and killed her. Released after twenty-seven years of prison and now fifty-eight years old, he lives in a Watts shack that is "just a space between two empty stores."[16] Like his namesake, Socrates is in pursuit of the truth. After he came out of jail, as he tells Oscar Minette, the owner of the Capricorn Bookshop, "my main problem was that I was never sure what was right." What's right, he learns, arises from a sea of existential circumstances and involves improvisation and luck. Without wanting the part, Socrates becomes a moral force in his neighborhood in *Always Outnumbered*. He teaches a young boy named Darryl about the significance of death, rids the neighborhood of a killer, creates a situation whereby a man learns to value his wife, takes in a two-legged dog that he ironically names Killer (the dog is, perhaps, a metaphor for himself), and helps his friend Right Burke face death with dignity. He gives a life lesson to Wilfred, who boasts that he robs white people while disguising himself as a poor man. "They scared'a me 'cause you out there pretendin' that you're me robbin' them," he explains, demonstrating that all actions inevitably involve unseen others.[17] In the collection's first story, Edward Hopper's famous painting of an angry black woman in a red dress hangs on Socrates's wall; she is a reminder of Socrates's violent crimes. In *Walkin' the Dog*, Socrates moves to a new home, taking with him the picture of the "disapproving woman dressed in red."[18] Her shadow is no longer that of Socrates's spiritual death.

In *The Right Mistake*, Socrates saves a house belonging to a South Central LA man from his treacherous wife and her lover. That house comes with an "add-on" house that the grateful owner gives to Socrates, who opens a school. He names it the Big Nickel, perhaps because anyone who comes will take away something small but valuable. The school is John of Patmos's twelve-gated city, open to everyone: Jews, Asians, blacks from all social strata, even killers like Socrates himself. The moral issues that arise in the house also remain open, for there are no final answers. Chaim Zetel, for instance, had a father who found broken things and fixed them, making a living from their restoration. Chaim continues his father's business, employing black kids as workers. The black murderer Ron Zeal complains that Chaim is exploiting black children, carrying on an economic tradition. Socrates does not solve the problem, but asks, "Tell me why it's okay for one black man to shoot down another one but it's wrong for Chaim here to make a buck while teachin' our youngsters a trade." The Big Nickel thus becomes the center of a moral community that transcends race. As Socrates says of one Asian member,

"Wan Tai is a brother ... so is Chaim and Antonio. You don't have to be black to be a brother an' you don't have to be white to be standin' in the way." That theme of the open community stands in opposition to Los Angeles' "Unreal City." As Socrates says, "Somebody dreamed up a prison for me and as long as I believe in his dream, and my nightmare, I'm never going to be free."[19] It is only by making a "mistake" (taking a risk) that people can make themselves "right" by escaping the dream. The truly strange is what people call "normal."

Best known as a poet, Wanda Coleman also writes brilliant, informal essays and short stories that deserve more attention, won an Emmy for her writing on the soap opera *Days of Our Lives* in 1976, and provided the text for the photo-documentary volume 24 *Hours in the Life of Los Angeles* (1984). In her satiric portrait, "L.A. Love Cry," she says that she hates her native city because to love it is to always love "unrequited ... [is] to always be hungry," yet she ends by admitting that she "can't leave" her city, and that she has "no regrets."[20] Playing at the intersection of the familiar and the strange in her short story "Hamburgers," Coleman refashions Hollywood's fascination with vampires into an LA story of a luxury automobile that lives "on blood." James Poke eats cheap hamburgers so he can make the monthly payments on a car he cannot afford. Eventually he moves out of his apartment to live in his car. One day the cops find him slumped over the steering wheel, dead from "malnutrition." No wonder he died someone says: "a car like dat runs on blood."[21] Los Angeles may promise the world, but the last thing it provides is spiritual nourishment.

Yet if Coleman explores the modern Gothic via Hollywood horror and Stephen King, she is also capable of summoning Frank Capra to Los Angeles. In her short story "My Son, My Son," a cabbie takes an old African-American woman to the airport to meet her perfect son (happily married, rich, a Stanford graduate) at Christmastime. She throws money at the cab driver, more than the fare. The son never shows up, suggesting that the woman is crazy and fabricated the story. The cabbie takes her back to her home in a posh section of black Los Angeles, and as the mad woman leaves, she throws more money into the cab, saying that "'no son of mine ... is going to go broke if I can help it!'"[22] The epiphany occurs as the cab driver realizes he has been blessed by the Virgin Mary. As an everyman, he is her "son."

and beyond ...

The black Los Angeles of many contemporary black writers is multilayered. The stark divisions of rich and poor corresponding to the division of white and black no longer express the complexity of black LA life. No one is better at depicting this world than Bebe Moore Campbell. In *Brothers and Sisters* (1994), she takes up the corporate world and the new black middle class. She uses cars to express social and economic ascent, not racial rage on the horizontal plane of Los Angeles' highways. Campbell's protagonist, Esther Jackson, was born on Chicago's South Side, but this energetic young woman is determined to make it in corporate Los Angeles. Already a bank manager, she wants to get into the more lucrative field of lending, lives in Park Crest ("the Black Beverly Hills"), and her motto is "no romance without finance." She drives a BMW and the arrogant doctor she wants to marry drives a Jaguar with a vanity plate that has his initials plus "MD."[23] When a friend sets her up with a bus driver, she rejects him. Then Tyrone comes into her life. He delivers parcels for UPS, sells T-shirts to make ends meet, and drives a five-year-old Audi. When he protects Esther during a holdup and exhibits aristocratic grace under fire, Esther revalues him.

Campbell's Los Angeles is the city of the Big Dream, but it is also a city in which dreams can disappear in a moment. Esther reflects that on the South Side of Chicago "all Hell could and did break loose but the ground, at least, stayed put. In Los Angeles ... she couldn't even trust the earth beneath her feet."[24] Earthquakes occur along Los Angeles' racial and economic fault lines as well. In the novel, the Rodney King beating is linked to the beating of Reginald Denny, the white truck driver pulled from his vehicle at a South Central LA intersection on the 1992 Justice Riots' first day. The beatings polarize the characters. Esther's white friend Mallory is sympathetic to Denny, whereas Esther and her black friends line up behind King.

At first, the vertical images in the novel seem to confirm race and class divisions. Preston Sinclair is the president of Esther's bank, and the view from his executive suite is pastoral: "He could see clear to the Pacific, and the sight of the sparkling blue water in the distance was surprisingly soothing, almost hypnotic." As he looks down on the city, however, Sinclair "knew that he wasn't immune to the chaos." No one is immune, not even Humphrey Boone, who rises from rags to riches. In an attempt to ease racial tensions in Los Angeles, Sinclair has made Boone, a black man, his regional manager, but Sinclair also comes to cherish Boone as a friend. From his office window, Los Angeles looks to Boone "like something that could be controlled, even conquered." Attracted to Mallory, he fails to see that she is beset by demons of her own – racial prejudices that the Justice Riots only exacerbate. Boone soon finds himself charged with sexual harassment, a charge not entirely justified. Strangely, he finds himself identifying with Denny, not King, as a man suddenly "pitched into the middle of a nightmare." The brilliance of Campbell's novels lies in her sympathy for good people who let the city's glitter cloud their judgment. Esther says of Tyrone that she could never marry a "man [who] didn't even have a MasterCard,"[25] but satire gives way to sympathy when the automobile that defines his status disappears at the end of the novel. What remains are the ambiguities of race and friendship and the possibility of redefining what community means in a city whose absence of tradition is for once an asset.

Also looking for fresh ways to discuss race, Paul Beatty creates a comic bildungsroman and send-up of the hard times school of black autobiography in *The White Boy Shuffle* (1996), the story of Gunnar Kaufman, a middle-class black kid "from a long cowardly queue of coons, Uncle Toms, and faithful boogedy-boogedy retainers." The radical change in Gunnar's life comes when his mother moves the children from Santa Monica back to the city, and he finds himself making a transition from surfer and skateboarder to life as a black urban male. Yet he emerges as a successful basketball player, and the theme of limited opportunity becomes the plight that "Successful niggers can't go back home and blithely disappear into the local populace. American society reels you back to the fold. 'Tote that barge, shoot that basketball, lift that bale, nigger ain't you ever heard of Dred Scott?'"[26]

Beatty's generation is strikingly savvy about popular culture, especially film. The protagonist of *Tuff* (2000) sees everything through its lens: "The symptoms of poverty are timeless, and Winston knew exactly who the weepy kid looked like: an extra from John Ford's *Grapes of Wrath*." Unread in print culture, he is a perceptive reader of obscure foreign films like Yasujiro Ozu's *There Was a Father* (1942). Of Paul Muni's character in *I Am a Fugitive from a Chain Gang* (1932), whose look at a black fellow prisoner suggests that he now knows what the other guy has experienced, he reflects: "sometimes you catch yourself feeling close to motherfuckers you not supposed to feel close to, but you can't afford to play the humanitarian role. But I realized I'm waiting for someone to look at me like that or for me to look at someone else like that. I'm not sure which."[27]

Gary Phillips is a self-described "sucker for pop culture" who writes comic books as well as novels featuring detective Ivan Monk. With a nod to Himes, the car in his story "53 Buick" is a Roadmaster with a bizarre history. It was driven to Los Angeles from New Mexico with a mysterious something in the trunk. In the year 2000, Monk is asked by the sister of a woman who used to date the car's former owner to find it. He died in 1968, and the car went missing. Monk finally tracks the Buick to its new owner, Jessie DeZuniga, who also wants to keep it hidden. When he finds Jessie with the car, his client appears, seizes the car at gunpoint and proceeds to open the trunk, only to be blinded by a "brilliant glow." Instead of being lethal, as it is in the films *Kiss Me Deadly* (Robert Aldrich, 1955) and *Repo Man* (Alex Cox, 1984), this substance powers the sisters and the old and new owners out Route 66 to a supernatural wonderland. "Before them lay hope and knowledge and the road," and they "went as if they had all the time in the world to get there."[28] What is hidden in the trunk is not the dark obscurity of the La Brea Tar Pits, which crime writer Gar Anthony Haywood's detective Aaron Gunner says drives "white people crazy" because they will never "know for sure what's down there,"[29] but the hidden power of the trickster who steals the enemy's symbols and transforms them into transcendent possibility.

These contemporary writers probe the changing racial landscape of Los Angeles along with the permeability of racial boundaries. Gunnar Kaufman's friend Scoby, having moved to Boston, is so homesick for Los Angeles that he tries to hire "some Puerto Ricans to act Mexican for a day."[30] Ivan Monk's live-in partner, Jill Kodama, is a third-generation Japanese American whose parents were interned during World War II. Paula Woods's detective Charlotte Justice uncovers a horrific past that is not black but Japanese in *Dirty Laundry* (2003). Nevertheless, this lure of mobility still pulls against a yearning for older forms of the black community, as it did for Easy Rawlins. In Haywood's novels, the Acey-Deuce tavern, Mikey Trueblood's barbershop, the HiNotes coffee shop, and Big Mother's gym all are centripetal refuges from the city's centrifugal anonymity. In a wonderful scene in *Brothers and Sisters*, the ambitious Esther enters a Korean doughnut shop where three aging black men hang out swapping lies, and she feels a pang of regret for a world she left behind to climb the socioeconomic ladder.[31]

Thus contemporary black writers often feel that they are travelers in more than one galaxy. In *The White Boy Shuffle*, Gunnar uses an astronomical metaphor to comment on the multicultural whirl of Los Angeles: "The web of amber streetlights looked like a constellation fallen to earth, awaiting some astronomer to connect the glowing dots to give form to its oracularity."[32] In Carol Reed's postwar film noir *The Third Man* (1949), the "dots" are disconnected people who, if removed or erased, would never be missed, or so says Harry Lime (Orson Welles) to his boyhood friend Holly Martins (Joseph Cotten) from a perspective atop a Ferris wheel. Beatty rewrites Graham Greene's script for *The Third Man* to make present the "dots" that white writers ignore. He is speaking not only for Los Angeles' black writers but for all those writers on the periphery of the city's official culture. The artist who would dare to represent Los Angeles must connect the multiple voices of the streets, films, songs, and other forms of mass culture to reveal the palimpsest, the utopian city within the City of Angels.

NOTES

1. Bebe Moore Campbell, *Brothers and Sisters* (New York: Berkley Publishing, 1995), p. 171.

2. Paula L. Woods, *Stormy Weather* (New York: Ballantine Books, 2003), p. 10.
3. Gary Phillips, *Perdition, U.S.A.* (New York: Berkley Publishing, 1997), p. 98.
4. Octavia E. Butler, *Kindred* (Boston: Beacon Press, 1988) pp. 191, 264.
5. Arna Bontemps, *God Sends Sunday* (New York: Harcourt, Brace, 1931), p. 53.
6. *Ibid.*, pp. 116, 118, 160, 161.
7. Carey McWilliams, *Southern California Country: An Island on the Land*, American Folkways (New York: Duell, Sloan & Pearce, 1946), p. 179.
8. Kevin Starr, *Embattled Dreams: California in War and Peace, 1940–1950* (New York: Oxford University Press, 2002), pp. 112–13.
9. Chester Himes, *If He Hollers Let Him Go* (Garden City, N.Y.: Doubleday, 1945), p. 17.
10. *Ibid.*, pp. 202, 153.
11. Walter Mosley, *Devil in a Blue Dress* (New York: W. W. Norton, 1990), p. 19.
12. Mosley, *White Butterfly* (New York: Pocket Books, 1992), p. 133.
13. Mosley, *Devil in a Blue Dress*, p. 55.
14. Mosley, *Black Betty* (New York: Pocket Books, 1995), pp. 155, 83.
15. Mosley, *Bad Boy Brawly Brown* (Boston: Little, Brown, 2002), p. 311.
16. Mosley, *Walkin' the Dog* (Boston: Little, Brown, 1999), p. 21.
17. Mosley, *Always Outnumbered, Always Outgunned* (New York: Pocket Books, 1998), pp. 162, 49.
18. Mosley, *Walkin' the Dog*, p. 216.
19. Mosley, *The Right Mistake* (New York: Basic Civitas Books, 2008), pp. 46, 93, 221.
20. Wanda Coleman, *Native in a Strange Land: Trials & Tremors* (Santa Rosa, Calif.: Black Sparrow Press, 1996), pp. 19, 22.
21. Coleman, *A War of Eyes and Other Stories* (Santa Rosa, Calif.: Black Sparrow Press, 1988), p. 102.
22. Coleman, *Jazz and Twelve O'Clock Tales* (Boston: David R. Godine, 2008), p. 132.
23. Campbell, *Brothers and Sisters*, pp. 380, 33, 103.
24. *Ibid.*, p. 14.
25. *Ibid.*, pp. 45, 46, 150, 512, 361.
26. Paul Beatty, *The White Boy Shuffle* (New York: Henry Holt, 1996), pp. 5, 119.
27. Beatty, *Tuff* (New York: Anchor Books, 2000), pp. 147, 100.
28. Gary Phillips, *Monkology: The Ivan Monk Stories* (Tucson, Ariz.: Dennis McMillan Publications, 2004), pp. x, 115, 116.
29. Gar Anthony Haywood, *Fear of the Dark* (New York: Penguin, 1988), p. 148.
30. Beatty, *White Boy Shuffle*, p. 203.
31. Campbell, *Brothers and Sisters*, p. 361.
32. Beatty, *White Boy Shuffle*, p. 159.

7

JAMES KYUNG-JIN LEE

Pacific Rim city: Asian-American and Latino literature

The Pacific Fish Center is an unlikely destination for Korean tourists, but in the summertime thousands bring their visiting relatives and friends from Korea to this ramshackle eatery on a well-trodden portion of Redondo Beach Pier, about a dozen miles south of Los Angeles International Airport. All sorts of bivalve mollusks, shrimp, and – most importantly for these customers – crab and lobster swim in individual tanks in the front of the restaurant, a marine manifestation of Southern California's seeming treasure. Here, one can enjoy seafood with plates of *kimchi*, the staple Korean side dish of spicy pickled cabbage, as well as *soju*, the fermented, potato-derived beverage that in Los Angeles is as commonly consumed as Japanese *sake*. Here, the tourists' server is unlikely to be Korean himself; rather, he will probably hail from El Salvador or Guatemala, but will still converse fluently in Korean with staff and clientele alike. While visitors to Los Angeles may initially marvel at such proficiency in someone who looks nothing like themselves, the longtime residents of Southern California's many Koreatowns will barely skip a beat, and instead complain that their steamed king crab hasn't arrived soon enough. The server will apologize and bark at a fellow Latino feverishly keeping up with similar orders to hurry up – in Korean.

Twenty miles eastward and inland, in an unassuming storefront sandwiched between a clothing store and another restaurant, young Koreans work late into the night creating a flyer in three languages: Korean, English, Spanish. The flyer is to be distributed at an afternoon protest rally in front of a Korean supermarket the next day, just when families drive from around the Southland to shop for their weekly staples. Members of Koreatown Immigrant Workers Advocates, also known as the "Alianza de trabajadores inmigrantes del Barrio Coreano" amongst Koreatown's mostly Spanish-speaking residents, infuriate the management of the supermarket targeted that day by calling on customers to boycott the store until its mix of Korean and Latino workers are afforded a living wage, more humane working conditions, and the right to unionize. But this evening preparations for the protest are underway; chief strategists of the event prepare speeches in at least two languages, while press releases are sent to the *Los Angeles Times*, *La Opinion*, and the *Korea Times*. Meanwhile, young children amusing themselves by playing hide-and-seek between the photocopy room and the executive director's office are corralled into the conference room so that they can learn the rally chants – "A Fair Share for Workers" and "Justice Now" among them – in Spanish, English, and Korean.

This scene may seem postmodern, but the common, sometimes intersecting histories of Asian-American and Latino/a workers facilitate a comparative reading of the literatures of these two LA communities. Karen Tei Yamashita redacts the cross-community interaction between two immigrant groups whose numbers have swelled in the last half-century in her novel *Tropic of Orange* (1997). One of its seven main characters is the memorable Bobby Ngu, to whom we are introduced early in the story as "Chinese from Singapore with a Vietnam name speaking like a Mexican living in Koreatown." Bobby is married but separated from Rafaela, the housekeeper at the partially built villa in Mazatlan, Mexico, owned by Gabriel, an aspiring Chicano reporter for the *Los Angeles Times*, who is casually dating Emi, a Japanese-American broadcast news producer who deliberately disassociates herself from Manzanar Murakami (whose first name reminds readers of the wartime internment camp where he was born), a homeless Japanese American whose vocation is to "direct" LA freeway traffic like a grand symphony, at least initially only in his own mind. The conceit of the novel, an orange plucked from Gabriel's Mexican courtyard traveling north to California utterly transforming the entire geography of North America, is a pseudo-apocalyptic allegory that employs the tradition of magical realism to introduce readers to cultural material as popular as news radio and the Internet, as historical as the Japanese-American internment, as mythic as the prophetic reconquest of the US Southwest from the cultural and material theft wrought by the 1848 Treaty of Guadalupe Hidalgo, and as avant-garde as the performance artist Guillermo Gómez-Peña, figured in the novel as the character Arcangel. Yamashita's Los Angeles is no multicultural paradise. Indeed, the cynical Emi exclaims in a sushi restaurant that "cultural diversity is bullshit," which infuriates a liberal white woman sitting next to her. Emi points to the chopsticks in the woman's hair, picks up two forks and asks her if one set of eating utensils might be substituted for another.[1] But neither is Los Angeles a dystopian Babel.

Tropic of Orange has been called a postmodern Asian-American novel, but beneath its surface cacophony lies an assertion of historical, cultural, and even political continuity. Although the deep chasms of culture and class, representation and resources, remain at the novel's end, Yamashita's multivalent, multivocal rendition of contemporary Los Angeles invites the reader to imagine the region's landscape as evoking, even if intermittently and imperfectly, an ethos of what Vijay Prashad calls "horizontal assimilation," the idea that different communities of color forge relations with each other against the grain of US white supremacy.[2] Migrants from Asia and Latin America may not have this relationship in mind when they cross the border or go through customs, and certainly the first words that each community learns of the other's language are the curse words they hurl in crowded apartment buildings, cramped work spaces, and dilapidated schools. But just as an excavation of relations between African-American and Asian-American communities makes for a more complex story than simple "black–Asian conflict," so Asian-American and Latino/a writers are at pains to understand and to show how the communities survive alongside one another, in what ways their communities bear responsibility when conflict emerges, whether it emerges from within or is instigated by an external force, and what kind of common language might emerge after the communities have fully incorporated each other's curse words into their vocabularies.

Certainly, the long and entrenched story of US white supremacy does not facilitate such cross-cultural knowledge. Rather, Asian Americans and Latino/as throughout the twentieth century suffered legal exclusion and persistent extra-legal violence that, although similar, often felt singular and deeply alienating. Edith Eaton, whose pen name was Sui Sin Far, was a daughter of an English merchant and a highly Westernized Chinese mother. She spent much of her literary and journalistic career documenting and fictionalizing the travails of Chinese immigrants who lived in the early part of the century, an era of profound discrimination and legal exclusion. Edith and her sister Winnifred, whose pen name was the Japanese-sounding Onoto Watanna, are considered the two mothers of Asian-American literature. Edith often embedded social critique in genre fiction and picturesque essays in terms that might pass the unsuspecting eye. For a brief period, she wrote about Los Angeles' Chinese community under her pen name for the *Los Angeles Express*. These ostensibly colorful portraits of a section of Los Angeles largely closed to the white community include discussions of well-worn images of Chinatown – brothels, laundries, curio merchants, missionary schools, and, of course, restaurants.

"In Los Angeles' Chinatown" (1903) depicts a Chinese community largely at home in the United States, a "heathen" people well on its way to Christian and American assimilation. Eaton transcribes a translation of "Now I Lay Me Down to Sleep" sung by Chinatown's children, briefly notes the "joss houses" that stand near the Christianized families, and encourages her readers to consider what about Chinese food is "interesting": "Chinese food, though rather insipid to the palate, is good and nutritious … There is nothing on a

Chinaman's table to remind one of living animals and birds – no legs, heads, limbs, wings or loins – everything is cut up small. The Chinaman comes to the table to eat – not to work." This tone of reserved sympathy that anticipates the reader's recoil from a culture often deemed inassimilable and alien persists throughout Eaton's writing about Los Angeles' Chinatown, and it is easy to miss the essay's satirical moments: while she seems to be at pains to describe its inhabitants as Christian, Eaton implies that the "heathen Chinese congregation" largely ignores the proselytizing efforts of missionaries and their Chinese preachers, and largely prefers the joss houses in order to honor ancestors. And while it would appear that children run rampant in this small space within Los Angeles, she dashes this halcyon scene of Chinatown by the story's end: "Notwithstanding what is said to the contrary, the Chinese are good livers, and there are few dyspeptics among them, their food being the kind that digests easily. According to Chinese statistics there are about 4,000 Chinese in Los Angeles, including about seventy-five women and from fifty to sixty children."[3] A subtle reminder of late-nineteenth-century exclusion laws that barred Chinese from entering the United States – targeted first and foremost at women to prevent the reproduction of Chinese-American *families* – Eaton's final sentence elucidates the effects of exclusion, a community largely bereft of its future. What begins as a tale of Chinese-American life thriving from liberal American benevolence becomes a trenchant critique of the enervation brought about by US law.

Critics have on occasion sensed in Eaton's writing a kind of missionary zeal in her advocacy for Chinese Americans, a literary social gospel that sometimes condescends toward the people for whom she writes. Still, Eaton demonstrated self-consciousness in her understanding of the pervasive and insidious quality of white supremacy, which affected not only the Chinese but other people deemed nonwhite. In her autobiographical story "Leaves from the Mental Portfolio of an Eurasian" (1909), Eaton writes poignantly about her struggles as a half-Chinese person, from the overtly racist childhood fights she and her siblings suffered to the more insidious conundrum of wondering whether she should publicly identify as Chinese in potentially dangerous situations. At one point in the story, she recounts meeting another "half Chinese, half white girl" whose face is "plastered with a thick white coat of paint" in order that she might pass as a woman of "Spanish or Mexican origin."[4] This is a curious suggestion given that Mexicans on the US side of the border were already being divorced from their "Spanish" or European-hybrid origins by Anglos intent on widening the racial gulf between them. Still, this moment may be read not only as capitulation to European standards of beauty, but also as an early expression of the kind of "horizontal assimilation" Prashad describes. Japanese and Mexican immigrants in Oxnard were as early as 1903 forming multiracial labor unions in defiance of the national tendency to exclude workers of color. This historical example provides an alternative lens through which to consider Eaton's Chinese character's attempt to pass as "Spanish or Mexican": this phrase may carry a recognition of shared conditions that counters the character's apparent acceptance of white supremacy, as it certainly does in more recent fiction.

Half a century later, the ghosts of Oxnard must have haunted José Antonio Villarreal when he published what would become a classic in Chicano/a literature, *Pocho* (1959). Set in the agricultural region of Santa Clara, *Pocho* employs a conventional bildungsroman structure to chronicle the life of Richard Rubio, a young Mexican American growing up in the chaotic era of the Great Depression. Economic crisis accentuated the racial division between whites and Mexicans, and Villarreal's novel charts the irony of this dominant racial understanding of Mexican as "dirty" for young Richard: even as his Mexican identity is denigrated by bosses and teachers, Richard finds solace in the burgeoning community that emerges in Santa Clara, as the Depression forces Mexicans into migrant labor settlements. In a sense, poverty and racism produce the coherent community that consolidates the Mexican identity that Richard deploys dialectically once he enters the white worlds of school and the Navy. While not deviating far from the tradition of the bildungsroman, Villarreal does provide elements of three historical circumstances that at least hold at bay a complete acquiescence to unfettered American belonging. First, we early learn that Richard's father participated in Pancho Villa's uprising against a corrupt Mexican government. From this legacy, Richard learns of the politicized Native, anti-Spanish, identity that would play a large role in post–World War II Mexican-American and, later, Chicano/a identity. Second, the Mexican community emerging in Santa Clara during the Depression is perhaps Villarreal's redacted insertion of the Bracero Program of 1942, which invited thousands of Mexicans as temporary guest workers into California and other states during the war. Finally, as young Richard reaches adolescence, his developing sense of Mexican camaraderie is buttressed by interracial friendships with an Italian American, other white characters, and, significantly, Thomas Nakano, a Japanese American. In Nakano we find echoes of Oxnard, ones that the novel may be at pains to foreclose, but that are never as far away from Villarreal as one might imagine.

Pocho's story ends with the United States at the brink of World War II, but it was written in the middle of the Cold War. Although the anti-Communist blacklisting of McCarthyism was on the wane by the time Villarreal published his novel, the effects of this ideological noose continued to be felt and would not be fully broken until Vietnam sent students and activists into US streets proudly chanting "Ho-Ho-Ho Chi Minh!" to protest that war. Certainly,

Richard's induction into the Navy (whose recruits targeted Mexican Americans during Los Angeles' Pachuco Riots) signals the circumscription of a nascent Chicano/a identity that necessarily wore overtly American garb.

We see elements of McCarthyite pressure at the end of *America Is in the Heart* (1946), the autobiographical novel written by Carlos Bulosan, a Filipino immigrant who was a migrant worker, labor activist, and writer; during his years in Los Angeles he became friends with journalist and labor advocate Carey McWilliams, who provided an introduction for the reissue of *America*, and novelist John Fante. Bulosan's protagonist fantasizes about a maternal America warmly embracing him and providing a faith in his adopted land that no one could take away, yet this claim of allegiance seems opposed by almost every event in the novel. The story opens with young Allos experiencing firsthand the effects of US imperialism in the recently acquired territory of the Philippines: the dispossession of peasants of their land, a corrupt and uncaring *comprador* Filipino middle class, the rapid disintegration of the Filipino family, all of which compel Allos and other young men to journey eastward to the land American missionaries promise them offers equality and opportunity.

Immediately upon landing, Allos, now renamed Carlos, experiences instead what he views as the worst and therefore most honest expressions of US society. When not cheating or being cheated by fellow Filipinos at gambling or being chased by violence-prone police furious at the prospect of brown men sexually coupling with white women, Carlos moves from town to town, farm to farm, to survive in a land that he thinks produces many deaths – psychic in his case but actual for many of his compatriots. At a crucial moment, Carlos experiences a kind of conversion, but one not so much religious as a newfound devotion to socialism, when he meets Pascual. In this encounter, what began as a narrative of failed education becomes Bulosan's actual project: a socialist bildungsroman in which the protagonist's capacity to transcend his social limits is made possible by what he describes as a fraternity of fellow laborers caught in the vise of US capitalism's fascist elements. The alignment of big business and fascism demonstrates Bulosan's facility with Popular Front rhetoric during that brief period when the American Communist Party tempered its aspirations of international solidarity with US nationalist rhetoric. To work against fascism, in Popular Front discourse, was actually to embrace communist ideals as ideals *within* the American democratic tradition. While *America* ends with a once-again renamed Carl unable to establish this brotherhood of workers and waxing nostalgically about the America found only in one's heart, he does manage to forge brief contacts that bind, in these cases, Filipinos and Mexicans in a crucially important and successful strike. Like the Japanese-Mexican Labor

Association of 1903, such glimmers are only provisional, but Bulosan is at pains to describe how they measure the distance formerly alienated workers have traveled to march together.

Villarreal and Bulosan both offer a curious, marginal figure quickly glossed over, one whose significance and impact would be felt only after McCarthy-era repression gave way to a period more willing to experiment with alternative, even militant ways of living. In *Pocho*, Richard regards with oscillating degrees of desire and repulsion the "pachuco," the figure often described as a Chicano gang member whose style of dress and language deliberately flaunts both American and Mexican social protocols. Speaking in "polyglot speech ... unintelligible to anyone but themselves," and dressing – "to the point of being ludicrous" – in what would become known as zoot-suit style, pachucos "were a menace, and the name alone classified them as undesirables, but Richard learned that there was much more to it than a mere group with a name ... And because theirs was a spontaneous, and not a planned, retaliation, he saw it as a vicissitude of society, obvious only because of its nature and comparative suddenness."[5] Likewise, in *America Is in the Heart*, when Carlos meets his brother in Los Angeles, the industrious adolescent who left the Philippines has donned the zoot suit, frequents dance halls, and forces his brother to drink hard liquor for the first time. Carlos reflects, "I found my brother Macario in a strange world. I could stand the poverty and hunger, but this desperate cynicism disturbed me. Were these Filipinos revolting against American society in this debased form?"[6]

Neither narrative grants the pachuco much credence as a figure from which to forge an identity that could adequately stand up against what Bulosan and Villarreal viewed as the deleterious effects of racial inferiority pervading both the Mexican-American and Filipino-American communities. *Pocho* views the struggle over identity as one that must reconcile a Mexican past with an American present; Bulosan seeks to envision a different "America" that fuses interracial solidarity, labor struggle, and socialism. But the figure of the pachuco, the openly rebellious figure who at once spit in the face of America and was its most profound expression, would seize the imagination of a later generation.

Oscar Zeta Acosta was born in El Paso, Texas, and raised in a small town in California's San Joaquin Valley, but his arrival in Los Angeles as a newly minted lawyer during the Chicano/a Movement of the 1960s and 1970s marked him as an indelible voice of a tumultuous era. The two narratives for which he is best remembered – *Autobiography of a Brown Buffalo* (1972) and *Revolt of the Cockroach People* (1973) – feature Buffalo Brown, a radical attorney modeled on himself. (Acosta enjoys a second fictional life as gonzo-journalist Hunter S. Thompson's self-described three-hundred-pound Samoan attorney.) *Revolt* attempts to encapsulate in narrative the explosive energy that transformed a "Mexican" community into one self-consciously "Chicano." Almost deliberately offensive in its sexism, vitriol against the Catholic Church, and the hyperbolic heroism that Acosta attributes to his protagonist, *Revolt* profanely chronicles the events of the late 1960s that culminate in the Chicano Moratorium of August 1970, a massive antiwar march that crystallized a rebellious Chicano identity at the very moment the protagonist's own life and identity disintegrate.

Brown's loss of selfhood is quite telling: it is as if Acosta suggests that the development of a viable Chicano identity (Acosta's vision was decidedly masculinist) compels an incorporation of social energies that exceed, even violate, the contours of the personal. The novel is thoroughly satirical, particularly toward the institutions that claim moral certainty – the church and the law – but at the core of the novel and its sharp critique resides a deeply romantic vision of collective consciousness embodied in the outbursts of public rebellion against the forces that hold back this revolutionary identity.

Villarreal's pachucos become Acosta's "cockroaches," figurations of unde-sirables that Los Angeles' social, cultural, and political institutions seek to eradicate at all costs. The best expression of the cockroach is the pachuco's direct descendant, the *vato loco* (crazy guy) whose psychic alienation mirrors the distance between the affluence of Anglo Los Angeles and the impoverish-ment of the Mexican sections of town like East Los Angeles, with its "streets of dogs and cats and trash, narrow jungle paths of garbage cans, beat-up jalopies, mudholes and dogshit."[7] *Vatos locos* spend their days, high on "pills, dope and wine," marking up walls in their neighborhood, and while Acosta's protago-nist's regard for them is not unqualified, it is the *vato loco*'s obsession with territoriality and space – thus the constant tagging – that serves as the primary lens through which Acosta views the struggle of Chicano/as in Los Angeles. The novel rails against the white, touristic versions of Mexican culture at Olvera Street (part of the original pueblo that was "reconstructed" by Anglo boosters in the 1930s) and the multi-million dollar Cathedral of St. Vibiana, whose opulence, along with the wealth of its parishioners, seems completely discor-dant in light of the poverty of Mexican Catholics.

The focus on space as the fulcrum of political and cultural struggle culminates in Acosta's depiction of the Chicano Moratorium, whose large-scale protest escalates into either a riot (mainstream media accounts) or police brutalization of marchers (Oscar's version). Acosta's prose bites bitter irony as it describes the aftermath: "Whittier Boulevard is burning. Tooner Flats is going up in flames … Here a police van overturned, its engine smoking. There a cop car, flames shooting out the windows. Cops marching forward with gas masks down the middle of the debris. An ordinary day in Saigon, Haiphong, Quang Tri and Tooner Flats."[8] By likening East Los Angeles to a geography of war, in this case the very war in Vietnam that brought out 30,000 protesters in the first place, Acosta implies that the struggle over space for Chicano/as is as much a project of anticolonialism as the war fought by the Vietcong in Southeast Asia. There is indeed something to the *vato loco*'s protection of Chicano space against the institutionalized "gangs" of the LA police whose primary job is to protect the territories of white Angelenos from the "cockroaches."

Meanwhile, student strikes at San Francisco State College and UC Berkeley generated a parallel Asian-American Movement that was, like its Chicana/o counterpart, simultaneously political and cultural. However, at the same time the nation watched Watts explode in black rebellion against police brutality and intransigent poverty, the United Farm Workers strike and boycott in Delano, and President Johnson respond by declaring a War on Poverty, a new image of Asian Americans was produced to counterpoint the demands of black and brown insurgency. In December 1966, *U.S. News and World Report* published an article, "Success Story of One Minority Group in the U.S.," that featured Chinese Americans as paragons of minority economic mobility who achieve success "by dint of [their] own hard work" and "not a welfare check."[9] The emergence of the Asian American as "model minority" in the mid-1960s superseded almost overnight the earlier image of the Asian as inassimilable "menace" to US society, and it framed Asian-American experience in ways that directly delegitimized other minorities' quests for radical social change.

Amy Uyematsu wrote poems during this period, but much of her literary work would not be published until much later. Her first collection of poetry, *30 Miles from J-Town* (1992), includes "Deliberate," a remembrance of how young Japanese Americans struggled to express visibly "Yellow" identity as demonstrably nonwhite:

> So by sixteen we move in packs
> learn to strut and slide
> in deliberate lowdown rhythm
> talk in a syn/co/pa/ted beat
> because we want so bad
> to be cool, never to be mistaken
> for white, even when we leave
> these rowdier L.A. streets –
> remember how we paint our eyes
> like gangsters
> flash our legs in nylons
> sassy black high heels
> or two inch zippered boots
> stack them by the door at night
> next to Daddy's muddy gardening shoes.[10]

While the ostentatious flirting with a resistant identity not unlike those of the pachucos and *vatos locos* dominates the poem, the final image of her father's gardening shoes perhaps best captures the larger project of the literary arm of the Asian-American Movement. Moving out of wartime internment camps, Japanese-American Nisei men turned to landscaping and gardening, an unassuming industry, as a primary mode of reentry into California's labor pool and the American social body. Here, however, Uyematsu's speaker ironically recasts the "gardening shoes" as an emblem not of assimilation but of quiet struggle, one as defiant as the "sassy black high heels" that the daughter wears. Indeed, for Uyematsu it is the task of the artist to give the silent gardening shoes new valence; the means to accomplish this was to find a language, one that her speaker finds in the "syn/co/pa/ted" beats of the working-class rhythms of black and brown Los Angeles. Asian-American Movement writers like Uyematsu consciously wrote in a revisionist vein to find in the historical narrative of post–World War II assimilation the seeds of radical rebellion that helped to shape an identity expressive of resistance.

A generation earlier, Hisaye Yamamoto cast the silence of the "gardening shoes" in a scene on a westward-bound bus in Los Angeles. In "Wilshire Bus" (1950), Esther Kuroiwa travels along the eponymous boulevard and encounters a racist white man taunting an elderly Asian couple, whom she assumes is, unlike Esther, Chinese American. But when the man yells "So clear out, all of you, and remember to take every last one of your slant-eyed pickaninnies with you!" just before exiting the bus, Esther realizes that her silence during the man's tirade implicates her in the man's epithets, which leaves her "once again in her life with the infuriatingly helpless, insidiously sickening sensation of there being in the world ... nothing solid."[11] Feeling helpless "once again" evokes the ghost of the traumas that Japanese Americans underwent during internment, but this time Esther's "sickening sensation" comes from the realization of how easily the helplessness of their racial victimhood could turn Japanese Americans into unwitting perpetrators of injury toward others; all this while the bus travels down Wilshire Boulevard, picking up and letting off passengers in patterns that correlate to Los Angeles' residential segregation. The "deliberate" effort to move "Daddy's gardening shoes" beyond their silence in Uyematsu's poem thus stems from her recognition of the equivocal benefits and clear dangers of not clearly stating what it means to be Asian American, which we see in Yamamoto's story.

The expressive energies of the Chicana/o and Asian-American movements that emerged so forcefully in the late 1960s would exhaust themselves by the end of the 1970s. The neighborhoods from which the movements derived their cultural material were often erased by the creative destruction of urban renewal, which razed the physical markers of communities' stories. Equally important was a demographic change in both communities that eroded the cores of their newly forged radical traditions. The Hart–Celler Immigration and Nationality Act of 1965 ushered a mass influx of new migrants from both Latin America and Asia, and profoundly remapped the demographics for both Asian Americans and Latino/as, especially in Southern California. Both the cultural displacement of "urban redevelopment" and the shape of "new" immigration of people from places beyond Mexico, China, Japan, and the Philippines have compelled a reimagination of both Latino/a and Asian-American Southern California.

Helena Maria Viramontes's collection *The Moths and Other Stories* (1985) addresses both of these forces. "The Cariboo Café" embarks on a tripartite narrative to depict the parallel struggles between longtime Chicano residents and new immigrants who we might infer hail from the then-politically repressive state of El Salvador. Recasting well-known legends of "fallen" Mexican women such as La Llorona from masculinist Chicano renditions of womanly betrayal of *la causa*, Viramontes offers a seemingly disjunctive story from three narrative perspectives to shed slanted light on the struggles that Salvadoran migrants suffer as they flee *La Migra* (the Immigration and Naturalization Service), the US equivalent of the *polie* (the repressive arm of the Salvadoran state). Viramontes carefully plays on the blunt racial lumping that *La Migra* exacts on this now expanded Latino/a community in Los Angeles, as her Salvadoran characters fear deportation "back" to Tijuana, Mexico.

In another story, "Growing," Viramontes provides a broader history of Pacific Rim migration by placing young Chicano/as and the East LA barrio in which they play baseball amidst other, buried stories of immigrants, in this case, Chinese:

> She pitched and Chano made the connection quick, hard, the ball rising high and flying over Piri's, Lourdes', Naomi's and Lucía's heads and landing in the Chinese Cemetery… Lourdes searched frantically for the ball, tip-toeing across the graves saying, excuse me, please excuse, excuse me, until she found the ball peacefully buried behind a huge gray marble stone, and she yelled to no one in particular, CATCH IT, SOMEONE CATCH IT.

Lourdes's injunction to "no one in particular" to catch the baseball that landed on another buried immigration story gains additional resonance when read alongside "Neighbors," a story that ostensibly pits an aging Aura Rodríguez, defending the "perimeters" of her East LA home, against the "tough-minded young men who threw empty beer cans into her yard." Aura makes a fatal mistake: she calls the police, whose brutal response against

the gang makes the eventual confrontation between its younger members and
the old woman as fateful as the story suggests it is violent. But Viramontes
carefully demonstrates that this internecine and intergenerational conflict is
largely a product of the spatial destruction of the neighborhood by "company
men [who] tore into the shabby homes" to make way for a freeway.[12]
Likewise, Lourdes's search for the baseball invokes the utter transformation
of the Chicano community, uprooted to make way for Dodger Stadium in the
Chavez Ravine barrio. For Viramontes, both spatial transformation and new
immigration displace the desire for American "belonging" that we see in
Villarreal's work or Chicano/a reclamation in Acosta's, and her stories
emphasize the shared fragility of identities of survival that has the threat of
death and alienation at its core.

The layers of immigration history that create the palimpsest of Southern
California's racial geography require a more complex language of cultural
identity and authenticity that recognizes contemporary identity as a hybrid
product of multiple cultures and the dynamics of cultural forces and personal
choices. Contemporary mixed-race authors have described Los Angeles as a
mélange, but one that is conflictual. Sesshu Foster paints a haunting, sometimes inchoate and byzantine scene. One prose-poem "love song" to East Los
Angeles highlights this place in all its brutal humanity, especially in the wake
of the 1992 Justice Riots:

> Los Angeles is my city, I sucked on her neck, gave her purple hickeys before she
> backhanded me out a car at 35 MPH on a turn in Highland Park. From a street
> corner, all the Chinese signs in Alhambra declare her love. Korean signs of
> Koreatown are just another word for feelings. Beautiful hair of Vietnamese
> noodles. Wonderful smile of oranges sold at East L.A. on-ramps. Big bottles
> of pigs' feet & giant kosher dills on the counter at every corner store… Babies,
> shot in the head, not knowing how to love, how to write their names. They cry
> too much. Their parents cry too much in churches.[13]

Borders between Asian and Latino/a Los Angeles blur in Foster's poems: a
poem that features Chuy from El Salvador is followed immediately by a
verbatim reproduction of the military exclusion order that sent the
Japanese-American community of Los Angeles' Little Tokyo to internment
camps.

Meanwhile, Brian Ascalon Roley's satirical bildungsroman of Asian-
American masculinity, *American Son* (1999), features two half-white, half-
Filipino brothers living in the working-class section of Los Angeles' Westside.
The socially awkward, model-minority protagonist daily confronts his older
brother, who acts and dresses like a twenty-first-century iteration of a *vato
loco* in order to forge a resistant urban manhood in a place where such

braggadocio is perhaps the only cogent, even if limited, response to the idealized form of affluent white masculinity the brothers can never achieve. Affluence and poverty collide in *American Son*, refuting common images of the beachfront communities as inhabited solely by the wealthy. The rich do exist, but in a more intimate proximity to the have-nots than they like to imagine:

> Abbot Kenny Street's New Age boutiques and artist's stores look funky and bright with afternoon shoppers. At night here it is empty except for the black kids who hang out at the liquor stores and the Lee Fan kick-boxing students who are not afraid of the black and Mexican gangs that come here to shoot each other and sometimes die.[14]

If Foster's *City Terrace* embraces the discontinuous histories of different groups that make up this space, Roley's portrait of West Los Angeles highlights the limitations of cross-cultural fertilization to mitigate the rage of social deprivation.

Even as they acknowledge identity's element of performance, these writers resolutely refuse the idea that identities are changed with such facility as to become fashionable accessories easily acquired and discarded. Rather, they remain deeply engaged with the material conditions that produce such identities and out of which some transformation of the city and its existing spatial order (a legacy of discrimination and economic disfranchisement) might be possible. Indeed, as both Latino/as and Asian Americans continue to encounter one another on the corners, and in the apartment buildings and storefronts of Southern California, the axis of East–West struggle that was once the domain of Asian-American concern and the axis of North–South struggle that dominated Chicano/a and Latino/a imaginations are aligning together. Thus, it is no surprise that Bobby in Yamashita's *Tropic of Orange*, the "Chinese from Singapore with a Vietnam name speaking like a Mexican living in Koreatown," struggles to reunite with his Chicana wife, Rafaela, and half-Asian, half-Mexican son, Sol; the magical geographies of the two axes coincide as Bobby literally (in this magical realist trope) carries the Tropic of Cancer north.

The promise of Asian-American and Latino/a reimaginations of Los Angeles lies precisely in acknowledging *both* the power and the fictitiousness of the borders and boundaries that separate one community from another, and in this acknowledgment creating possibilities for new social imaginaries in response to Bobby's questions, which in many ways are the questions that Asian-American and Latino/a writers have asked relentlessly through the years: "What are these goddamn lines anyway? What do they connect? What do they divide? What's he holding on to? What's he holding on to?"[15]

As Bobby lets go of the line that separates him from his family, for a brief moment borders are crossed to facilitate the family's reunion. While the line reconnects to reestablish the boundaries of culture, class, and nation – the present social imaginary – this provisional break is perhaps Yamashita's prophetic hope for what the cultures of these two communities colliding in Los Angeles might bring about or at least augur.

NOTES

1. Karen Tei Yamashita, *Tropic of Orange* (Minneapolis: Coffee House Press, 1997), pp. 15, 128–9.
2. Vijay Prashad, *Everybody Was Kung Fu Fighting: Afro-Asian Connections and the Myth of Cultural Purity* (Boston: Beacon, 2002), p. x.
3. Sui Sin Far, *Mrs. Spring Fragrance and Other Writings*, ed. Amy Ling and Annette White-Parks (Urbana: University of Illinois Press, 1995), pp. 199–200, 200.
4. *Ibid.*, p. 227.
5. José Antonio Villarreal, *Pocho* (New York: Anchor Books, 1959), p. 150.
6. Carlos Bulosan, *America Is in the Heart* (Seattle: University of Washington Press, 1973), p. 133.
7. Oscar Zeta Acosta, *The Revolt of the Cockroach People* (New York: Bantam, 1974), p. 35.
8. *Ibid.*, p. 217.
9. "Success Story of One Minority Group in the U.S.," *U.S. News and World Report*, Dec. 26, 1966, 73.
10. Amy Uyematsu, "Deliberate," in *30 Miles from J-Town* (Brownsville, Or.: Story Line Press, 1992), p. 16.
11. Hisaye Yamamoto, "Wilshire Bus," in *Seventeen Syllables and Other Stories* (New Brunswick, N.J.: Rutgers University Press, 2001), p. 37.
12. Helena Maria Viramontes, "Growing," in *The Moths and Other Stories* (Houston: Arte Público Press, 1988), p. 41; "Neighbors," *ibid.*, pp. 102, 106.
13. Sesshu Foster, *City Terrace Field Manual* (New York: Kaya, 1996), p. 51.
14. Brian Ascalon Roley, *American Son* (New York: W. W. Norton, 2001), p. 140.
15. Yamashita, *Tropic of Orange*, p. 268.

8

JULIAN MURPHET

The literature of urban rebellion

Pseudo-events

Los Angeles' "coolie riots" of 1871, in which nineteen Chinese were "hanged and shot in one evening," never attained literary memorialization;[1] but they confirmed a trend that was to become typical of Los Angeles, where riots tended to be upsurges of public violence against scapegoat minorities. The first such pseudo-event to receive literary attention was the "Red hysteria" of 1919. As Los Angeles adapted to the afterglow of the Great War, the anti-Bolshevik propaganda emanating from Washington percolated down into everyday acts of violent anti-Leftism. Police Chief George K. Home raided the Industrial Workers of the World hall on October 2, and crowed to the press that the "cleanup" would continue "until the last of their number has been placed behind bars or driven from the city."[2] Servicemen and citizens took this task into their own hands: "about twenty-five men in full uniform of the Army and Navy together with a few civilians raided the IWW headquarters ... while a 'defense' meeting was in progress, drove out the occupants, hospitalized four, and demolished the furniture and equipment. Five of the alleged IWW members were arrested and charged with inciting a riot."[3]

The incident was processed into the climax of Upton Sinclair's 1927 epic, *Oil!*:

> There came rushing down the street a squadron of motor-cars, two abreast and blocking the way entirely; and from them leaped a crowd of some fifty men, carrying weapons of various sorts, clubs, hatchets, pieces of iron pipe. They made a rush for the entrance [of the IWW hall], and a moment later the music ceased, and there came a sound of shrieks, and the crash of glass and battering of heavy blows.[4]

Within minutes, "like the passing of a tornado" the mob violence is over, and the protagonist enters the dance hall to discover the beaten bodies of working men, and children thrown into a boiling coffee urn. The attackers are revealed to be sailors from the nearby fleet responding in "patriotic indignation" to false rumors of an IWW raid. Sinclair's brief vignette discloses the truth about collective violence in Los Angeles prior to 1965: far from being a manifestation of the political will of the oppressed, mass violence tended to be administered from above, or by "patriotic" citizens reacting to a simulacrum of a threat. It is felt in "that horrible drumming of blows – you couldn't tell whether they were falling on furniture or on human bodies" that Sinclair adduces to clinch the scene's affective intensity, somewhere between sound and tactility; a rain of anonymous terror on unprotected flesh.[5]

Los Angeles' tendency toward the pseudo-event was confirmed by the so-called Pachuco Riots of 1943. If the patriotism aroused by World War I had been projected inward against Moscow's localized Red threat, the strategy was not repeatable in a World War II context where the Soviet Union was a valued ally. In early June 1943, large numbers of servicemen and sailors stationed in Los Angeles repeated history by seizing on new forms of "anti-Americanness" parading the streets. The chief offenders in the altered urban everyday life of wartime, the subject of numerous editorials and denunciations by public authorities, were not Reds but zoot-suiters, youth gangs sporting loudly colored, oversized drape suits with "ankle-tight pegged cuffs, reet pleats, peg tops, lids, and DA hairstyles" in defiance of official prescriptions of austerity and patriotic homogeneity.[6] These suits and the youth fad associated with them were national phenomena, but in Los Angeles the principal protagonists were working-class Chicanos from the growing barrios in East LA.

When the servicemen took to the streets on June 3, however, commandeering taxis and blitzing the barrios with the idea of "destroy[ing] every zoot suit in Los Angeles County," ethnicity was not the organizing frame of the attacks. The initial assessment of the violence as "race riots" may have been well intentioned, but it was misguided to the extent that it attributed entrenched local motives to recruits from all over the country with no prior exposure to Los Angeles' peculiar racial topography. Instead, the violence, which was unusual in consisting of "no looting, burning, raping, or killing," was projected from one (military) youth group at another (civilian) youth group on the basis of *style* and what it communicated at an unconscious level of cultural politics.[7] For several nights, the servicemen and gangs of civilian abetters roamed the streets beating zoot-suiters, stripping them bare, and shaving their hair – symbolically castrating their sexual dandyism. Yet such a style war would finally be inextricable from ethnicity, as the literary work in which this pseudo-event found its ultimate expression would make clear.

Luis Valdez

Luis Valdez, who cut his theatrical teeth on the California farmworkers' struggles of the 1960s, turned to the subject matter of the Pachuco Riots in the late 1970s, at a time when Mexican Americans had established their way of life as the "second" culture of the region. Far from wanting to consign the pseudo-event to a sociological curiosity of the war years, Valdez sought to recuperate the utopian dimension of the zoot-suit craze, and thus to reposition the militarist reaction as a limit placed by the establishment itself on the constitutional "freedom of expression." It was important to uncouple that utopian dimension from any too-easy correspondence with Chicano identity per se – to erect formal barriers between the embodied representative of the "zoot"-effect, and the play's more abstract endorsement of the expressive effect. From his involvement in political community theater, Valdez assumed a Brechtian distance between characters and audience; from his sense of Chicano-Mayan/Aztec ethnic traditionalism he adapted *corrido* musicality, group dance, and a mythic iconicity; and from mainstream entertainment theater he took the lure of attractive young characters, courtroom and prison settings, and a kinetic forward drive.

It was with these hybrid techniques that Valdez pinioned his historical material in *Zoot Suit* (1978). He avoided the pitfalls of essentialism by positioning his young hero-protagonist, Henry Reyna, along the fault line between his own ethnic identity and his patriotic enlistment in the Navy. The temptation to play Anglo servicemen against Chicano civilian youth as stereotypical presences is deconstructed in advance by the sense of affinity the hero has with each group. His pachuco self is incarnated alongside him in the allegorical figure of El Pachuco, whose admonitions drive a wedge between Henry's national and ethnic identities: "this isn't your country. Look what's happening all around you. The Japs have sewed up the Pacific. Rommel is kicking ass in Egypt but the Mayor of L.A. has declared all-out war on Chicanos. On you!"[8] Meanwhile, the Irish police prey on the young man's familial pride as a second-generation American: "I'm thinking of your family, Hank. Your old man would be proud to see you in the Navy."[9] Valdez concentrates most of the play's energies in this contradictory interior zone, wisely preferring to avoid direct representation of the riots. The dramaturgical method tends toward 1930s Newspaper Theater: the curtain consists of a giant facsimile of a newspaper front page; scenes follow one another according to testimony, memory, and symbolic intensity rather than literal consecution; and the choral figure of El Pachuco himself constantly interrupts and comments on proceedings.

The riots are felt all the more accurately in their symbolic dimension by keeping the stage action psychological. For the symbolism of these riots overrode their literalness to the very extent that what was being attacked was not the *actual* bodies of persons, but their very *style* as *personae*. Thus the prologue spoken by El Pachuco:

The Pachuco Style was an act in Life
And his language was a new creation.
His will to be was an awesome force
Eluding all documentation ...
A mythical, quizzical, frightening being
Precursor of revolution
Or piteous, hideous heroic joke
Deserving of absolution?
I speak as an actor on the stage.
The Pachuco was existential
For he was an Actor in the streets
Both profane and reverential.[10]

What was aspired to, and what was attacked, during the riots was this quotidian actor-character, which El Pachuco himself embodies throughout the play. The violence was projected against something that existed not in flesh and blood, but in attitude, gesture, and dress; and so it is that, in the most powerful scene, as news of the riot seeps into prison and Henry imagines it, we are given a dumb show:

EL PACHUCO *is overpowered and stripped as* HENRY *watches helplessly from his position. The* PRESS *and* SERVICEMEN *exit with pieces of* EL PACHUCO's *zoot suit.* EL PACHUCO *stands. The only item of clothing on his body is a small loincloth.* HE *turns and looks at* HENRY, *with mystic intensity.* HE *opens his arms as an Aztec conch blows, and* HE *slowly exits backward with powerful calm into the shadows. Silence.* HENRY *comes downstage.* HE *absorbs the impact of what* HE *has seen and falls to his knees at center stage, spent and exhausted.*

Here we are reminded that Henry is "*dark, Indian-looking, older than his years*" (twenty-six), as Valdez pulls the rug out from any simplistic essentialism. The moment audaciously alters the theatrical elements in play. It also, mutely, harkens back to a "precursor of revolution" in the richness of Native-American style obliterated by European settlement. If I suggest that the play is offered in tacit solidarity, not with a 1943 pseudo-event, but with the nascent youth culture of punk – with its Mohawk haircuts, savage face adornments, and torn clothing – which was just establishing a beachhead in Los Angeles during the writing of this play, then that is to recognize how mobile and resourceful the play's symbolic elements are, and to commemorate youth culture's fractured assaults upon establishmentarian anti-style throughout the twentieth century. Utopia leaves its traces in the inventiveness with which youth "find[s] a style of urban survival / in the rural skirts and outskirts / of the brown metropolis of Los."[11]

Watts, 1965

In the war-stimulated boom of the late 1940s and 1950s, something else was happening to the racial complexion of that "brown metropolis": it was becoming still darker. The booming military–industrial complex lured thousands of poor Southern blacks to the Southland through Watts, the unofficial Ellis Island of black Los Angeles. By the mid-1960s, as the great period of full employment had come to an end, Watts itself was 87 percent black and working class, living in overcrowded conditions and vigilantly patrolled by the nation's most notorious police force. Cut adrift physically by the new freeway system, Watts stewed in its own juices in what Thomas Pynchon called "a country which lies, psychologically, uncounted miles further than most whites seem at present willing to travel."[12] On August 11, 1965, Marquette Frye was pulled over for speeding down Avalon Boulevard, and the pressure under which the community had been suffering suddenly erupted. "The rioting continued for six days, leaving 34 dead, over 1000 injured badly enough to require treatment, nearly 4000 arrested, and 1000 buildings damaged or destroyed, at a probable loss, in 1965 dollars, of $40 million."[13]

In her recollections of the riots, Wanda Coleman, Watts's premier poet, recalls: "All whites and light-skinned blacks mistaken for whites were being forced out of the 'cordoned off' area. My husband didn't dare to go out in daylight for fear we'd be separated. There was little to do but watch the televised coverage. Frequently we saw the same scene unfold on the streets below as took place on camera."[14] There is much at stake in these spare sentences. We sense the degree to which the city's geographically segregated racial demographics are internalized to the community's own means of managing civil unrest; we see how "cordoning off" works on two or three distinct levels, right down to the disjunction between husband and wife; and above all we glean an insight into Los Angeles' mediation of itself as spectacle, so that even someone caught directly in the middle of a genuine urban event has to access it first of all through the television, and then, belatedly, sees the "same scene unfold on the streets." Coleman's record of poetic work, an extensive formal meditation on existential antagonisms from the broadest social scale right down to the most intimate spaces of the self, is deeply scarred by the violence of 1965. Her poems are dispassionate tabulations of the fact-metaphors that govern everyday life in a space torn apart by rebellion, exposing the true fault lines of race and class:

> i drip blood
> on my way to and from work
> i drip blood

> down the aisles while shopping at the supermarket
> i drip blood
> standing in line at the bank ...
> the wolf will come for me sooner or later
> i know this
> the wolf makes no sexual distinctions
> i am the right color
> he has a fetish for black meat ...[15]

It is not enough to decode "the wolf" as a symbol of white Los Angeles; the poem works because it is also meant as the irrational upsurge of something immanent. The wolf ravages from within, he is the very condition of possibility of the riot as such, making "black meat" the material of his own, non-subjective urban frenzy.

Coleman's verse is disposed around a sense of the black body as the site of everyday violence in Los Angeles, and as that which fails to register in the ceaseless streams of unreality emanating from Los Angeles' culture industries.[16] In this respect, it borrows from the Black Arts Movement, but Coleman's corporeality is more versatile than most contemporary black aesthetics. Witness her "Essay on Language," in which the tongue is heralded as a common denominator of African Americans:

> and so we found

> thru deceit, ways to keep our tongue alive. to let it live within us
> though departed from our source. to become the tongue itself
> (attitude) so that it speaks even in our bodily movements. so that it
> seduces english, snaking back to ourselves. so that the dominant
> tongue, once infected with our hunger will one day succumb without
> divining what has passed (unspoken).

This utopian prophecy touches base in a bodily specificity – "my tongue alive in my particular vocalizations, chorusing with like others also singing"[17]– which, as style, belies the medium of print and aligns its authenticity with the art of performance, music, and spoken word poetry.

We thus reconfirm Valdez's intuition about the Pachuco Riots, that they would attain optimum expression in the medium of live performance. The longer Los Angeles' status as the nation's dream capital persisted, the more the rhythms of the human body were felt as a source of legitimacy amid the irreality of nascent postmodernity. When screenwriter and novelist Budd Schulberg, moved by the plight of the ghetto and all the "unheard voices" of which the riots had given evidence, opened up a writers' workshop in the very heart of Watts, he had assumed that print would be the best medium for a wider communication. The results of that workshop were published as *From the Ashes: Voices of Watts* (1967), and included the work of eighteen writers reflecting not so much on the urban violence itself as, again, the existential conditions in which it had taken root. Alvin Saxon, also known as Ojenke, contributed his landmark poem "Black Power," and Johnie Scott offered his autobiographical essay "The Coming of the Hoodlum." But the most significant of Schulberg's initiates were the Watts Prophets: Anthony "Amde" Hamilton, Richard Dedeaux, Otis O'Solomon, and Dee Dee McNeil. The Prophets built their word-art around spoken performance, often set to music. Inspired by the local avant-garde jazz scene, the Prophets "took poetry from the podium to the stage," as Dedeaux has said. "We added dimensions to it. We started putting movement to it, drama, and the call and response."[18] This fleshing out of text into drama and performance was critical, and it gave radical power to the language of such raps as "Freedom Flame/What Is a Man":

> Putting us in a cage was a mistake.
> All that did was intensify hate.
> And now shackled to our cages you expect us to wait
> While you fool around on the moon?
> And from there look for another place to conquer
> While I throw another log on the fire.
> ...
> The flames are at their peak can't wait.
> Too many broken promises, too many black babies asking why.
> Too many restless armies in the ghetto.[19]

The riots endure in this kind of speech as an incendiary metaphorics, a linguistic legacy of rebellion, duplicated in the stridency and timbre of the voice that articulates it. It is here that urban violence is subjectified, not as memory, but through an ongoing stylistic fidelity to its causes, the enraged and restless voices incited by unkept promises and unanswered questions. Tongue, lips, teeth, and larynx: Los Angeles' first popular riots are faithfully assumed as a responsibility in *this* medium above all, where a human body and the abstract codes of "english" are mutually "seduced" – the Voice.

1992 Justice Riots

Twenty-seven years later, when Los Angeles endured the most destructive event of its history (and the costliest national rebellion since the Civil War), the embodied word once again suggested itself as the logical form that any adequate representation of it would take. The trigger for these riots was televisual: a police beating of a black man, Rodney King, was videotaped and sent to a news agency, before becoming the primary evidence against the officers involved in a major criminal case. When the jurors acquitted the officers of all charges, violence broke out in a new and unpredictable urban pattern, reflecting the fact that racial tensions were no longer described along a monochromatic axis. "Groups once the majority of inhabitants in certain areas were by 1990 just one of several minorities there."[20] Hispanic and Asian layers diffracted the bipartite tensions of 1965 into a fully multicultural urban revolt against all kinds of perceived injustice. But the place of the media was all important, since the motor of perpetuation and extension was the screened spectacle of an unchained urban violence, filmed from helicopters, by which all of Los Angeles was transfixed.

The artist best positioned to "represent" the complex events of 1992 was Baltimore-born dramatist Anna Deavere Smith. Smith's long-term theatrical project, "On the Road: In Search of American Character," consists of a sequence of one-woman shows organized around the same methodological principles. Smith interviews many subject-participants in significant incidents, and then "performs" them verbatim in edited sequence to project a sense of the multiplicity internal to any event. The essence of Smith's art is to hone in on the voice, somewhere between a bodily and a linguistic process, as the venue of something that is neither of these two things: *character*. Smith is interested in linguistic events, not as semantic occurrences, but as *excesses* of meaning – those moments at which, during a speech act, words and body make a detour, and betray some underlying fixation or unconscious drive. While her works may appear to privilege the consciousness of the individual, in actuality it is the dimension of anonymity within the individual that she maps. Smith puts it this way: "The point is simply to repeat [the speech act] until I begin to feel it and what I begin to feel is his song and that helps me to remember more about his body ... My body begins to do the things that he probably must do inside while he's speaking."[21] Smith suggests that the wellspring of urban rebellion lies here, at this unconscious layer of what one "must do inside" while speaking.

In adapting her project to the specific requirements of Los Angeles in 1992, Smith wanted to dismantle the expectation of an eye-in-the-sky "unifying voice" to explain the savagery of the riots. The voices of *Twilight: Los Angeles, 1992* (1994) are plural, and to that extent faithfully echo the prevailing ideological matrix of multiculturalism; blacks, whites, Chicano/as, Koreans, intellectuals, spectators, policemen, gangbangers, and so on – *Twilight* provides a reasonable cross-section of the riots' constituency. But more than that, the play testifies to a certain plurality and inconsistency within each "individual," who cannot adequately know or represent herself, let alone a racial collective. Looking at the instructive prologue to the piece, by "Rudy Salas, Sr.," we note that Mr. Salas performs much more than his self or his "people" when he speaks of the legacy of white police harassment. Speaking of his grandfather who rode with Pancho Villa in the Mexican Revolution, he then reflects:

> So I grew up with all this rich stuff at home
> (*Three quick hits on the table and a double sweep*)
> and then at school,
> first grade, they started telling me
> I was inferior
> because I was a Mexican,
> and that's where
> (*He hits the table several times, taps, twenty-three taps until line 'the enemy' and then on 'nice white teachers' his hand sweeps the table*)
> I realized I had an enemy
> and that enemy was those nice white teachers.
> I wonder what it is,
> why
> did I have this madness
> that I understood this?
> It's not an enemy I hated.
> It's not a hate thing,
> the insanity that I carried with me started when I took the beating
> from the police.
> Okay, that's where the insanity came in.
> In forty-
> two,
> when I was in my teens
> running around as a zoot-suiter,
> one night the cop really tore me up bad.[22]

Here is a possible genealogy of urban rebellion in Los Angeles – not the expression of an ethnic essentialism, felt as some kind of inner truth of being, but inferiority repeatedly branded via publicly sanctioned violence. This is felt immediately as a "madness," a schism within consciousness, which at this traumatic point cannot rationally reflect upon "why" it is so, but breaks down into gestures and tics. The "understanding" Mr. Salas has of his condition is just that irrepressible tapping and sweeping of his hands, an "insanity" of the body that is the distillate of the beatings he took as a zoot-suiter in his teens. The body performs more than it knows, speech deviates from its wonted course, and ethnicity is broken down into its component parts as a defensive reaction against being "torn up bad" by social discrimination. The deepest literary lesson of urban rebellion in Los Angeles is this dismantlement of identity in the name of preconscious drives circling the void of a "city without a center." From the very beginning, all serious literature written from this city has shown the impossible everyday tensions that result from that restless circling, from Nathanael West's *Day of the Locust* to Chandler's Marlowe's frantic mapping operations, Pynchon's politicized archaeologies, Ellroy's combustive jazz prose, and beyond: if this is not all literature of urban rebellion, it is literature that registers the tectonic frictions of a long history of urban unrest.

NOTES

1. Henry Norton, *The Story of California from the Earliest Days to the Present* (Chicago: A. C. McClurg & Co., 1924), p. 294.
2. "Every Red an Active Criminal, Say Authorities; Arrests Started," *Los Angeles Times*, Oct. 2, 1919, 2:1.
3. Woodrow C. Whitten, "Criminal Syndicalism and the Law in California: 1919–1927," *Transactions of the American Philosophical Society*, New Series, 59.2 (1969), 38.
4. Upton Sinclair, *Oil!* (New York: Penguin, 2008), p. 529.
5. *Ibid.*, pp. 529–30.
6. Mauricio Mazón, *The Zoot-Suit Riots: The Psychology of Symbolic Annihilation* (Austin: University of Texas Press, 1984), pp. 7–8.
7. *Ibid.*, pp. 79, 85.
8. Luis Valdez, *Zoot Suit and Other Plays* (Houston: Arte Público Press, 1992), p. 30.
9. *Ibid.*, p. 32.
10. *Ibid.*, pp. 25–6.
11. *Ibid.*, pp. 81, 80.
12. Thomas Pynchon, "A Journey into the Mind of Watts," *New York Times Magazine*, June 12, 1966, 78.
13. David O. Sears, "Urban Rioting in Los Angeles: A Comparison of 1965 with 1992," in Mark Baldassare, ed., *The Los Angeles Riots: Lessons for the Urban Future* (Boulder, Colo.: Westview Press, 1994), p. 238.
14. Wanda Coleman, *Native in a Strange Land: Trials & Tremors* (Santa Rosa, Calif.: Black Sparrow Press, 1996), p. 79.
15. Coleman, *Mad Dog Black Lady* (Santa Rosa: Black Sparrow Press, 1979), p. 17.
16. Pynchon, "A Journey," p. 84.
17. Coleman, "Essay on Language," *Kenyon Review* 14.4 (1992), 122–3, 123.
18. CD liner notes, The Watts Prophets, *Things Gonna Get Greater: The Watts Prophets 1969–1971* (San Francisco: Water 157, 2005).
19. The Watts Prophets, "What Is a Man," *ibid.*
20. Peter A. Morrison and Ira S. Lowy, "A Riot of Color: The Demographic Setting," in Baldassare, ed., *The Los Angeles Riots*, p. 23.
21. Anna Deavere Smith, *Fires in the Mirror: Crown Heights, Brooklyn and Other Identities* (New York: Anchor Books, 1993), p. xxv.
22. Smith, *Twilight: Los Angeles, 1992* (New York: Anchor Books, 1994), p. 2.

9

WILLIAM MARLING

City of sleuths

The prototypical Los Angeles detective was invented in San Francisco by Dashiell Hammett. Whether his name was the Continental Op or Sam Spade, he was hard-boiled, with a blue-collar attitude, edgy repartee, and a close connection to his setting. Hammett used him to portray the city, its political corruption, its fog and docks and hills, its cab drivers and efficiency apartments. By 1925 the Op was already a working stiff who suffered for his drinking bouts. With a few changes, he became Sam Spade, the iconic hero of *The Maltese Falcon* (1930). In this novel and *The Glass Key* (1931), Hammett showed that the detective novel could be political allegory, cynical love story, or tale of tragic friendship. "Once a detective story can be as good as this," wrote Raymond Chandler in "The Simple Art of Murder" (1944), "only the pedants will deny that it *could* be even better."[1]

Los Angeles crime writers also drew inspiration from Raoul Whitfield, who moved to Los Angeles in 1929, drawn by the aviation and film industries. He developed Mel Ourney, an ex-con and sometime detective whose search for stolen emeralds combines geographic sweep and dubious morality in *Green Ice* (1930), and Ben Jardinn, who tracks the killer of a conductor murdered while leading a concert in the Hollywood Bowl in *Death in a Bowl* (1932). Using the pen name Ramon Decolta, Whitfield also created Filipino detective Jo Gar, one of the first ethnic detectives. Another important precursor was Paul Cain, whose *Fast One* (1932) featured Gerry Kells, a minimalist version of Sam Spade so terse, so tough that one critic wrote he seemed to have been created with a scalpel.

The Great Depression was key to the creation of Los Angeles as a distinct detective terrain, for it led to a reevaluation of American myths about self-creation, honesty, and upward mobility. When outsiders such as James M. Cain moved to Los Angeles for work in film, they tried to impose their preconceptions on the city. Meanwhile writers of longer residence, such as Chandler and Horace McCoy, offered local interpretations of the region for the national understanding. The result of this ideological jostling was that the "land of sunshine and oranges" was soon recast as "mean streets." The outsiders made astronomical salaries: Hollywood paid Hammett $1,000 a week to live in a penthouse at the Biltmore with a cook and driver. James M. Cain moved from the *New York World* for $400 a week.[2] Their tone was literary and disillusioned, but the locals struggled in a pulp jungle. Chandler wrote his first stories for a penny a word. Horace McCoy, a bohemian aviator, wrote simultaneously for six pulp magazines to pay his bills. Down on his luck, he hired out as a bouncer at a marathon dance contest, which he later turned into *They Shoot Horses, Don't They?* (1935).

During the Depression, Southern California fared better than other regions. Earlier municipal reforms protected Los Angeles from the depths of corruption seen in many cities, and crime in the city was rather minor. As David Fine notes, the "noir" that LA novelists created was "contrapuntal," a reaction against two fatigued metaphors: the Romantic view rooted in the Spanish past and the "Progressive" view of the city's boosters. Annoyed by both versions of Los Angeles, the noir writers focused on the finiteness of the "man-made landscape – the roadside motor court, the dance hall at the edge of the ocean, the car on the Coast Highway – as images of deception, metaphors for betrayed hope."[3]

James M. Cain initially praised California's roads and schools, its courteous citizens and kind climate. But he was suspicious of the lack of smokestack industries supporting the good life: he felt local economic life lacked "voltage" and began to look for a narrative that would epitomize his unease. His first success was "The Baby in the Ice Box," which he sold to the studios. Then, with screenwriter Vincent Lawrence's aid, he retold New York's 1927 Gray–Snyder murder in *The Postman Always Rings Twice* (1934).

Not a detective novel per se, *Postman* is the first major work of LA noir. It is a confession, told by the criminal, Frank Chambers, who kills the Greek owner of a roadside restaurant for his sensual wife, Cora. The force that brings him to justice is the insurance industry; as the judge explains to Frank, "They'll spend five times as much as Los Angeles County will let me put into a case. They've got detectives five times as good as any I'll be able to hire. They know their stuff from A to izzard, and they're right on your tail now. It means money to them." Cain's style was widely copied: he avoided "he said" and "she said" speech tags, and his characters' dialogue was brilliantly self-revealing. "They threw me off the hay truck about noon," is Frank Chambers's opening line, and he says that Cora's lips "stuck out in a way that made me want to mash them in for her."[4]

Cain followed with *Double Indemnity* (1936), which hewed more tightly to the Gray–Snyder case. Insurance salesman Walter Huff and blonde bombshell Phyllis Nirlinger plot to kill her husband, but to make it look like an accident and collect the double indemnity due in an accidental death. As quasi-detective, Huff's boss, claims investigator Barton Keyes, tracks down the murderers. Listening to his intuitions, Keyes unravels Huff's perfect crime. The settings are quintessentially LA – a supermarket, a drugstore on Sunset and Vine, the Hollywood Hills – and driving is at once leisure, rendezvous, and means of crime.

Across town, Chandler and Erle Stanley Gardner were grinding out stories and meeting for dinner with veteran genre writers Dwight Babcock, Cleve Adams, and W. T. Ballard, who invented the first "studio detective," an investigator who works for a movie studio. They called themselves the Fictioneers. Gardner had moved to California when young and became a lawyer in Oxnard, then a wide open town of bars, brothels, and immigrants. After trying various protagonists and professions, Gardner hit on defense lawyer Perry Mason in *The Case of the Velvet Claws* (1933). Mason works at a modest LA office with his secretary, Della Street, and investigator Paul Drake. In print Mason is closer to the pulp magazine tradition and blunt about his line of work: "I'm a specialist in getting people out of trouble... If you look me up through some family lawyer or some corporation lawyer, he'll probably tell you that I'm a shyster. If you look me up through some chap in the District Attorney's office, he'll tell you that I'm a dangerous antagonist."[5] He juggles, conceals, and even creates evidence, misleads the police, breaks into apartments, and tampers with witnesses. He is always justified by the outcome, and excused by judges, for "If facts can be shuffled in such a way that it will confuse a witness who is not absolutely certain of his story ... I claim the attorney is within his rights."[6]

In most ways, Mason is a generic, methodical version of Spade, one who talks, rather than punches, his way through cases. In other respects he is the foundational character of the LA police procedural, which develops after 1945. Like procedurals, Gardner's novels are highly structured. The first quarter presents the charges against Mason's client, while the second shows contrary evidence produced by Drake or contradictions uncovered by Mason. The second half, set in court, reveals the pettiness of human desires and grievances, or the fallibility of perception and everyday logic. The Perry Mason novels are not rich in landscape, however. Except for some Westerns and *The Case of the Drowsy Mosquito* (1943), Gardner's settings are generically Southern Californian.

The opportunity to make Southern California geography work for detective fiction fell to Raymond Chandler, who brought an outsider's eye (he was raised in England and Ireland) and a classical education. When he fell for a married woman and lost his high-paying job in the oil industry during the Depression, Chandler enrolled in a correspondence course to learn to write fiction. He imitated Gardner's stories, taking five months to write his first story for the hard-boiled magazine *Black Mask*, for which he earned a penny a word.

Chandler arrived before the explosive growth of Los Angeles, and as part of an elite – he socialized with the "Arroyo Culture," the Pasadena-centered community of writers, artists, and craftsmen influenced by Charles Fletcher Lummis and the Craftsman style – he maintained a foreigner's sense of the exotic. He found the orange groves, oil derricks, film studios, tycoons' mansions, and Chinatowns visually important in a way Gardner had missed. He thought the scandals of Teapot Dome and the Julian Trust, of Mabel Normand and Fatty Arbuckle, not to mention the booze smuggling and gambling boats off the coast, evidence of a general moral slipperiness.

Indicative of his literary background and chivalric attitude, Chandler named his first detective after the author of *Le Morte d'Arthur*. Mallory works in a city where "the languid ray of a searchlight prodded about among high faint clouds ... The car went past the oil well that stands in the middle of La Cienega Boulevard, then turned off onto a quiet street fringed with palm trees."[7] Blackmail and kidnapping became Chandler's favorite plots, the first threatening reputation and the second the body, both prized commodities in Los Angeles. But he wrote slowly, so Chandler needed a novel to make ends meet. He fused four early stories to make *The Big Sleep* (1939), in which he fleshed out his legendary detective Philip Marlowe thus: "I'm thirty-three years old, went to college once and can still speak English if there's any demand for it. There isn't much in my trade. I worked for Mr. Wilde, the District Attorney, as an investigator once ... I'm unmarried because I don't like police-men's wives." And he adds, "I was fired. For insubordination. I test very high on insubordination." This insubordination, crossed with irony, proved attractive for a readership that worked in offices and on assembly lines but rebelled against the faceless nature of life. So did his style: a big man for the time at six feet and 190 pounds, he smokes Camels at work and a pipe at home, drinks American whiskies or bourbon. He drives a convertible with a secret compartment for a gun and sometimes a bottle of rye, even though he lives in an efficiency apartment with little more than a Murphy bed and "a few books, pictures, radio, chessmen, old letters, stuff like that."[8]

Like Cain, Chandler had an eye for California oddities. In one short story he featured the Santa Ana winds, which fan fires and supposedly encourage crime. In several he used rain as an emblem of strangeness. His settings include the La Crescenta flood plain in the San Fernando Valley, Japanese truck gardens in Orange County, Santa Monica, the foothills, and the flophouses of the Central District, the Skid Row area east of downtown. Chandler also polished the detective novel's repartee, incorporating self-deprecation, literary allusions, and a metaphoric exuberance that has seldom been matched.

Chandler pushed the LA detective novel toward an archetypal crime, the LA Murder. Beginning with "Try the Girl" (1937), his revealed stories – what the denouement reveals actually to have occurred, as distinct from what appears to be the case as the narrative unfolds – focus on a female murderer who manipulates men for economic gain. In his first novel, *The Big Sleep*, Marlowe works for General Sternwood, an oil pioneer whose daughter Carmen murders her sister's husband. Marlowe is hired to find out who is blackmailing the Sternwoods, who turn out to be the objects of extortion, pornography, gambling, and kidnapping plots. These threats come from a hierarchy of criminals who are uniformly sleazy, but more talk than action. All their rackets are united, in Marlowe's opinion, and depend on the complicity of government and the easy morals of the aristocracy. Chandler made LA geography political on Marlowe's first visit to the Sternwood mansion, where he finds the general rusticating in his greenhouse of orchids and saving his strength "as carefully as an out-of-work showgirl uses her last good pair of stockings." The detective notes that he

> could just barely see some of the old wooden derricks of the oil-field where the Sternwoods had made their money. Most of the field was public park now, cleaned up and donated to the city by General Sternwood ... The Sternwoods, having moved up the hill, could no longer smell the stale sump water or the oil, but they could still look out of their front windows and see what had made them rich. If they wanted to. I didn't suppose they would want to.

The novel ends at the oil field, where the body of Rusty Regan, dumped into the sump, now is "sleeping the big sleep."[9] The Sternwoods' aristocratic "degeneracy" serves as a cautionary example, distancing Marlowe from the Romantic and Arroyo interpretations of LA history.

A new interpretation of LA crime crystallized in *Farewell, My Lovely* (1940). The perps are no longer the Old Guard, but newcomers like mobster Laird Brunette, grotesque giant Moose Malloy, corrupt police chief Wax, and psychic Jules Amthor. Opposing them are "the Folks" – older, earlier, white migrants like Chandler himself. They include Lieutenant Randall Nulty, Mrs. Florian, Mrs. Morrison, Red Norgaard, and Ann Riordan, who is "the kind of girl Marlowe would have married, had he been the marrying kind."[10] In Chandler's view, the Folks were threatened by the avaricious behavior of new arrivals, such as Mrs. Grayle, who use any means to work their way up the economic ladder.

This novel's settings are among the most original and distinctive of any LA detective novel. Santa Monica, which Chandler had always disliked, becomes

"Bay City." Run by corrupt Chief Wax, Bay City is now the focus of fraud. Farther up the coast, in what would be Malibu, are the celebrity psychic, Amthor, his "Hollywood Indian" Second Planting, and fey middleman Lindsey Marriot. What is clear is that Chandler plotted a political geography of the LA Basin. Marlowe lives and works in Hollywood and downtown, while Santa Monica lies at the end of a vector of development that pushed out Wilshire Boulevard around 1921. The only real crime arises from gangster Tony Cornero's two gambling boats three miles offshore, in international waters, accessible from Venice Beach, to the south, which Chandler stigmatized with a carnivalesque atmosphere of cheap, and possibly homosexual, sexuality. The real subject of Chandler's ire is development of the sort represented by the Huntington (Pacific) Palisades, at the end of Wilshire Boulevard. Just north of here Marlowe smirks on seeing "a broad avenue lined with unfinished electroliers and weed-grown sidewalks. Some realtor's dream that turned into a hangover there."[11] Marlowe prefers the older, aristocratic community of Hancock Park and Anne Riordan's middle-class Los Angeles. Thus did Chandler create the first LA detective novel in which we must read geography as a historical and socioeconomic system.

Neither *The High Window* (1943) nor *The Lady in the Lake* (1945) advanced Chandler's art, but they did specify this geographic reading. Set in Pasadena, *The High Window* thematizes the blankness (its most common trope is "nothing") of a young woman from South Dakota who emigrates to Los Angeles. Better is *The Lady in the Lake*, split between Bay City and Little Fawn Lake (Big Bear Lake); it features mountain cabins, San Bernardino motels, and long drives to the mountains and high desert, as well as another of Chandler's dope-dealing doctors, Dr. Almore, and a small-town drunk, Bill Chess. The clientele and terrain presage the work of Ross Macdonald, who reworked the plot in *The Zebra Striped Hearse* (1962).

Chandler then roused himself to write a classic American detective novel, *The Long Goodbye* (1953). Preserving the traditional functions of the genre and role of the detective as knight, this work explores the alienation of modern man through three central characters: the rogue Terry Lennox (a version of Chandler in his youth), Philip Marlowe (an idealized Chandler), and hack novelist Roger Wade (Chandler's blackest self-portrait). This path-breaking detective novel also manages to be self-critical autobiography and sociological commentary. While its back story lies in World War II Europe, the novel's present extends to Tijuana, and even Otatoclan, Mexico, where Terry Lennox hides, further expanding the geographic and racial compass of the LA crime novel. As in *The Big Sleep*, the oligarchy are still culprits, but they are placed deeper in the background. The metaphors are toned down, the number of digressions and soliloquies increased – the latter bitter but sharply observed. The bane of this world-weary Marlowe are huge enterprises – press, law, courts, police, and crime – that form a monolith in which good and evil are indistinguishable. Everything in the Southland is now big and interconnected: press baron Harlan Potter summers with Nevada gambling chief Chris Mady. Marlowe still works on the sixth floor of the Cahuenga Building and plays chess, but he lives in a spacious house in Laurel Canyon; a Japanese gardener cuts his oleander bushes. If the novel is weary and cynical, it is nonetheless "the vision of a complete novelist."[12]

Using the pen name Ross Macdonald, Ken Millar developed the capacity for social analysis and criticism implicit in *The Long Goodbye* in his seventeen Lew Archer novels. Archer still resembles Spade and Marlowe – he's single, a brawler who smokes and drinks and likes women – but the roots of his cases run deep into family dramas and generational conflict. Millar was born in the United States but raised in Canada, to which his parents returned when he was four. So he, too, brought an outsider's perspective to Los Angeles. Millar led a Dickensian childhood – his impoverished mother took him on the streets to beg and almost put him in an orphanage. Despite academic talents and literary ambition, Millar drank and fought continuously; he stole from school lockers and stores, and had what biographer Tom Nolan calls "homosexual incidents with other boys." In his early teens he read *The Maltese Falcon* and discovered that "like iron filings magnetized by the book in my hands, the secret meanings of the city began to organize themselves around me."[13]

Millar named Lew Archer after Sam Spade's partner, Miles Archer, and made him a Gemini (or twin). That his initials form *L. A.*, where he worked at 8411 ½ Sunset Boulevard, is a happy coincidence. For his cases, Archer often goes to Santa Teresa (Santa Barbara), where the rich exploit the poor, especially the Mexicans. Knopf didn't think much of Millar's first novel, *The Moving Target*, so Millar used the pseudonym of "John Macdonald." This was the ignoble birth of what the *New York Times* would later call "the finest series of detective stories ever written by an American."[14] With his sixth novel, *The Drowning Pool* (1950), John Macdonald was given the middle name Ross, to avoid confusion with John D. MacDonald; "John" was dropped beginning with *The Barbarous Coast* (1955).

Millar began to study the rich of Montecito for *The Drowning Pool* and even joined the Coral Casino Beach Club, eavesdropping on its members, teaching himself to platform dive, and swimming a daily half mile in the sea. "Montecito was a hotbed of hard drinking, wife-swapping, and all kinds of scandalous stuff," said a friend. "This was a dangerous social set," writes Nolan, "witty and accomplished, but reckless in pursuit of pleasure."[15] Tragedy among the privileged, the sort that Macdonald wrote about, struck the Millars when their daughter drove a car into three boys, killing one. They hired counsel and clammed up, an irony not lost on the writer, who had criticized such behavior and used hit-and-run accidents as a paradigm of local immorality in his novels.

Meanwhile, other Los Angeles writers developed the "police procedural." Police work had been the subject of dime novels in the 1880s, and after World War II there were millions of ex-soldiers interested in military policing and questions of public order. The LAPD novel owes its existence to Jack (John Randolph) Webb, who grew up in Los Angeles' Bunker Hill neighborhood. After serving in the Pacific, Webb turned to San Francisco radio in 1946. A role as a crime lab technician in *He Walked by Night* (1948), based on the murder of a California Highway Patrolman, gave him the kernel of *Dragnet*, which he developed with the aid of LAPD Sergeant Marty Wynn and Chief William H. Parker, whom Webb made into an icon of fair and efficient Anglo-Saxon policing. *Dragnet* ran on radio from 1949 to 1954 and on television from 1952 to 1959 and 1967 to 1970 starring Webb as Sergeant Joe Friday. Its sign-on – "The story you are about to see is true. Only the names have been changed to protect the innocent" – became legendary. Webb intended to show the reality of police work and to depict policemen as working-class heroes, but his only literary effort, *The Badge* (1958), was almost adulatory. The LAPD was then lionized in popular narrative for the next four decades in television series and movies like *Adam-12*, *The Terminator* (1984), *Blue Thunder* (1983), *Die Hard* (1988), *The Shield*, *Lethal Weapon* (1987), and *Rush Hour* (1988). This era was dominated by three police chiefs – William Parker (1950–66), Edward Davis (1969–78) and Daryl Gates (1978–92) – under whom the force became more than 80 percent white and suburban.[16] From the 1965 Watts riots onward, it was also identified as racist. During the 1965 Watts riots, Parker called participants "monkeys in the zoo,"[17] and Gates, who created the first SWAT team in the United States, was forced to resign in 1992, after civil disturbances that arose in response to the acquittal of the LAPD officers who beat Rodney King by a mostly white, suburban jury.

During the Davis epoch, however, the LA police procedural was transformed by Joseph Wambaugh, a patrolman and detective from 1960 to 1974. *The New Centurions* (1971) follows young men through the police academy, their first assignments, and into the Watts riots of 1965. From idealists they evolve into corrupt warriors who feel they have been sent futilely into the trenches. The novel strides back into the Central District and ethnic neighborhoods that Chandler visited but that Macdonald ignored. In *The Blue Knight* (1972), Wambaugh depicts the last three days in a twenty-year veteran's police career. Bump Morgan had accepted free meals, roughed up informers, and solicited prostitutes, believing that he was the law. Occasionally he arrested someone, but his informal justice was more feared, until he perjured himself during a trial, which provides the matrix of the novel.

Even darker was *The Choirboys* (1975). Ten cops from the Wilshire Division meet after hours in Los Angeles' MacArthur Park to relieve their stress through "choir practice": drinking, storytelling, group sex with barmaids, and violence. They accidentally kill a gay teenager while drinking, and the resulting investigation provides the structure of the novel. The officers range from brutal "Rosco" Rules, who hates Los Angeles and lives sixty miles east near Chino, to culturally confused Francis Taniguchi, raised in the barrio and trying to prove that he is a Chicano. Not only is *The Choirboys* the most informed and savage depiction of the LAPD ever written, it shows the police and those they "defend" to be only slightly different than those they arrest, with race the most common determining factor.

Wambaugh became so notorious that he had to take a leave of absence, during which he wrote *The Onion Field*. The true story of officers Ian Campbell and Karl Hettinger, this novel is often compared to Truman Capote's *In Cold Blood*. In 1963 the officers pulled over a car in Hollywood, only to be taken hostage by a pair of small-time criminals who had just robbed a liquor store. They were driven to an onion field near Bakersfield, where Campbell was killed. Though convicted, the criminals were never executed. "I was put on earth to write this story," Wambaugh said. "Nothing could ever stop me ... I felt it was my sole reason for living."[18] Wambaugh also created *Police Story*, a television series that reversed the tone and themes of *Dragnet*.

Overlapping the police procedural is the LA historic crime novel, mastered by James Ellroy, who also subverted the heroic LAPD procedural. At his best, Ellroy evokes the sights, sounds, and feel of Los Angeles in the 1940s. Born in Los Angeles, Ellroy lived with his mother, who "drank Early Times bourbon and chased men"[19] before she was strangled after leaving a bar with a man and woman. The next year his father gave Ellroy *The Badge*, by Jack Webb, which included a summary of the "Black Dahlia" case: Elizabeth Short, a starlet and sometime prostitute, had been found naked in 1947, her body cut completely in half. Ellroy would link these cases, neither ever solved, in his best work, known as the L.A. Quartet. The first novel, *The Black Dahlia* (1987), is the best known. An extraordinary re-creation of LA police politics, racial and sexual attitudes, and slang of the 1940s, Ellroy's novel is true to the facts of the crime, but fictionalizes the solution. Ellroy also perfected an LA crime scene – the "body dump" – whose liminal location has had a strong pull on the imagination of crime in Los Angeles. *The Big Nowhere* (1988) is a lesser novel, but *L.A. Confidential* (1990) and *White Jazz* (1992), a stream-of-consciousness tour de force, are significant works. In *L.A. Confidential* (also a

1997 film) one of the characters moonlights as technical advisor to *Badge of Honor*, an allusion to *Dragnet*.

The world of LA minorities, initially marginalized by the Masons and Marlowes and then repressed by the LAPD procedural, was reclaimed by Ezekiel "Easy" Rawlins, the African-American detective of Walter Mosley. The background of *Devil in a Blue Dress* (1990), from details of the 1940s to the protagonist's early job in an aircraft plant, is indebted to Chester Himes's *If He Hollers Let Him Go* (1945), but from there Mosley recaptures the Central District of Chandler and extends the geography of the LA detective to the black communities of Watts and Compton. Worried about paying his mortgage, Easy takes $100 to find a blonde, Daphne Monet, who favors nightclubs on the black side of town. She has stolen $30,000 of her white patron's money which, after an immersion in the world of sexual debauchery and race politics that leads her to kill one man, she splits with Easy and his violent sidekick, Mouse. Easy has a distant and antagonistic relationship with the LAPD; instead, Mosley thematizes Easy's pride in home ownership and ends the novel with him watering his yard and pondering the morality of the justice that has transpired. In *A Red Death* (1991), Easy owns apartment buildings he bought with stolen money that he recovered and kept. Pursued by the Internal Revenue Service, he cooperates by spying on a union organizer, and again extortion and murder have underworld roots. The third Easy Rawlins novel, *White Butterfly* (1994), is set in 1956. Easy helps police investigate the murders of four young women, one of whom, a UCLA student and daughter of a city official, led a double life as a stripper. These novels prize the vernacular details of African-American life, but emphasize the constant compromises required to "get along with the Man." Mosley's recent work has departed from the genre; his mantle has been taken up by Gar Anthony Haywood, whose detective Aaron Gunner operates from an office behind a Watts barber-shop in *Fear of the Dark* (1989) and *All the Lucky Ones Are Dead* (2000). Haywood's novels are more driven by dialogue and less violent than Mosley's. Most recently Paula Woods has brought the African-American LA sleuth novel full circle, with black LAPD Detective Charlotte Justice, the protagonist of *Inner City Blues* (1999), *Stormy Weather* (2001), *Dirty Laundry* (2005), and *Strange Bedfellows* (2006).

Lucha Corpi and Michael Nava have created Chicana/o detectives. In Corpi's *Eulogy for a Brown Angel* (1992), Detective Gloria Damasco and her friend find a four-year-old boy dead during the 1970 Chicano Moratorium in Los Angeles. She returns to the case eighteen years later, employing a "dark gift" that allows her to dream and to see answers to problems. *Cactus Blood* (1995) is set in Delano during the farmworkers' strike of 1973, and *Black Widow's Wardrobe* (2000) delves into folklore. Nava weaves Chicano history and folklore in his stories of detective Henry Rios, a gay lawyer, who moves from San Francisco to Los Angeles in *How Town* (1990) and investigates the city in *The Hidden Law* (1992), *The Death of Friends* (1996), *The Burning Plain* (1997), and *Rag and Bone* (2001).

Other contemporary LA crime writers include Sue Grafton who, like Ross Macdonald, works in Santa Barbara (Santa Teresa); however, her detective, Kinsey Millhone, lives in the converted garage of octogenarian Henry Pitts, drives a beat-up Volkswagen, dresses in jeans, eats junk food, and jogs for exercise. Millhone is a loner with a code, who works for just causes. Grafton doesn't stretch the genre and her narratives are notably lacking in violence, but her revealed plots insightfully question gender roles and explore social issues. *T Is for Trespass* (2007) alternates points of view between Millhone and the culprit, Solana Rojas, a "chameleon" who assumes the identities of others in order to steal from them.

The contemporary LA detective novel shows breadth and depth. Michael Connelly, who worked as a crime reporter for the *Los Angeles Times*, updates the romantic LA detective to include the reality of time cards and weekend rotations in his twelve "Harry Bosch" LAPD novels published between 1996 and 2008. Another police procedural writer, T. Jefferson Parker, has written fifteen novels set mostly in Orange County or San Diego. Better known is Jonathan Kellerman, whose child psychologist detective Alex Delaware stars in twenty-one novels. Denise Hamilton, another ex-*Times* reporter, has written five detective novels about reporter Eve Diamond, who investigates crime in the local Latino, Asian, and Russian communities. Los Angeles' Orthodox Jewish community provides the settings for Faye Kellerman's seventeen novels about police detective Peter Decker and Rina Lazarus, and Rochelle Majer Krich has nine Jewish-themed PI novels. There is a throwback: Stuart Kaminsky's Toby Peters is a private detective who investigates film stars in 1940s Hollywood. Kem Nunn has pioneered a "surfer/noir" variation of the detective in a trilogy (*Tapping the Source*, 1984; *Dogs of Winter*, 1997; and *Tijuana Straits*, 2004) that pursues the environmental themes to which Macdonald, an avid birder, turned in *The Underground Man* (1971), which is set during the 1964 Coyote Canyon fire, and *Sleeping Beauty* (1973), whose central event is the 1969 Santa Barbara oil spill.

Although Los Angeles gained a place in detective fiction rather late, it has become an iconic locale. Films such as *Chinatown* have reinforced the mystique. Combining important industries such as oil, aviation, and cinema with terrain stretching from the Pacific over mountains to high desert, Los Angeles has offered writers endless possibilities. Its twentieth-century evolution into a highly multicultural city presages Los Angeles' continued importance in the genre.

NOTES

1. Raymond Chandler, "The Simple Art of Murder," in *Later Novels and Other Writings* (New York: Library of America, 1995), p. 990.
2. Diane Johnson, *Dashiell Hammett: A Life* (New York: Random House, 1983), pp. 90–108; Roy Hoopes, *Cain* (New York: Holt, Rinehart & Winston, 1982), p. 214.
3. David M. Fine, Introduction, *Los Angeles in Fiction: A Collection of Original Essays*, ed. Fine (Albuquerque: University of New Mexico Press, 1984), p. 18.
4. James M. Cain, *The Postman Always Rings Twice*, in *Crime Novels: American Noir of the 1930s and 40s*, ed. Robert Polito (New York: Library of America, 1997), pp. 49, 1, 2.
5. Erle Stanley Gardner, *The Case of the Velvet Claws* (New York: Fawcett, 1985), p. xx.
6. Gardner, *The Case of the Long-Legged Models* (New York: Fawcett, 1994), p. 98.
7. Raymond Chandler, "Blackmailers Don't Shoot" (1933), in *Stories and Early Novels* (New York: Library of America, 1995), p. 13.
8. Chandler, *The Big Sleep*, in *Stories and Early Novels*, pp. 594, 708.
9. *Ibid.*, pp. 593, 602–3, 764.
10. Chandler, quoted in Phillip Durham, *Down These Mean Street a Man Must Go: Raymond Chandler's Knight* (Chapel Hill: University of North Carolina Press, 1963), p. 39.
11. Chandler, *Farewell My Lovely*, in *Stories and Early Novels*, p. 810.
12. Frank MacShane, *The Life of Raymond Chandler* (New York: Random House, 1976), p. 207.
13. Tom Nolan, *Ross Macdonald: A Biography* (New York: Scribner, 1999), pp. 27, 31.
14. *Ibid.* p. 11.
15. *Ibid.* p. 110.
16. Jim Newton, "ACLU Says 83% of Police Live Outside L.A.," *Los Angeles Times*, March 29, 1994, B1.
17. See Anthony Oberschall, "The Los Angeles Riot of August 1965," *Social Problems* 15.3 (1968), 322–41.
18. Wambaugh, quoted in Evan Hunter, "Author Interview," *Playboy*, July, 1979, 69.
19. James Ellroy, "The Sub-Definitive Ellroy on Ellroy," *Richmond Review* 2003, www.richmondreview.co.uk/features/ellsound.html.

IO

DAVID SEED

Los Angeles' science fiction futures

Los Angeles is the home of the world's oldest science fiction association, founded in the mid-1930s by Forrest Ackerman. The Los Angeles Science Fantasy Society quickly became an important forum for writers. Ray Bradbury joined the society in 1937 and has repeatedly acknowledged his debt to figures like Leigh Brackett, the filmmaker Ray Harryhausen, Robert Heinlein, and Henry Kuttner, who all offered advice on his fiction. Once established, Bradbury advised younger figures. Although Bradbury has stated that this environment of writers' mutual aid has been lost, the society continues to serve as an important focus for science fiction activities in the city. Los Angeles also has been the site of collaborations like that between Larry Niven and Jerry Pournelle, and individual contacts like Octavia Butler attending Theodore Sturgeon's writing classes at UCLA.

Los Angeles has been virtually synonymous with the film business since the 1920s, and LA science fiction novelists like Steve Erickson acknowledge the influence of Hollywood. Aldous Huxley deploys cinematic techniques to explore the future of what he saw as film city in *Ape and Essence* (1949). Bradbury came to Los Angeles in 1934 and consistently celebrates the creative energy of Hollywood cinema; he received a star on the Walk of Fame in 2002. In his Hollywood novel, *A Graveyard for Lunatics* (1990), Bradbury describes Los Angeles as a surreal city where anything can happen. The popular culture historian Ron Goulart's satire *The Tin Angel* (1973) takes a different tack in ridiculing the media publicity machine. Set in 1999, the novel focuses on the animal talent section of Metro-Italian-American Talent, in particular on Bowser, a cocker spaniel who can play the piano and who has been fitted with a voice box. Goulart ridicules the showbiz of Hollywood, where ratings are all and where every event has to be filtered through the media. One performer's funeral cortege even includes the "corpses" of his two dummies. The tin angel of the title obviously glances at the City of Angels, but it is a commodified spiritual image for promoting another LA business: undertaking, as managed by the U.S. Transition Service. Goulart's futuristic satire closely resembles Norman Spinrad's sardonic reduction of Los Angeles to the pornography capital of the world and mockery of the local "guru business" in stories like "All the Sounds of the Rainbow" (1973). Here the promise of Los Angeles lapses into cynical exploitation from pornography, pop music, and cults alike.

Satire, however, is not the main characteristic of novels about the future of the city. In his classic study *Ecology of Fear* (1998), Mike Davis argues that LA disaster narratives "track national discontents" and also "mobilize deep-rooted cultural predispositions," giving expression to the underside of the American Dream.[1] As early as 1909, in Homer Lea's *The Valor of Ignorance*, which describes a Japanese invasion, novels had begun to imagine the future of Los Angeles as one of disaster caused by invasion, earthquakes, or, later, nuclear attack. They constitute an insistently localized form of an old American literary genre: the jeremiad, which warns of the terrible consequences of national failure. The shared perception of Greater Los Angeles as a place of promise and the location of booming businesses, from gene research to NASA and media technology, has led writers to extrapolate ominous futures from the very prosperity of the region, frequently identifying the fate of the city with that of the United States. Indeed, in Dean Owen's *End of the World* (1962) a nuclear strike on Los Angeles marks the demise of humanity itself.

An unusual ecological variation on disaster is given in Ward Moore's *Greener Than You Think* (1947), where the agent of disaster is a new kind of "devilgrass" that spreads rapidly and reaches a height of sixteen feet. Moore presents a cautionary tale of horticultural experimentation getting out of control, incorporating two of the standard satirical ingredients of these narratives: evangelists' attribution of events to God's wrath and the media's exploitation of the growing drama by pronouncing the death of the city. Unlike the spectacle of destruction evoked in accounts of earthquake or nuclear attack, Moore's description of downtown Los Angeles under the stranglehold of the surrounding grass is one of desertion. Ironically, the fabric of the city remains intact, but Los Angeles has become paralyzed and emptied of humanity, briefly a ghost city before the grass closes in.

As early as 1927, the British author Aldous Huxley identified the future of the United States with that of the world and ten years later made Hollywood his permanent home. From this base he meditated with increasing gloom on the totalitarian tendencies in nationalism and the development of new weapons in biological and atomic warfare. The product of these reflections was his 1949 novel *Ape and Essence*, which is set in Los Angeles in 2108 in the wake of World War III. The main narrative, in the form of a screenplay, assembles a montage of the twin themes of nationalism and perverted science in order to dramatize fear as the new basis of modern life. Huxley describes a rediscovery expedition of scientists from New Zealand, left untouched by the war, which finds Los Angeles reduced to a "city of two and a half million skeletons."[2] Like many subsequent post-nuclear narratives, *Ape and Essence* shows how the United States has lapsed into a new barbarism where people live partly by scavenging for valuables in the city's graveyards. Life does go on in Los Angeles, although its population has been decimated and a threatening new orthodoxy has come into operation according to which babies deformed by radiation or biological agents have to be "purified," that is, disposed of. The echoes of Nazi eugenics would have been unmistakable in 1949. The life of the inner city continues, though transformed so that examples of preindustrial life are ironically juxtaposed against the background of lost LA modernity and communal ovens are being stoked by armfuls of books from the local library in the crudest commodification of the past. The city has reverted to a culture dominated by a demonic cult. Huxley opens up no possibility for renewal in *Ape and Essence*; the novel closes with the protagonist and his lover departing Los Angeles to find a better place elsewhere.

Robert Heinlein's "The Year of the Jackpot" (1952) combines nuclear attack with satirical gibes against the religious cults of Los Angeles. The story opens with a young woman stripping her clothes off at a bus stop. Coincidentally the man who saves her from arrest (Potiphar Breen) is a mathematician developing a theory of cycles, one "confirmed" by the recurrence of stripping throughout Los Angeles. He reads this as a sign of cultural breakdown and, although Heinlein ridicules local messianic cults, the story develops this theory into full-scale apocalypse. Torrential rains flood the city, its main water supply is ruptured, Los Angeles is nuked, a spectacle witnessed from nearby hills. Heinlein's ironies also target the CONELRAD emergency radio service, which denies the nuclear attack. The story ends on an austere note of spreading death and growing national disorder.

Huxley's and Heinlein's satirical extrapolations do not reflect the real fears of nuclear war, which had become acute by the early 1960s. This urgency is reflected in the imminence of the post-nuclear futures imagined from the 1960s until the end of the Cold War. Robert Moore Williams's *The Day They H-Bombed Los Angeles* (1961) takes place in 1970 and seems at first to be an exercise in making concrete the dreaded possibility of attack. When the bombs fall, protagonist Tom Watkins (conveniently a former drill sergeant) immediately sets about organizing the group of survivors in his shelter, a group that includes a Hollywood star and an FBI agent. So far the story seems to be one of survival, but then strange things begin to happen. A scientist claims incredibly that it was Americans who bombed the city. When the group tries to leave the "contaminated area," as it is called, they are confronted with military barricades and a warning that they will be shot if they try to cross them. The second oddity is that some humans are seen behaving in a strange, zombie-like manner. Indeed, these figures herd together and communicate like wolves howling to each other. By this point the novel's subject has veered away from survival to alien take-over, fueled by a mysterious molecule that has infected the city from the Pacific. Through ironic plot twists, Williams closes the circle of causality around the United States. It was they who bombed Los Angeles, and it was probably due to their nuclear tests in the Pacific that the molecule was created.

Whitley Strieber and James Kunetka's 1984 novel of post-nuclear reportage, *Warday and the Journey Onward*, describes an investigative tour of the United States after a widespread nuclear attack in 1988, which has left Los Angeles relatively unscathed. The nation has fragmented into regions and California has become a police state run by martial law. Thus Los Angeles outwardly presents an appearance of normality, though stringent penalties are enforced on illegal immigrants, which is what the two protagonists are. Apart from the militaristic regime, a new apocalyptic folklore is emerging in Los Angeles, like the belief that "there is a gigantic beast with bat wings and red, burning eyes that has attacked adults and carried off children. The creature stands seven feet tall and makes a soft whistling noise. It is often seen on roofs in populated areas, but only at night."[3] Another "rumor" is the emergence of different kinds of human mutations attributed to radiation. Strieber and Kunetka's documentary method skillfully understates these possibilities by embedding them within official reports of war damage, at the same time implying that these beliefs are the signs of repressed war psychosis breaking through the surface prosperity of the city.

In Fritz Leiber's *The Wanderer* (1964) and Larry Niven and Jerry Pournelle's *Lucifer's Hammer* (1977) the nuclear threat is replaced by a new comet discovered to be heading straight for Earth. In Leiber the first reaction from Angelenos is to bring the freeways to a standstill as they try to flee the city. Local radio constantly reassures that there is no atomic attack. Ironically, the visitation is if anything worse because the comet induces fires and massive tidal waves – and it is manned. One Angeleno is taken into the craft and given a bird's-eye view of Los Angeles going up in flames. In *Lucifer's Hammer*, as soon as news of the comet breaks it becomes an extended media event – the subject alike of a TV show and apocalyptic warnings by a radio evangelist. In the event, the comet's fragments do strike Earth, triggering tidal waves and a massive earthquake. Indeed, the descriptions of collapsing buildings, ruptured freeways, and massed corpses are among the most powerful in the novel. The expectation of cataclysm is one of the hallmarks of the novel's Angelenos, who repeatedly recognize apocalypse: when floods knock out the railway and freeways a US senator declares, "the United States has ceased to exist."[4] The aftermath shows precious little sign of survival and the novel ends with a showdown at a nuclear power plant between a white saving remnant and its ethnic foes. Niven and Pournelle (who served as adviser to Mayor Sam Yorty in 1969–70) returned to Los Angeles, but one transposed 14,000 years into the past, in *The Burning City* (2000), which drew on the 1992 Justice Riots.

The science fiction future identity of Los Angeles is sometimes seen as defined by expansive business. Where Huxley places World War III as the crisis of social upheaval, Philip Wylie attributes the turning point to ecological disaster in his 1971 novel *Los Angeles: A.D. 2017*, which quotes Calvin Coolidge's aphorism, "the business of America is business." The narrative opens before the crisis with a secret meeting of businessmen, scientists, and the military. It isn't clear exactly what the agenda is here, although the ostensible reason is to discuss impending ecological problems. The protagonist, the media magnate Glenn Howard, then falls asleep in the early 1980s and wakes in 2017 to discover that Los Angeles has become a subterranean city run on commercial lines ("USA, Incorporated") with strict security guards. The resulting society, where once again Los Angeles is taken as an emblem of the future nation, is a brave new world of streamlined technologies, where defectives and criminals are "erased" and where citizens are classified from A to D. The crowning irony comes when it is revealed that life on the surface is actually possible, but that the authorities are maintaining an ecological lie to stay in power. In a final ironic twist, Howard returns to the Los Angeles of the 1970s complete with smog and pollution. Wylie evokes the consequences of willful commercial exploitation that transforms the American landscape into a wasteland scattered with rusting ruins.

Niven and Pournelle present big business as an invasive force in their 1982 novel, *Oath of Fealty*, which applies Paolo Soleri's arcology theory of building to promote population density. A massive, high-rise housing complex called Todos Santos has been built in one of the poorest areas of Los Angeles, from which it is completely separate. The complex is virtually a self-contained environment with its own security apparatus, food and electronics factories, and shopping malls. The novel dramatizes the tensions between the administration of Todos Santos and City Hall, which come to a head when the son of an LA City Council member is killed by security guards when he and his friends gain entry to the complex. *Oath of Fealty*'s Los Angeles is separated along vertical and horizontal axes. Greg Bear's *Queen of Angels* (1990) narrates a murder mystery set in the Los Angeles of 2047, which has the same spatial division. High-rise buildings are the focus of wealth and power, gradually eating up the flatland slums of the old city. Referred to as "insulas," these coastal enclaves have a geometric appearance: "cubes and tubes and hexagons and towers filled with lemmings gathered from around the world."[5] Bear's dystopian, ironic turn against Los Angeles as a city of promise is reinforced by the city's participation in a nationwide surveillance network called Citizen Oversight, maintained through countless sensors, monitors, and cameras. Criminals are treated with "therapy," a compulsory form of brainwashing.

Totalitarian measures inform most of Philip K. Dick's novels. His California locations are usually Oakland or San Francisco (the film *Blade Runner* [1982] transposed the novel's location to Los Angeles from San Francisco), but in some novels he does portray Los Angeles. *Counter-Clock World* (1967), set in the 1990s, describes the arrival of a religious leader in Dodger Stadium, where he addresses a crowd of thousands. Memories of the Watts riots at time of writing explain the fear of racial violence throughout the novel, in which African Americans have been segregated into a distinct section of the United States. Los Angeles is seen as the key focus of a police state in Dick's *Flow My Tears, the Policeman Said* (1974), where by 1988 the United States has become governed by the police and National Guard. "Pol" and "Nat" checkpoints riddle the city, as the protagonist Jason Taverner discovers when he wakes one morning in an unknown hotel room without any identity cards. Not only that: every associate denies knowledge of him and he is thus compelled to go to the slums of Watts to get himself new cards. From a successful television vocalist he suddenly finds himself an "unperson," and Taverner's search for an identity enables Dick to demonstrate the workings of this dystopia. Police surveillance is carried out by micro-transmitters embedded in ID cards or on Taverner's person. African Americans have been decimated by compulsory sterilization. In this novel Los Angeles is described as a city of signs, of bright flashing lights illuminating the night, which reflect not so much commerce as the ubiquitous state monitoring system dedicated to shedding official light on every citizen. As in Kim Stanley Robinson's *The Gold Coast* (1988), drugs are in free circulation in Dick's *A Scanner Darkly* (1977) despite elaborate police surveillance. Set in 1994, the novel describes closely guarded LA shopping malls and the product uniformity of franchises like McDonald's, both within the context of California drug culture.

The LA freeway system is repeatedly used to embody the priority given to the automobile. As Mike Davis and others have pointed out, the term *freeway* encapsulates a double identification – with the road itself and the idea of unfettered movement – that is reversed in these novels' images of gridlock. The automobile is the focus of Ray Bradbury's quixotic opposition. One night in 1949 he was stopped by the LA police and questioned – for walking. This became the subject of his story "The Pedestrian" (1951), which evokes a city (clearly modeled on Los Angeles although never named) where streets have fallen into disuse because television completely determines the social lifestyle of suburbia. Bradbury developed this extrapolation in *Fahrenheit 451* (1953), a novel written in the UCLA library's basement, which anticipates the obsolescence of books. The novel articulates two perceptions which Bradbury had of Los Angeles: the gradual disappearance of bookstores and the priority given to the automobile. The streets have becomes racetracks where drivers try to kill animals and humans. Bradbury's support for a city monorail, his criticism of the inefficiency of freeways, and his desire to see Los Angeles rebuilt eliminating the automobile help explain the particular force in the novel of the nuclear strike that destroys the city. Like Dick and other contemporary science fiction writers, Bradbury evokes Californian suburbia as an alienated, center-less expanse, where people depend on the automobile and develop anxieties over conforming to the local lifestyle. In 1970 Bradbury published an article subtitled "A Dream for Los Angeles" (revised and retitled in 1995), in which he proposed an experimental city block filled with cafés designed as a collective meeting-place. This dream of the future partly expresses a nostalgia for lost small-town practices that features in many of Bradbury's writings.

Kim Stanley Robinson has also commented on a willful ecological blindness tantamount to a collective death wish, and in his Three Californias trilogy, set in Orange County rather than Los Angeles itself, he has warned of the consequences of uneven prosperity fed by the Cold War. *The Wild Shore* (1984), set in 2047, makes a grim opening to his sequence in describing a California devastated by nuclear war. Within the ruined landscape the broken freeways symbolize the loss of interurban mobility. In *The Gold Coast*, moving freeways are the main sign of this "autopia," promising electronically controlled travel, which fails intermittently when automobiles become dislodged from these moving tracks. Robinson incorporates historical chapters outlining the evolution of shopping malls, the arms business, and the displacement of ethnic groups to its extrapolation into 2027 California mass culture. *Pacific Edge* (1988) concludes the trilogy on a more hopeful note in 2065. The area round El Modena is being reconstructed in an eco-sensitive way, signaled initially by digging up local roads.

Bradbury, Robinson, and others evoke a future for Los Angeles determined largely by its systems of communication, where the city comes to resemble a huge, diseased organism. In Richard Kadrey's *Metrophage* (1988) the city is going through an entropic decline sardonically signaled in the city's new name, "Last Ass." In a context of rationing, humans have separated into different castes: the Piranhas live in the ruined buildings on street level, the Croakers (anarchists and doctors performing illegal medicine) in the sewers.

The spatial separation of the social groups gives direct physical expression to their respective socioeconomic positions and their group names strengthen the thematic link between consumption and predation. Kadrey stresses the physical cost of the city's decline through the trade in body parts, the volunteers for paid medical experimentation, and the paucity of accommodation. The Golden Age of Hollywood Pavilion, a complex of teflon-coated tents, houses some 2,000 vagrants. The city's infrastructure becomes an emblem of urban disease: "The sewers, laced within the body of the city, were the corroded veins of a sick addict."[6] *Metrophage*, like Pat Cadigan's *Synners* (1991), links the media to economic and political power. In Kadrey's novel, "the Spectacle" promotes expedient images from the government. Cadigan traces a process of hegemonic expansion in the entertainment colossus Diversifications Inc., which, like the Tyrell Corporation in *Blade Runner*, presides over Los Angeles as if with a mind of its own. In a novel packed with the discourse of linkage – system, wiring, and so on – the "complex mechanism" of Diversifications can be read as a self-expanding structure of connections.

Synners presents Los Angeles through multiple interlocking systems ranging from commerce through computing nets to the city's automated traffic control network called GridLid. As soon as this network is named, it becomes clear that it isn't functioning properly. Indeed, Los Angeles is described in relation to disaster, an earthquake (the "Big One") which has left its mark everywhere. Cadigan frames her narrative between this quake and a new cataclysm. An electronically transmitted virus penetrates the computerized traffic control system and other electronic networks, producing a massive failure. "GridLid" becomes gridlock. Yet the cause can never be defined; as one character insists, "It's not a virus or a bomb." Not surprisingly, the event becomes instant spectacle: "the machinery of the city was melting down, and they were all just watching it happen on TV." At the end of *Synners*, the identification between vehicle and free movement is dramatically disrupted as more and more characters circulate on foot. The circulation of traffic and information alike seizes up in an expanding blackout which takes out Los Angeles International Airport and converts Greater Los Angeles into an "electronic crater."[7]

Where Kadrey and Cadigan retain the integral identity of their future visions of Los Angeles, Neal Stephenson in *Snow Crash* (1992) depicts a totally fragmented cityscape. By the twenty-first century, the national government has collapsed and the city has become a patchwork of autonomous areas which maintain their own private security systems. Indeed, laws have lapsed and been replaced with the disparate practices of private agencies. Federal authority has been reduced to a heavily fortified enclave called

Fedland. The layout reflects Stephenson's perception that city-dwellers are constantly trying to flee the realities of the United States, leaving only the "street people, feeding off debris."[8] Thus all characters are transients, including a range of immigrants from all over the world. The protagonist Hiro (Hero) lives in a former storage facility and begins the novel as a pizza delivery boy, a Mafia franchise. His associate is the teenage girl Y.T. (Yours Truly), who travels around the city as a courier on an ultra-modern skateboard. The generic city street functions here as a channel of communication and as a means of establishing a rapid tempo to the action. The city street (very few are named) blurs into the virtual Street in Stephenson's "Metaverse," a virtual reality where characters' avatars continue the deals they pursue in real time. As in *Synners*, the novel's location is held together by a network of commercial, criminal, and communication systems, within which is circulating the Snow Crash of the title, an electronic virus which can invade a person's DNA.

Narratives of decline and collapse are not the only versions of Los Angeles' future. A small number of writers stress survival. Thus Carolyn See's *Golden Days* (1987) builds up a montage of this life in different decades, culminating in a nuclear strike. The narrator describes the mounting frenzy of pursuing "fun" throughout the 1980s until the Angelenos expected the end of the world, but never left. See explicitly challenges the stereotype: "it was the city that held us, the city they said had no centre, that all of us had come to from all over America because this was the place to find dreams and pleasure and love."[9] The refusal to leave is symptomatic of the narrator's determination to present a tale of affirmation. The purgation of Los Angeles is seen as a natural process akin to rebirth. The incorrigible pleasure-seekers are the least missed.

Cynthia Kadohata evokes a different future for the city in her 1992 novel, *In the Heart of the Valley of Love*: dystopian, to be sure, but leavened by the protagonist's tenacious hope. The year is 2052, and the novel presents a series of stories narrated by teenage Francie, whose Japanese mother and Chinese-black father emigrated from Chicago only to die in Los Angeles. The stories present contingent images of day-to-day life, but they offer Kadohata a powerful, understated means of presenting the remorseless decline of Los Angeles. Pollution has increased, public transport has declined, and the freeways, when not frozen in gridlock, have become the domain of street vendors. Indeed Los Angeles seems to be collapsing into a barter economy, where prosperity has become a thing of the past. Water and fuel are rationed; quality food is scarce; even the climate appears to have desiccated the city. The cityscape is filled with boarded-up buildings, and intermittent riots have become the rule. Francie's deadpan descriptions present as routine the grotesque and unpredictable outbursts of violence that she witnesses, where hostility has no obvious motivation, but simply characterizes the total estrangement of one Angeleno from another. Every negative characteristic of 1990s Los Angeles – street crime, residential decline, ethnic fragmentation – has been taken to its bleak predictable extreme.

The strength of Kadohata's novel – eye-witness immediacy – is shared by Octavia Butler's *Parable of the Sower* (1993), set in the period 2024–7. The novel is narrated by Lauren, a teenage African-American girl, who witnesses the collapse of California from a small community twenty miles from Los Angeles, the city described as a "festering sore." No single reason is given for social disintegration although the symptoms are graphically described; Lauren quickly establishes her credibility through the precision with which she reports on spreading violence, especially on her need to kill in self-defense. Her community lives within a compound fortified against the constant danger of attack, and the turning point comes when the street people (beggars, pyromaniacs, and others) destroy her house, forcing her to take to the road. One possible remedy to the general anarchy is considered. An LA suburb is privatized by a company, which means in practice that the inmates live within a kind of military camp. Lauren joins the thousands of migrants straggling along the highways, armed against attack by other transients and feral dogs. There is more progression than in Kadohata's novel since Lauren is determined to survive and even to found a small community, although Butler's sequel, *Parable of the Talents* (1998), shows that group falling victim to religious fanaticism.

Steve Erickson, an Angeleno born and bred, mounts a different challenge to the myth of Los Angeles. In an interview he stated: "I think most Los Angeles novels have been written as an aberration of America – have seen Los Angeles as this little port of weirdness in America, not connected with the rest [...] I wanted to write a Los Angeles novel [with] Los Angeles as the furthest psychological and geological extension of America."[10] The novel referred to here is *Rubicon Beach* (1986), which actualizes Erickson's repeated conviction that Los Angeles is a fluid city. Ex-convict Cale sails around a flooded city whose geography has become destabilized and which gives forth a surreal medley of sounds. Cale's identity and purpose are as fluid as the cityscape, where mansions and hotels are clogged with sea debris. The second section of the novel describes the city before its apocalyptic flooding as perceived by a Latina girl totally estranged, linguistically and culturally, from Los Angeles. Cale's "tour" of the city is repeated in the girl's discovery of the "invisible borders" operating in LA society.

Erickson's narratives typically assemble a montage of brief filmic scenes. Indeed, he enrolled as a film student at UCLA in 1968. His scenes pay scrupulous attention to perspective and image, both equally surreal.

Amnesiascope (1996), set in the "Last City of the Last Millennium," is narrated by a journalist and film critic gradually losing touch with any coherent memory. His mental collapse mirrors the entropic decline of Los Angeles from a major earthquake, floods, and constant fires which ring the city, covering everything with black ash. The cityscape has become a wasteland: the airport and baseball stadium are derelict and occupied by squatters; the subway tunnels are flooded. And once again, the city is identified with the nation: "LA is all that's left of America the Delirious," embodying the last traces of a film business playing to the national subconscious.[11] Given Erickson's repeated identification of the future of Los Angeles with that of the United States, it is a constant irony in his writings that they return to imminent endings.

However bleak the futures evoked, there is usually some possibility of survival by a saving remnant. One rare case where survival doesn't happen is Curt Gentry's *Last Days of the Late, Great State of California* (1968), where the entire seaboard west of the San Andreas Fault sinks into the sea after a massive earthquake. Gentry summarizes the history of postwar Los Angeles as a constant abuse of the environment, an appropriation of land for freeways, and a sequence of change so extreme that "nothing was permanent." The earthquake confirms this perception with a vengeance, destroying buildings and causing gridlock on the freeways. Gentry assembles excerpts from news reports tracing the progress of the damage, reports that culminate in the shocked exclamation of a pilot flying over the area: "'Oh, my God! *Los Angeles has vanished!*'"[12] Gentry both mocks and confirms the local prophets of doom, presenting the earthquake as Nature's revenge on ecological abuse and as retribution for long-standing political racketeering. The city of promise disappears, although the rest of the United States lives on.

The sheer variety of LA futures suggests that the fate of the city and of the nation has become an insistent, if somber, subject for debate. Although disaster and decline repeatedly figure in these accounts, paradoxically they are confirming a general perception of Los Angeles as the site of national experimentation. Writers' extrapolations of different social, residential, and communication structures lugubriously confirm that Los Angeles still offers the key to the nation's future. Continuing the tradition of the jeremiad, evocations of the city's future repeatedly contrast promise with failure and offer warnings of an "inadequate fate."[13]

NOTES

1. Mike Davis, *Ecology of Fear: Los Angeles and the Imagination of Disaster* (New York: Vintage, 1999), p. 354.

2. Aldous Huxley, *Ape and Essence* (London: Chatto & Windus, 1949), p. 143.

3. James Kunetka and Whitley Strieber, *Warday and the Journey Onward* (London: Hodder & Stoughton, 1984), p. 160.

4. Larry Niven and Jerry Pournelle, *Lucifer's Hammer* (London: Futura, 1978), p. 372.

5. Greg Bear, *Queen of Angels* (London: Legend, 1991), p. 101.

6. Richard Kadrey, *Metrophage* (London: Victor Gollancz, 1988), p. 42.

7. Pat Cadigan, *Synners* (London: Grafton, 1991), pp. 357, 321, 349.

8. Neal Stephenson, *Snow Crash* (London: Penguin, 1993), p. 179.

9. Carolyn See, *Golden Days* (Berkeley: University of California Press, 1996), p. 167.

10. Michael Ventura, "Phantasmal America," *L.A. Weekly*, Aug. 29–Sept. 4, 1986, www.steveerickson.org/articles/phant.html/.

11. Steve Erickson, *Amnesiascope* (New York: Henry Holt, 1996), p. 126.

12. Curt Gentry, *The Last Days of the Late, Great State of California* (New York: G. P. Putnam, 1968), pp. 184, 338.

13. David Minter, "The Puritan Jeremiad as a Literary Form," in *The American Puritan Imagination: Essays in Revaluation*, ed. Sacvan Bercovitch (Cambridge: Cambridge University Press, 1974), p. 48.

11

CHIP RHODES

Hollywood fictions

Near the end of Mel Brooks's *Blazing Saddles* (1974), a fight breaks out in a saloon. As the brawl escalates, a wall of the saloon is knocked down to reveal another movie being made, a high society musical in the Fred Astaire/Ginger Rogers vein. Soon hyper-masculine cowboys fight effeminate dancers in a clash of classic film genres. This scene reveals the basic theme of Hollywood-on-Hollywood movies: movies are not true-to-life; instead they conform to strict genre formulas to create their own "reality."

Movies about Hollywood are well known and popular. Films like *Singin' in the Rain* (Stanley Donen, 1952) and *Sunset Boulevard* (Billy Wilder, 1950) share *Blazing Saddles*'s delight in making viewers feel like insiders in the know about moviemaking. Even when there is an apparent critique of the film industry, it isn't genuine. At a silent film premiere, Gene Kelly's character is interviewed and delivers a stereotypical high-art story of his rise to fame that is undercut by the visual images of a child of the urban ghetto dancing in saloons and pool halls and then working as a stuntman before chancing into a starring role. The silent era, the film strongly implies, was a fake and elitist era but the new Hollywood of the sound era allows for genuine stories about real people. Similarly, *Sunset Boulevard* is brutally critical of the narcissism that characterizes the silent studio's star system. Norma Desmond now lives in a delusional world because she was ultimately nothing but the creation of the studios. While the silent era was unwittingly comical in *Singin' in the Rain*, here it is grotesque, but for the same reason. More recent films about Hollywood like the Coen brothers' *Barton Fink* (1991) and Robert Altman's *The Player* (1992) are certainly more genuinely critical of the film industry, only celebrating Hollywood's influence on culture in ironic and black comedic ways.

Novels about Hollywood are not as beloved or even particularly well known. According to Anthony Slide, by 1995 there had been 1,200 novels written about the US film industry.[1] Some scholars, including me, see a set of persistent preoccupations in these novels. The Hollywood novel is usually written by someone who has logged time as a screenwriter. In the conventional story, the Hollywood novel pits those who would defend art against those who treat movies as a business. F. Scott Fitzgerald's *Pat Hobby Stories* depict a once-talented, once-famous writer who has been reduced to a pathetic figure by drink and his inability to write the kind of formulaic story that the studios expect. These stories are often discussed precisely because they fit the stereotype of the author in Hollywood so well. But it is worth noting that in his last, unfinished novel, *The Last Tycoon* (1939), Fitzgerald provides one of the rare, positive fictional representations of Hollywood. He casts Monroe Stahr, a powerful producer, as the inheritor of the optimism of the American Dream most famously embodied by Fitzgerald's Jay Gatsby.

The Hollywood novel in the studio era

The first notable novel about Hollywood was Harry Leon Wilson's *Merton of the Movies* (1922). This light comedy tells the story of a young man who believes so optimistically and completely in the reality of filmmaking that he ends up tricked into doing lowbrow comedy because his attempts at high drama are so comically bad. But when the optimism of the 1920s gave way to the fear and desperation of Depression-era America in the 1930s, novels about Hollywood became much darker. These novels use the Depression as a backdrop to a darkness that comes from the ongoing conflict between two things that motivate its principal characters: art and sexual desire. These preoccupations provide the best way to appreciate the critique of American culture that the Hollywood novel delivers.

The seminal text for the genre of the Hollywood novel is Nathanael West's *The Day of the Locust* (1939). This novel remains one of the most insightful literary meditations on the substitution of simulations of reality for reality itself in an entertainment age. While predating Jean Baudrillard's theory of the "simulacrum," it presents Hollywood as a mélange of simulations – imitations that take the place of something more "real." Protagonist Tod Hackett is the novel's artistic conscience. He marvels at and mourns the fact that Hollywood has embraced simulations of everything from yachting hats to tennis outfits to architecture to much larger things like history, love, and genuine feelings. This replacement of the "real" with representations is also parodied by the British novelist Evelyn Waugh in his comic novel *The Loved One* (1948), which extends the culture of simulation to the well-known Forest Lawn mortuary, where artifice employed on corpses invariably improves and certainly outlasts the real "loved ones" of the novel's title.

The first chapter of *Locust* introduces Tod as a Yale-educated artist recruited to do set design for a studio. He is immediately confronted with an absurd image of a war movie being made with no fidelity to historical fact. Tod works throughout *Locust* on a painting entitled *The Burning of Los Angeles*. The painting reflects Tod's growing realization that desire unsatisfied turns into violence, a belief inspired by his relationship with Faye Greener, a beautiful would-be actress who is the personification of simulations in the novel. Tod's painting does not present the reality that the simulations ignore, however; it portrays what will surely happen in a world that generates desire for inaccessible objects. Just so, his painting pictures Faye running naked, blissfully unaware of the angry mob chasing her and hurling rocks. The fire that surrounds them all is a sign of the impending apocalypse. It also suggests the intimate link between desire and art. Tod has himself come to desire Faye in particular and Hollywood in general and thus feels the same desire leading to aggression. He has a rape fantasy about Faye when he realizes that he can never be her boyfriend. He is thus one of the masses with frustrated desire for what he can't have. But through his painting he achieves some critical distance by recognizing the consequences of this much unsated desire.

In *Locust*, Tod's desire transforms his art, but art can still show the origin and consequences of a culture fueled by manufactured desire that cannot ever be satisfied. Desire and art again function in tandem in Budd Schulberg's *What Makes Sammy Run?* (1941), but in a very different way. Al Manheim, the first-person narrator is ambivalently fixated on Sammy Glick, the ambitious young man who first comes to work at the newspaper where Al is a drama critic and swiftly and unscrupulously rises to become a successful Hollywood producer. Al disapproves of Sammy for two reasons: his unethical behavior in pursuit of success and his lack of respect for serious art. Yet Al's disapproval is so obsessive that the reader is invited to question how much Al unconsciously desires Sammy's success.

Sammy takes advantage of Al to facilitate his rise. Sammy also corrupts him, a dynamic that is one of the Hollywood novel's principal themes, according to Bruce Chipman.[2] This novel is curiously devoid of any of the tangible desire that was evident in *Locust*. But it is filled with evidence of repressed, socially unacceptable sexual desires. Al's fixation on Sammy comes out in many curious ways – in wish-fulfillment dreams in which Al is surrounded by hundreds of Sammys and in his pursuit of Kit, Sammy's ex-girlfriend, who is always described in masculine terms. When Al first dances with her, it reminds him of the time in Greenwich Village when he ended up dancing with a transvestite. Moreover, in their exchanges, Sammy consistently talks to Al like a lover, full of innuendo and awareness that Al's disapproval masks an intense attachment. Walter Wells was the first critic to question whether Al harbored repressed homosexual desire for Sammy. If he does, then Al's many commentaries on art's autonomy from entertainment have to be taken with a grain of salt. As for Sammy himself, the object of this desire, the novel's title alone is enough to suggest that Schulberg sees him not just as a product of Hollywood; he is a symptom of a nation that is driven by an "id" (to quote Kit) that wants fame and fortune.[3]

John O'Hara's *Hope of Heaven* (1939) shares much with Schulberg's *Sammy*. The novel's protagonist, Jim Malloy, is a screenwriter who continues to make a lot of money even though he is depicted as basically never working. His inactivity has left him without a clearly defined gender role and a troubled relationship with his girlfriend, Peggy, who was psychologically damaged by relationships with her father and brother that the novel strongly implies included sexual abuse. Their relationship fails, and it seems clear that the reason is a film industry that complicates traditional gender roles, frustrates genuine romantic expectations, and proffers material temptations that rob screenwriters of their artistic integrity.

Raymond Chandler's *The Little Sister* (1949) shares much thematically with *Sammy* and *Hope*, particularly the notion of the protagonist who is fully caught up in Hollywood culture. Chandler's plot is busy and convoluted, but it revolves around the Quests, a family from rural Kansas. One sister has come to Hollywood and changed her name to Mavis Weld. She has been followed by her brother Orrin, a photographer who tries to blackmail Mavis with a photo he took of her with a well-known mobster. The series of events that transpires as the protagonist and narrator Philip Marlowe looks for Orrin – involving shady hotel detectives and ice picks – eventually brings Marlowe into close contact with Dolores Gonzalez, an actress who plays the part on and off screen of a sexy Latina even though she is not a Latina and hails from Cleveland, and Mavis herself. He watches one of Mavis's movies and comes away smitten. He has a few highly dramatic arguments with her that are part acting and part seduction. They provide Marlowe with his first real motivation in a case that had originally found him at his most misanthropic because it only brought him into contact with swindlers. Now he wishes only to protect Mavis. Not unlike Tod's desire for Faye, Marlowe's desire for Mavis Weld is desire for an inaccessible object. But unlike Tod, Marlowe knows he will never possess the woman, and he evinces none of Tod's aggression. His aggression is displaced onto all those who have exploited Mavis, including a mobster she might be in love with. Desire in its more typically Freudian form is figured through Dolores's desire for Marlowe and her ex-husband Dr. Lagardie's obsession with her. Eventually, the doctor kills Dolores and then himself because he refuses to accept rejection.

While desire does propel the lives of characters in the thrall of the film industry, art is present in Chandler's novel only on the formal level. Marlowe is another unreliable first-person narrator, but the worldview he espouses throughout the novel is that of an alienated romantic aesthete who feels disgust at the simulations and standardizations of the city, particularly when they threaten his self-reliant individualism. That he falls in love with Mavis Weld, however, undercuts his autonomy; it suggests that Marlowe doesn't want to be alone. The novel doesn't pursue this question. Instead, it contrasts Marlowe's chivalric love with the shabby desire of Hollywood-centered culture.

After the "studio system"

Everything changed for the film industry in 1948, when the Supreme Court ruled that the major studios had been operating as a monopoly. The Paramount Decision marked the end of the production-driven monopoly that lay behind the Hollywood novel. During the 1950s, the film industry gradually began changing; the major studios reluctantly sold off theaters and dealt with the advent of television. The novel that best captures this decade of transition is Norman Mailer's *The Deer Park* (1955). One of Mailer's stranger novels, *Deer Park* reflects the eventual dissolution of self that too much time in Hollywood produces. The novel also suggests something transitional in terms of how the writer thinks about art and desire. It provides a vision of decadence, corruption, and sexual deviance that is taken to a higher level by Mailer than anyone previously. Hollywood is a community suffering from moral depravity for which sexual deviants, whores, gamblers, pimps, and drug dealers are no more responsible than producers, actors and actresses.

Deer Park is set in Desert D'Or, a fashionable California resort along the lines of Palm Springs, so the entire environment is one of leisure and pleasurable pursuits. It is also, as Carolyn See writes, a world in which nothing is what it seems and everyone "pretends to be something other than themselves."[4] Like *Hope of Heaven*'s Jim Malloy, *Deer Park*'s protagonist is a writer. Sergius O'Shaughnessy is a veteran who arrives impotent from his war experience and seeks to write the "great American novel." But the environment is not conducive to his artistic ambition. Among the temptations he faces is a generous offer from a Hollywood producer for the rights to his life story as the basis for a movie. This temptation, the novel strongly implies, threatens his robust, masculine creativity. It is striking, though, that O'Shaughnessy overcomes his impotence after a sexual dalliance with a famous film actress, suggesting how disingenuous this particular critique of Hollywood can be.

By the time the Hollywood novel moved into the 1970s, the New Hollywood had taken over. In the New Hollywood, multinational corporations like Sony own the studios. But at the same time, the deregulation of the industry opens up a space for independent filmmakers. This change enabled the rise to prominence of auteurs like Robert Altman, Francis Ford Coppola, and Martin Scorsese. Just so, the Hollywood novel's depiction of art and desire changed as well.

Joan Didion's vision of an institutionalized actress, Maria Wyeth in *Play It As It Lays* (1970), is unsparing in its representation of the cultural wasteland that is Hollywood. The opening interior monologue is set in the mental hospital where Maria, the protagonist, resides after a series of events have led her estranged husband and friends to commit her. Maria is notable among our many protagonists because she is a woman and an actress, not a male writer or artist. She is also notable for her psychological state. While most of the characters in this novel teem with desire, either normative and aggressive or "abnormal," and others try to pass themselves off as romantics, Maria is remarkable for her total lack of desire. She lives without any emotional reaction to much of her life. She is, however, haunted by the institutionalization of her daughter, Kate, and by an abortion. But Didion doesn't try to generate any sympathy for Maria; she presents Maria as an utter absence throughout the text. Her chosen activity of driving the freeways day after day suggests that she finds all participation in the world pointless and random. The only tangible desire in evidence in the novel is the casual sex among Hollywood denizens, but none of it has consequences. It is as if the uncontrollable sexual desire to which previous authors attributed so many of Hollywood's crimes against art and morality no longer exists.

Maria's lack of belief in any code of values shows up in her approach to aesthetics as well, particularly the independent movie that launched her film career. Made by her husband, Carter, when he was a film student in New York, the film simply follows Maria through what is intended to be an average day in her life. Maria doesn't feel any identification – good or bad – with the movie, just a sense that the character in the movie seems to have "no knack for anything."[5]

Play It As It Lays certainly takes the dissolution of self to its logical extreme. It is also perhaps the novel that best represents the auteur era because its writing coincided with the careers of so many directors who would soon achieve great personal fame. Artistically ambitious directors could get funding to make movies well outside the studios' purview, and these films were often debacles financially (*Apocalypse Now* [Coppola, 1979]) and artistically (*Heaven's Gate* [Michael Cimino, 1980]). Maria's husband is one of these celebrated auteurs; his depiction is a pretty clear mockery of those in Hollywood who considered themselves pure artists.

As this era of bloated budgets and larger-than-life directors gave way to the 1980s with its shift toward multinational corporations that would not indulge maverick directors, the power of agents and bankable stars began to rise. Talent packages from influential agents like Michael Ovitz were often necessary to get movies made. Fewer movies were given the green light in this era in which studios could make only as many movies as their parent companies would permit and therefore only wanted films that had blockbuster potential. In this Reagan-era economic climate, Bruce Wagner's trilogy of novels of Hollywood became the appropriate fictional response. His first novel, *Force Majeure* (1991) is the most important and the one that follows most consistently in the tradition that began with West's *Locust*.

Force Majeure is told in free indirect discourse, in which the narrator knows and records the thoughts of only one character. The protagonist is Bud Wiggins, an unsuccessful screenwriter who was briefly hot until his promising screenplay was shelved after a new studio head deemed it unacceptable. He is now back living with his mother. The world Bud inhabits in Hollywood, the only world he has ever known, is utterly a world of simulations in which one must be able to convince others one is successful in order to become successful. Still, Bud does not wholly give up on the existence of something real beneath the images. Two figures in the novel who fascinate Bud are the Rav, a Holocaust survivor, and Rachel, a Vietnam vet who has written an autobiographical long poem. Both turn out to be frauds who have assumed identities for gain. Against this backdrop, Bud's own family history is heavily mediated through the films that have shaped his way of narrating his life. Even his dreams that involve early-childhood events are remembered through the nuts and bolts of filmmaking. In one dream, "Little Bud stared at the foot in the shoe (CAMERA PUSHES IN TO EXTREME CLOSE-UP OF BOY) ...The torpid screenwriter turned over in bed and thought: Jesus. That was a fetish."[6]

Art is much discussed by Bud and others, but those who sanctify art are also phonies. Bud has contempt for characters like Perry Bravo, a criminal who has literally gotten out of prison because he has the backing of Hollywood heavyweights. Perry's approach to literature is presented as all posturing. Even Bud uses art as a pretext to rehearse his personal obsessions. Bud's failings as a writer seem partly the result of random luck and partly the result of his psychosexual problems. When he has a chance to have sex with a famous actress, the great desire of Marlowe and Sergius O'Shaughnessy, he cannot follow up even though he tries to remind himself that "Joan Krause desires you, you are a gifted writer."[7] From there, things get more disturbing. He has sex with a powerful male producer while *The Best Years of Our Lives* plays in the background. The incident produces no response, not disgust or awakened desire. At the novel's end, Bud is on the verge of having sex with the "bicycle girl," an eight-year-old girl he meets when he has taken a job going door-to-door.

While Didion's Maria has no desire and only has one sexual experience in the entire novel, Bud does all of it – but stumbles into most available forms of sex with no sense that they are anything more authentic than the simulations of desire that surround him. In a curious reversal, Bud's descent into peder-asty and the aimless sexual liaisons along the way seem more effect than cause. While the unsettling, conflicted, and triangular nature of sexual desire was often the cause of artistic corruption in the past, here it seems that Bud's failure as a screenwriter of some artistic ambitions generated the humiliation that led to his sexual transgressions.

As desire has moved from orthodoxly Freudian to something random but hardly conventional, the conception of art likewise seems to have lost what-ever critical distance it once maintained by the time the New Hollywood supplants the "golden era." Elmore Leonard, who has written about Hollywood frequently, changes all that in a remarkably straightforward way. In *Get Shorty* (1990), Leonard returns the Hollywood novel to the basic narrative strategy of realism, simplifying both aesthetics (tell the real story, not the formulaic one) and desire (keep desire and romance in their proper, subordinate place).

The novel tells the story of loan shark Chili Palmer, who chases to Los Angeles someone who faked his death to get out from under his debt. Once there, Chili figures out that anyone can make it in Hollywood because "there's nobody in charge," a simple but accurate description of the process of making movies in the New Hollywood.[8] The story Chili wants to get made into a movie is his story, which the reader already knows. The novel is pure satire, and there is much fun made of Harry Zinn, the independent producer Chili teams up with to pitch his movie. Harry may be independent, but the films he makes are comically bad B movies. Leonard's critique of the way the film industry represents human motivation seems to be rooted in a rejection of the Freudian subject whose motives are always traceable to psychosexual origins. The Hollywood novel of the studio era used Freud's idea of the psychologically conflicted self to challenge the sanitized images of self found in mainstream films. In the New Hollywood, Hollywood novelists tend to represent sexuality either on the far end of the spectrum or as troublingly absent. Leonard relocates desire and love in its proper, realist place – as simply a piece of the puzzle.

Thus we have come full circle, returning to the simple world of *Merton of the Movies*, before Nathanael West made things dark and disturbing. In both *Get Shorty* and *Merton*, a fundamental distinction between image and reality drives the narrative and provides the critical framework necessary to expose

Hollywood as a physical place that is also a microcosm of the national culture. One possible reason for this return to realism is that realism was born in the nineteenth century in large part as a substitute for romance fiction, which placed love at the center of human existence. Freud introduced to the United States the notion of a subject driven by doomed, aggressive desire; Hollywood exploited that desire by feeding its audience film romance. Hollywood novels, however, demystify desire and thereby provide critical commentary on this, what Robert Sklar has called, "movie-made America."[9] If writers had chosen to focus on only one dimension of Hollywood, the Hollywood novel would be far less interesting.

NOTES

1. Anthony Slide, *The Hollywood Novel: A Critical Guide to Over 1200 Works with Film-Related Themes or Characters, 1912 through 1994* (Jefferson, N.C.: McFarland, 1995).
2. Bruce L. Chipman, *Into America's Dream-Dump: A Postmodern Study of the Hollywood Novel* (Lanham, Md.: University Press of America, 1999).
3. Budd Schulberg, *What Makes Sammy Run?* (New York: Vintage, 1993), p. 193. See Walter Wells, *Tycoons and Locusts: A Regional Look at Hollywood Fiction of the 1930s* (Carbondale: Southern Illinois University Press, 1973), pp. 145–8.
4. See Carolyn See, "The Hollywood Novel: The American Dream Cheat," in *Tough Guy Writers of the Thirties*, ed. David Madden (Carbondale: Southern Illinois University Press, 1968), pp. 199–217.
5. Joan Didion, *Play It As It Lays* (New York: Noonday Press, 1990), p. 21.
6. Bruce Wagner, *Force Majeure* (New York: Random House, 1991), p. 3.
7. *Ibid.*, p. 264.
8. Elmore Leonard, *Get Shorty* (New York: HarperCollins, 2002), p. 157.
9. Robert Sklar, *Movie-Made America: A Cultural History of American Movies* (New York: Random House, 1975).

12

MARK SHIEL

The Southland on screen

Surely no single city has such a close relationship with motion pictures as Los Angeles, which has appeared on screen in myriad guises for over a century since a film crew employed by Thomas Edison's Edison Manufacturing Company arrived in December 1897. *South Spring Street, Los Angeles, California* (1898), a twenty-five-second "actuality" film shot by Frederick Blechynden, captured a sense of Los Angeles as a metropolis-in-the-making by presenting a view of pedestrian and horse-drawn traffic on that busy downtown commercial thoroughfare. Painters and photographers had long flocked to Southern California for its climate, sunlight, Mediterranean landscapes, and the romantic appeal of its Spanish and Mexican heritage. D. W. Griffith first captured these ingredients on celluloid in *Ramona* (1910), a fifteen-minute adaptation of Helen Hunt Jackson's novel. Offering a utopian image of the region as a combination of flower-filled garden and expansive wilderness waiting to be exploited, *Ramona* assisted the civic boosters in marketing Los Angeles as an ideal place in which to live and work. *Ramona* was remade in 1916, 1928, and 1936, while another romantic Mexican legend, that of Zorro, was adapted for the screen in 1920, 1925, 1937, 1946, and 1949.

Following the establishment of film studios early in the second decade of the twentieth century by pioneers such as William Selig, Thomas Ince, Carl Laemmle, and Mack Sennett, images of Los Angeles achieved widespread and repeated dissemination in the hundreds of short slapstick comedies played by Charlie Chaplin, Harold Lloyd, Laurel and Hardy, and other comedians. Made quickly and cheaply, and with small and mobile casts and crews, many of these films were shot, in part or in whole, on location in the streets of Los Angeles and adjacent municipalities. Indeed, they derive much of their humor and distinctive imagery from the fact that Los Angeles was then a young city going through a phase of particularly rapid growth. The films of Chaplin, Lloyd, and Laurel and Hardy are notable for their depiction of suburban bungalows in the local Craftsman style, with well-tended lawns and driveways overlooked by pretty verandas that often serve as ready-made stages for dramatic action between the star and his sweetheart, wife, or mother-in-law, as in Chaplin's *Cruel, Cruel Love* (George Nichols and Mack Sennett, 1914), Lloyd's *I Do* (Hal Roach, 1921), and Laurel and Hardy's *Should Married Men Go Home?* (Leo McCarey and James Parrott, 1928). Such homes proliferated in reality and on the screen as the population of Los Angeles rocketed from 319,000 in 1910 to 1.24 million in 1930. Suburban domesticity was matched in settings involving nature on a grander scale where the new suburban masses passed their leisure time. Public parks, especially Echo Park in Edendale, were favored locations, as were the oceanfront amusement parks on the piers at Santa Monica and Venice Beach. The somewhat smaller number of films made in downtown Los Angeles typically make significant use of that district's landmark high-rise, neoclassical commercial buildings, metropolitan ambience, and crowds. In *Safety Last!* (Fred C. Newmeyer and Sam Taylor, 1923), filmed on location on Broadway, Harold Lloyd plays a lowly department store sales assistant who climbs up the face of the building in which he works as part of a stunt to publicize the store, impress his boss, and win the affections of his leading lady.

While all slapstick comedy involves frenetic action culminating in moments of danger and comic release, slapstick comedy filmed around Los Angeles is especially notable for its extended chase sequences along the city's long avenues and boulevards, and through the mazes of streets in the recently subdivided suburbs. In films like *Making a Living* (Henry Lehrman, 1914) and *Mabel's Busy Day* (Mabel Normand, 1914), Chaplin's stock character, the Tramp, is typically pursued on foot by the police for some misdemeanor, or by a rival suitor for the affections of a woman.[1] But Harold Lloyd and Laurel and Hardy more frequently take to the automobiles (and sometimes horses and electric streetcars) that raced through the distinctive commercial strip development that typified LA streets even then, often coming to a head in a wreck at a busy intersection. The special iconic power that the automobile possesses in cinematic images of Los Angeles today began to be established at this time.

Early Chaplin films such as *A Film Johnnie* (George Nichols, 1914) and *The Masquerader* (Chaplin, 1914) contribute to another iconic image of Los Angeles – the land of cinematic make-believe – that proliferated in the following two decades in a large number of feature films whose action takes place primarily in the movie studios. These films familiarized the world with a kaleidoscopic locale consisting of cavernous studio buildings and back lots filled with timber sets depicting everything from Wild West saloons and Manhattan jazz clubs to Babylonian palaces, Parisian streets, and the trenches of World War I. Amidst these synthetic surroundings, the automobile is a much less prominent feature, more likely to pull up sedately to the red carpet outside Grauman's Chinese Theater on the night of a movie premiere. Equally, whatever danger the protagonists face is more likely to be moral than physical. These films balance a celebration of Hollywood's romance with recognition of the potential pitfalls of its vanity and material wealth. *The Extra Girl* (F. Richard Jones, 1923) portrays Sue (Mabel Normand), a naive young woman newly arrived from rural Illinois, who seeks stardom only to find herself working as a seamstress in the costume department, where she is chastened by various comic mishaps before returning home. At a time when the Hollywood studios were responding to a series of sex scandals and were defending themselves from accusations of moral depravity by conservative Christians, the formula was also employed in *Souls for Sale* (Rupert Hughes, 1923), *Hollywood* (James Cruze, 1923), and *Merton of the Movies* (Cruze, 1924). However, each of these films lightens its theme with comic relief. The corruption of innocence, kindness, and beauty by the false pretenses of the movies was explored with greater melodramatic intensity in the following decade in *Hollywood Boulevard* (Robert Florey, 1936) and *A Star is Born* (William Wellman, 1937; remade in 1954 and 1976). *What Price Hollywood?* (George Cukor, 1932), which set a precedent for them, stars Constance Bennett as a waitress who works in the Brown Derby restaurant, a favorite haunt of actual movie personalities. She falls in love with a handsome actor and becomes a star with his support before he declines into alcoholism and eventual suicide.

These films present Hollywood as a semi-autonomous town whose film industry is a family or community unto itself, albeit dysfunctional, that could take or leave the city around it. Their titles and scripts more frequently refer to Hollywood than to Los Angeles, aiding the studios' efforts to promote "Hollywood" as a brand name. Despite the disappointments and tragedies of their narratives, Hollywood appears as a liminal space between reality and fantasy in general, filled with a superabundance of stars that gives it a spectacular aura. The films' narrative critiques of Hollywood are counterbalanced by a fascination in their mise en scène and cinematography with the allure of ritzy nightclubs and movie premieres, the streamlined art-moderne offices of movie executives, the ornate mansions of Beverly Hills, and secluded Malibu beach houses.

Moreover, such critical representations are matched by more positive images: *Show People* (King Vidor, 1928) and *Hollywood Cavalcade* (Irving Cummings, 1939) use slapstick comedy as the basis of nostalgic celebrations of the creativity of the silent-film pioneers. *Crashing Hollywood* (Lew Landers, 1938) presents a gangster film comedy about mobsters delighted to be hired by a movie studio to lend authenticity to its gangster film scripts. *Hollywood Hotel* (Busby Berkeley, 1937), a musical, stars Benny Goodman and his band in a fairy tale of romance and celebrity that unfolds on Hollywood Boulevard, at the Hollywood Bowl, the Café Trocadero, and the Orchid Room of the Hollywood Hotel, a venue famous for its live-radio broadcasts. *Hollywood Canteen* (Delmer Daves, 1944) recounts the somewhat other-worldly experience of two ordinary GIs who arrive in Los Angeles, on leave from the South Pacific, where they meet movie stars in the flesh at the Hollywood Canteen, a dance hall established by the film industry to support enlisted men and to raise money for wartime charities.

The spectacularization of Hollywood – and, by extension, of Los Angeles – as a landscape of make-believe achieves even more exaggerated form in the Technicolor images of *Singin' in the Rain* (Stanley Donen, 1952). But by this time, such images are in the minority, held in check by the downbeat revision of the city's cinematic vision in film noir. Recognition of Southern California's propensity for violent crime had never been entirely absent, as *Studio Murder Mystery* (Frank Tuttle, 1929) and *Blood Money* (Rowland Brown, 1933) demonstrate. In the 1940s, however, film noir became the dominant mode for cinematic representation of the landscapes and society of Los Angeles as the result of a unique combination of circumstances: the directors and screen-writers from Germany and other parts of Central Europe who fled the rise of fascism and who imported their expressionistic visual style to Hollywood cinema; the lingering effects of the Great Depression, which radicalized many people in Hollywood and led them to favor a socially responsible realism in the arts; the critical encounter of these progressive voices with the long-standing utopian mythology of Los Angeles as a sun-tanned bastion of the American Dream; and the economic boom of Los Angeles during and after World War II, which gave it a new strategic importance in the Cold War and emboldened those on the political right to prosecute what they saw as un-American behavior. In fact, the rot had set in even before the United States declared victory in World War II. Barbara Stanwyck, playing herself, smiled sweetly at the young GI who gazed at her, starry-eyed, in *Hollywood Canteen*. But that same year in *Double Indemnity* (Billy Wilder, 1944) she was a murdering adulteress, Phyllis Dietrichson, the quintessential femme fatale, who resides in a Spanish-style villa in Glendale, overlooking down-town Los Angeles where the insurance salesman Walter Neff, her lover and accomplice in the murder of her husband, works in George H. Wyman's landmark art-nouveau Bradbury Building.

Not every film noir makes as much use of location filming in Los Angeles as does *Double Indemnity*. The low-budget B movie *Detour* (Edward G. Ulmer, 1945) uses brief, rear-projection shots of Hollywood Boulevard and a cramped indoor set representing a cheap hotel room to achieve an effective characterization of Hollywood as a tawdry dead-end town for the couple of killers (played by Tom Neal and Ann Savage) who hide there in fear of the law. The star vehicle *The Big Sleep* (Howard Hawks, 1946), one of many adaptations of Raymond Chandler's Philip Marlowe novels, entails investigations by Marlowe (Humphrey Bogart) that spread in a wide arc from downtown to Hollywood, Santa Monica, and the Lido Pier at Malibu, but all of them were re-created on sound stages at the Warner Bros. studios in Burbank.

Location filming did become more and more prevalent, however, and the increasing attention given to the real city outside the studios' walls, together with its physical size and contrasting spaces, helped to accentuate the themes of confinement and reactionary violence that underpin film noir as a whole. In the opening scenes of *The Pitfall* (André De Toth, 1948), the protagonist declares while trapped in heavy traffic, "Sometimes I get to feel like a wheel within a wheel within a wheel," a feeling only partly relieved by the sunlit, palm tree-lined comfort of the suburban street where he lives, the scenes of boating at Santa Monica, and the affair he has with a blonde he meets at work. In *In a Lonely Place* (Nicholas Ray, 1950), gruesome shots of a woman's murdered body dumped in the dirt of Benedict Canyon are followed by scenes of screenwriter Dixon Steel (Humphrey Bogart) dining at a swanky Hollywood club and answering questions in the manicured Spanish-style headquarters of the Beverly Hills Police Department. In *Kiss Me Deadly* (Robert Aldrich, 1955), the dilapidated tenements of Bunker Hill are offset against the urbane modernity of the detective protagonist, Mickey Spillane's Mike Hammer, and his minimalist apartment on Wilshire Boulevard. In *Plunder Road* (Hubert Cornfield, 1957), the Harbor Freeway and LA Civic Center are contrasted as icons of modern technology to the remote spot in rural Nevada where the protagonists rob a train of gold bullion.

While the majority of film noirs use location filming to depict the actual streets and buildings of Los Angeles with a new degree of detail, a significant number, often referred to as "police procedural films" – including *He Walked by Night* (Alfred L. Werker, 1948) and *Dragnet* (Jack Webb, 1954) – give increasing prominence to representations of the professional ability of the police to marshal information, coordinate investigations, and apprehend criminals across the urban landscape. Images of the invasion of suburban domestic space became widespread in this period, automobile use became unnervingly routine or compensatory for some psychological lack, and a growing sense of the insufficiency of material wealth, the persistence of sexual obsession, and the loss of Southern California as utopia was evident. In the late 1950s and 1960s, as the middle-aged and middle-class audiences to whom film noir was primarily addressed deserted cinema-going in favor of television, the cinematic representation of Los Angeles would come to be shaped by the experiences and attitudes of Southern California teenagers and young adults who were alienated from the region's boosterist mythology but who responded with an intensified hedonism and deliberately subcultural or countercultural behavior.

Rebel Without a Cause (Nicholas Ray, 1955) drew public attention to the then-urgent issues of teenage rebellion and juvenile delinquency that manifested themselves acutely in Los Angeles because of its good weather and especially high rates of automobile ownership. Revolving around the dysfunctional family life of Jim Stark (James Dean), his romance with the maladjusted Judy (Natalie Wood), and friendship with the loner Plato (Sal Mineo), *Rebel* was produced by Warner Bros. in rich color and CinemaScope widescreen. But films with youth subculture themes and settings were more often produced on low budgets by independent companies in the exploitation film industry and usually adopted a less moralistic tone. This is evident in Roger Corman's *A Bucket of Blood* (1959), a parody of the beatnik artists' scene in Venice Beach that revolves around a young layabout with no talent who becomes a celebrated sculptor by literally killing his subjects, covering them in plaster, and displaying them for the appreciation of none-the-wiser beatniks, who philosophize about their existential meaning. In a different vein, a series of films like *Beach Party* (William Asher, 1963) and *Beach Blanket Bingo* (William Asher, 1965) were aimed at teenage audiences with an appetite for high school girls in bikinis, muscular college men in shorts, seaside romance, rock 'n' roll, surfing, and the Southern California sun. However, the relative naiveté of what Mike Davis has called Southern California's "Endless Summer" of the early 1960s was displaced later in the decade by images of an increasingly large and anti-establishment youth counterculture that asserted itself in drinking, brawling, and sacrilege in biker films such as Corman's *The Wild Angels* (1966), hippie fashions and music in *Mondo Mod* (Bethel Buckalew, 1967), and political demonstrations in *Wild in the Streets* (Barry Shears, 1968).[2] These films are positioned ambivalently between celebration and condemnation of their subjects, but they are certainly united by a recognition of the particular prominence of young people as a demographic group, and of youth culture as a new phenomenon in Los Angeles, a city whose population growth after World War II was the most rapid of any in the United States, and that was now the center not only of American feature film production but also of television production and music recording. While films with very low budgets continued to use sets for interiors, the majority of films further increased the prevalence of location shooting by describing places in and around Los

Angeles that were apart from the mainstream of everyday life: the beatnik cafés of Venice, the beaches of Malibu, the hippie nightclubs of the Sunset Strip, and the back roads of the Hollywood Hills.

A less ambivalent, less sensationalist cinematic critique of Los Angeles also emerged in the late 1960s, incorporating the modernist influences of European art cinema. Many of the most aesthetically innovative and thematically ground-breaking films of the time were made by foreigners who gravitated to Los Angeles because they saw in it a telling landscape of the future. This was the case with *Point Blank* (John Boorman, 1967), *Model Shop* (Jacques Demy, 1969), *Zabriskie Point* (Michelangelo Antonioni, 1970), and *The Outside Man* (Jacques Deray, 1972), all of which portray the city as a place of latent or actual armed aggression, hard-edged modern commercial architecture, garish color, and constant automobile mobility. In *Point Blank* and *The Outside Man*, these features are presented within the format of an updated film noir (or "neo-noir") narrative, while in *Model Shop* and *Zabriskie Point*, the intense anomie generated by Los Angeles' synthetic surfaces is explicitly linked to the ongoing war in Vietnam and the antiwar movement then active in the city.

In an era when for the first time more Americans lived in suburbs than in cities and the countryside combined, many films also implied that Los Angeles was the nation's limit case of rampant urban growth, suburban conformity, and televisual superficiality, all of which led to crises of identity and mental breakdown. This is true of perhaps the most famous film of the era set in Los Angeles, *The Graduate* (Mike Nichols, 1967), which focuses on the frustration felt by college graduate Benjamin Braddock (Dustin Hoffman) in the face of the staid middle-class marriage and career in the plastics industry that his parents have mapped out for him. Notably, in *The Graduate*, as in many other films of the era, the activity of driving at high speed through Los Angeles and on its freeways becomes a prominent subject for representation in its own right, as Benjamin rejects the mansions and swimming pools of Beverly Hills by driving off in his red Alfa Romeo Spider sports car. Inverting such images of mobility, on the other hand, Peter Bogdanovich's *Targets* (1968) recounts in a deliberately cold and distant manner the developing obsession with guns of an outwardly typical San Fernando Valley teenager, much less well off than Braddock, whose disgust with his parents leads him to kill them in cold blood before taking off on a shooting spree, sniping at passing cars on the Ventura Freeway and at the audience in a drive-in movie theater in Van Nuys. The sense of Los Angeles as an exemplar of late-twentieth-century middle-class urban living and urban angst is further explored in myriad permutations by John Cassavetes' *Faces* (1968), Paul Mazursky's *Alex in Wonderland* (1970), Robert Altman's *The Long Goodbye* (1973), Roman Polanski's neo-noir *Chinatown* (1974), and Hal Ashby's *Shampoo* (1975).

The fact that many of these films involve no shooting in studios at all testifies as well to the collapse of the Hollywood studio system. Film production on location by independent companies became the standard practice, while the studios concentrated on financing and distribution. These films render Los Angeles as a patchwork of horizontal, high-speed, and depthless landscapes by employing a panoply of mobile cinematographic techniques such as aerial shots, hand-held cameras, cameras mounted on vehicles, and rapid zooming and panning, to a degree never before seen in American narrative film. Moreover, their spectacle of the city as dystopia is heightened by the fact that, in contrast to film noir, but like *Rebel Without a Cause*, they were made in color and widescreen.

Despite their progressive deconstruction of Los Angeles' inherited cinematic image as a place of opportunity, beauty, and wealth, however, most of the action in these films unfolds in the relatively comfortable locales of Venice Beach, Santa Monica, Hollywood, Beverly Hills, and Malibu, and most of the films pay no attention to issues of social and economic inequality between Los Angeles' historically dominant white middle class and its many minority populations. These would come to the fore in a creative explosion in the 1970s, beginning with the thriller *Sweet Sweetback's Baadasssss Song* (Melvin Van Peebles, 1971), filmed on an extremely low budget in the Watts ghetto recently torn apart by the rebellion of 1965. Centered on a black male hustler sympathetic to the Black Panthers, *Sweet Sweetback* is politically confrontational on behalf of black nationalism and the urban poor, and aesthetically avant garde not only in its *cinéma vérité* documentation of sections of Los Angeles previously absent from the screen, but also in its use of jump-cutting, psychedelic effects, multiple exposures, and the techniques of mobile cinematography evident in the art films of the day.

Sweet Sweetback and a number of less radical, more formulaic films in the "blaxploitation" cycle that it inaugurated, including *Coffy* (Jack Hill, 1973) and *Foxy Brown* (Hill, 1974), emerged in the aftermath of the studio era, during which those narrative films set in Los Angeles that feature racial minorities at all often relegated them to the background, derogatory roles, or romantic stereotypes. Chinese immigrants appear as idlers in the Chaplin comedy *Caught in a Cabaret* (1914), Mexicans as poor peasants and swashbuckling Romeos in *The Mark of Zorro* (Rouben Mamoulian, 1940), African Americans as comic buffoons in *Safety Last*, menial workers in *Double Indemnity*, and jazz musicians in *The Strip* (Lásló Kardos, 1951). Cinematic representations of Los Angeles' race relations became more nuanced at the end of the 1950s; the very late film noir *The Crimson Kimono* (Samuel Fuller, 1959), for instance, was shot in Little Tokyo and sympathetically portrays the friendship of two police detectives and Korean War veterans, one Anglo, the other Japanese American.

After *Sweet Sweetback*, on the other hand, a significant number of independent films about the African-American experience of Los Angeles were made by black filmmakers, from *Killer of Sheep* (Charles Burnett, 1977) and *Bush Mama* (Haile Gerima, 1979) to *Illusions* (Julie Dash, 1982). A series of popular comedies about pot-smoking Latino dropouts began with *Cheech & Chong: Up in Smoke* (Lou Adler, 1978), pointing a satirical but light-hearted finger at the police and US immigration service, while a tough representation of the hardships encountered by illegal immigrants to Los Angeles from Guatemala appears in the magical realist *El Norte* (Gregory Nava, 1983). Representations of Latino Los Angeles increase in number and reputation in the next twenty years, mapping out previously neglected parts of the city like East Los Angeles in *Born in East LA* (Cheech Marin, 1987), reflecting on the modern past of the Latino community in historical dramas such as *American Me* (Edward James Olmos, 1992) and *My Family* (Gregory Nava, 1995), and drawing attention to continuing social problems such as gang violence in *Mi Vida Loca* (Allison Anders, 1993). At the same time, Los Angeles became an important center for filmmaking in the nationwide movement known as New Black Realism. *Boyz N the Hood* (John Singleton, 1991), *Menace II Society* (Albert and Allen Hughes, 1993), and *Higher Learning* (Singleton, 1995), were shot on modest budgets in a relatively flat, televisual style but became particularly controversial because of their resolute focus on the deprivation, endemic drug use, and street violence that continued to blight the African-American ghettoes of South Central Los Angeles before and after the Justice Riots of 1992. Indeed, the new attention to Los Angeles' racial inequalities was strengthened by contributions from white filmmakers who focused on the issue primarily from the point of view of white protagonists, as in *Colors* (Dennis Hopper, 1988), *Grand Canyon* (Lawrence Kasdan, 1991), and *Falling Down* (Joel Schumacher, 1993).

On the other hand, the smaller number of films about Asian-American Los Angeles remain relatively traditional in their preoccupation with heroism and legend in martial arts films from *The Karate Kid* (John G. Avildsen, 1984) to *Rush Hour* (Brett Ratner, 1998), and in *Brother* (Takeshi Kitano, 2000), the story of a Japanese *yakuza* gangster lost in Los Angeles, although occasional films such as *Come See the Paradise* (Alan Parker, 1990) have focused more critically on the detention of Japanese Americans during World War II. Whichever community they focus on, all of these films explore the value and sustainability of ethnic minority communities in a polyglot city shaped by continuing de facto neighborhood segregation, the forces of globalization, and what many of these films depict as the LAPD's heavy-handed tactics.

In the last quarter of the twentieth century, Los Angeles' new global prominence combined with a sense of its propensity for catastrophe, whether riots, earthquakes, or wildfires, and Hollywood's increasing reliance on blockbusters and special effects, to foreground an image of Los Angeles as disaster zone. Disaster films from *Earthquake* (Mark Robson, 1974) to *Volcano* (Mick Jackson, 1997), both of which take place entirely in Los Angeles, and key sequences in *Armageddon* (Michael Bay, 1998) and *Deep Impact* (Mimi Leder, 1998), foreground the spectacle of Los Angeles' annihilation, the collapse of its commercial buildings, homes, and freeways, and play with the idea that Los Angeles, which began as desert, might one day return to that form. That possibility had already been a subject for cinematic speculation in *The War of the Worlds* (Byron Haskin, 1953) and *Them!* (Gordon Douglas, 1954), science-fiction films that involve threats to Los Angeles by mutant aliens from outer space, and play upon its relative proximity to the wildernesses of the desert Southwest, where the shady military–industrial complex that overshadowed American life during the Cold War carried out secret operations at Area 51 and Los Alamos. Futuristic projections of Los Angeles' possible destruction preoccupy another wave of science fiction films in *The Omega Man* (Boris Sagal, 1971), *Escape from the Planet of the Apes* (Don Taylor, 1971), and *Conquest of the Planet of the Apes* (J. Lee Thompson, 1972), but intensify in the scale of their spectacle and their box office success in subsequent decades with *Blade Runner* (Ridley Scott, 1982), *The Terminator* (James Cameron, 1984), *Terminator 2: Judgment Day* (Cameron, 1991), and *Escape from L.A.* (John Carpenter, 1996).

Blade Runner's city emphasizes Los Angeles' Asian and Latino populations juxtaposed with landmark LA buildings such as the Bradbury Building on South Broadway and Frank Lloyd Wright's Ennis house in Los Feliz. However, as an entirely high-rise and densely urban city, with no suburbs or beaches, filmed entirely at night, *Blade Runner*'s Los Angeles is much less immediately recognizable. *Terminator 2* was filmed on location across the LA region and mostly by day, the entire film being one long chase sequence in which a good android from the future (Arnold Schwarzenegger) and the young boy whose life he is trying to save, are pursued by an evil android disguised in the black uniform of an LAPD patrolman. While the film was most remarked upon for its pioneering computer-generated imagery and its budget of over $100 million, it arguably derives more meaning from the real city it maps out, through a shopping mall and suburban streets in Sherman Oaks, along storm drains and freeways, out into the desert, and back for a showdown in a Fontana steel mill.

However, the reliance of science fiction films on special effects and relentless spectacular action has arguably constrained the effectiveness of any critique of the excesses of the city that the films may want to propose. This might also be said of the numerous big-budget crime thrillers that stylize Los

Angeles as a city dominated by sleek corporate architecture and disturbed only by automatic weapons fire and gargantuan explosions, as in *Die Hard* (John McTiernan, 1988), *Heat* (Michael Mann, 1995), *Speed* (Jan De Bont, 1994), and *Collateral* (Mann, 2004). In the last twenty years, representations of Los Angeles have proliferated in a variety of genres. Its distinctive landscape and social environment have been affectionately ridiculed in comedy films such as *Naked Gun: From the Files of Police Squad!* (David Zucker, 1988), a ridiculous pastiche of a 1950s police procedural film, *L.A. Story* (Mick Jackson, 1991), in which Steve Martin is a television weatherman with a PhD, and *The Last Action Hero* (McTiernan, 1993), in which a little boy is magically inserted into the narrative of an action adventure film. The city's racial diversity continues to play a prominent role in films like *Baby Boy* (John Singleton, 2001), *Real Women Have Curves* (Patricia Cardoso, 2002), and *What's Cooking?* (Gurinder Chadha, 2000). Movies about the movies, such as *The Player* (Altman, 1992), *Swimming with Sharks* (George Huang, 1994), and *L.A. Confidential* (Curtis Hanson, 1997) mix themes of thwarted artistry, ruthless ambition, and murder to standardize an image of the Hollywood film industry as dystopia. And the insights of European filmmakers visiting Los Angeles have been extended by the German director Wim Wenders, whose *End of Violence* (1997) is a meditative thriller that posits the existence of a network of surveillance cameras secretly monitoring every block of Los Angeles for evidence of crime or nonconforming behavior.

Surely the most prominent recent tendency, however, is represented by the numerous off-beat LA dramas emanating from the "indies," from *Short Cuts* (Altman, 1993), *Pulp Fiction* (Quentin Tarantino, 1994), and *The Big Lebowski* (Joel Coen, 1998), to *Magnolia* (Paul Thomas Anderson, 1999), *Mulholland Drive* (David Lynch, 2001), and *Crash* (Paul Haggis, 2004). In these films, features of Los Angeles that were remarkable in earlier films – palm trees, sunshine, the ocean, highways and freeways, gas stations, mini-malls, motels, parking lots, and the automobile – are ubiquitous and banal. Multiple narrative strands bring together disparate quirky characters from various parts of Los Angeles and adjacent cities, and extended driving sequences in which little happens but mundane conversation or presentation of the passing landscape underline the endlessness in every direction of Los Angeles' low-rise, low-density, and commercialized built environment.

However, these films do not generally seek to critique this environment, nor do they show much consciousness of the racially and socioeconomically exclusive character of the West LA and San Fernando Valley settings that dominate their mise en scène. Rather they proceed on the basis of an ironic knowing of the city's history and dysfunction, and within these terms they arguably serve to acclimatize audiences to the present-day landscapes, lifestyles, and rhythms of Los Angeles by acknowledging its commodification of everyday life, its tendency to sudden and random violence, and its apparently limitless size. Notably, the aerial shot of the city at night, appearing as a flickering matrix of lights as far as the eye can see, has become one of the most regular visual metaphors, while the most striking narrative device has been the use of chance as a determining factor. An earthquake occurs at a strategic moment in *Short Cuts*, relieving the building tension that permeates the relationships of the underpaid waitress, uptight cop, drunk hippies, world-weary nightclub singer, and children's party clown whose several trajectories the film loosely describes, while in *Magnolia* a similar function is performed by a heavy shower of frogs falling from the sky. What ultimately unites these films, then, and marks them as a tremendously important stage in the history of Los Angeles' cinematic image, is an effort to demonstrate that the myriad individuals who make up the region's current population of over twelve million people can achieve meaningful interpersonal connections despite the postmodern tendency of all human interaction to seem like a series of unrelated transactions, and despite the apparent separation of each individual from the next in the city's endless physical terrain.

NOTES

1. Chaplin *does* take his family from their bungalow for a scenic drive in *A Day's Pleasure* (1919), but this is the exception to the rule.
2. Mike Davis, *City of Quartz: Excavating the Future in Los Angeles* (New York: Verso, 1990), p. 65.

13

BILL MOHR

Scenes and movements in Southern California poetry

Critical accounts of American poetry all too frequently privilege San Francisco, Berkeley, and Oakland, overlapping sites that evoke West Coast poetry's most memorable events and movements: the Berkeley Renaissance, the San Francisco Beat scene, and most recently, Language writing. Yet the outsider impetus behind William Everson's observation that the West Coast canon prizes creativity, and the East Coast canon judgment, applies equally to Los Angeles, although the fractal energy of the city's poetry scenes is less easily mapped out. While surveys of fiction probably work best by focusing on individual authors, the development of American poetry for much of the past half century is intimately linked to communities of writers and publishers. The viability of the network of workshops, public readings, magazines, and presses in 1970s and 1980s Los Angeles, for instance, depended on the availability of production facilities such as NewComp Graphics at Beyond Baroque, in the beachfront city of Venice, to help poets demarcate their communities in a self-reflective, organic manner.

Fervently embracing the antinomian tendency in American poetry first enunciated by Roy Harvey Pearce, these intersecting communities and coteries produced poetry far exceeding in quantity and quality the writing produced about Los Angeles in the form of occasional poems by temporary residents or those living at a bemused distance. This survey will therefore focus on the scenes and communities that have flourished and intermingled in Los Angeles since World War II. This emphasis is not meant to dismiss the notable, if very brief, presence of poets such as W. B. Yeats, Hart Crane, or James Dickey, or to erase the youthful years of Robinson Jeffers from the history of the region, but almost all the writing that will inform the poetic patrimony of Los Angeles has emerged in this more recent period.

Underground magazines and the jazz scene of Venice West, 1948–1968

Throughout the entire period under consideration, poets in Los Angeles, Long Beach, and adjacent cities usually launched their magazines independent of institutional support or the pliant resources of financial as well as cultural capital. By the mid-1950s, Los Angeles was home to an impressive range of literary magazines, not the least of which was James Boyer May's *Trace*. Started in 1951 as a directory of little magazines, *Trace* lasted almost six dozen issues. Its roster of contributors included poets such as William Pillin, Bert Meyers, and Alvaro Cardona-Hine, who appeared in *California Quarterly*, founded by blacklisted poet Tom McGrath in 1951, or *Coastlines*, which was launched by his protégés Gene Frumkin and Mel Weisburd in the mid-1950s and lasted until 1964. *California Quarterly* dedicated its pages not only to subversive LA poets such as Don Gordon and Edwin Rolfe, but also to circumventing the official censorship of the McCarthy period. Witch hunts had successfully prevented distribution of the classic working-class film *Salt of the Earth*, but *California Quarterly* retaliated by devoting an entire issue in the summer of 1953 to Michael Wilson's screenplay.

In 1958 the editors of *Coastlines* hosted a reading by Allen Ginsberg at a house in Los Angeles that served as their headquarters, where Ginsberg obliged a heckler by taking off all his clothes to demonstrate what he meant by "nakedness," or risking sincerity in poetry and life. One of the young poets in attendance, Stuart Perkoff, had already established a community of Beat poets in the beachfront community of Venice, which his erstwhile mentor, Lawrence Lipton, described as the "slum by the sea."[1] Operating out of residential enclaves and coffeehouses, Venice West became prominent enough to be cited in Donald Allen's introduction to *The New American Poetry*. Perkoff and Bruce Boyd, who were part of its core group, had poems in that anthology, alongside Ginsberg, Frank O'Hara, John Ashbery, Denise Levertov, Charles Olson, and Robert Duncan. Although Perkoff's *Voices of the Lady: Collected Poems* would eventually be published by The National Poetry Foundation in 1998, most of the LA Beats – poets like John Thomas, William Margolis, and Charlie Foster – remain inexcusably absent from virtually all surveys of Beat literature. The pairing of poetry readings with jazz music, however, served as a precursor to spoken word poetry in Los Angeles and its kinship with punk and rap music.

By the early 1960s, the aspirations of Venice West, based on an idealistic program of voluntary poverty, had succumbed to the ravaging allure of drugs. Other communities in Los Angeles whose poverty was involuntary, however, finally rebelled. In the aftermath of the 1965 Watts uprising, East Coast institutions attempted to wield their largesse in hopes of stifling militant trends in African-American communities and forestalling any foothold by the Black Panther Party and other radical organizations. The Ford and Rockefeller foundations bolstered the contributions of Hollywood figures like Gregory Peck and Budd Schulberg in the development of the Watts Writers Workshop and the Inner City Cultural Center, which published poetry in its house organ magazine, *Neworld*. Though the Watts Writers Workshop produced work in many genres, including playwriting, the poetic legacy of this workshop remains its most significant accomplishment; several alumni are still writing today, including Eric Priestley, K. Curtis Lyle, Ka'mau Da'oud, Otis O'Solomon, and Quincy Troupe.

Beyond Baroque and the Venice Renaissance, 1968–1985

Venice did not remain dormant for long. In 1968, former high school English teacher George Drury Smith bought an abandoned building on West Washington Boulevard and began publishing a new literary magazine, *Beyond Baroque*. When subscription money failed to materialize, Smith started a print shop and opened the storefront area to the Venice community. Within a few months, detective fiction writer Joseph Hansen and a poet friend, John Harris, launched a free Wednesday night poetry workshop; it remains the longest continuously running free poetry workshop offered by any significant alternative literary arts organization in the United States. Beyond Baroque also continued to produce a magazine under a variety of names, including *NeWLetterS*, *New*, and *Obras*. It underwent several production variants, including a newsprint format that was distributed for free. One editor, James Krusoe, began a Friday night reading series in 1972; within two years, crowds overflowed onto the sidewalk, and an outdoor sound system was erected to broadcast the performances.

By the time Dennis Cooper, the editor and publisher of *Little Caesar* magazine and its offshoot small press, took over the reading series in late 1979, Beyond Baroque was no longer a pass-the-hat affair. Inspired by punk music's rebellious self-resourcefulness, Cooper combined his interest in the New York School poets and Language writing with a firm allegiance to promising local poets like David Trinidad and Amy Gerstler, who went on to win a National Book Critics Circle Award. Simultaneously with Cooper's inauguration, Beyond Baroque moved its small press library and the type-setting equipment of NewComp Graphics from its confined quarters to the two-story complex of the Old Venice City Hall. Cooper's term as artistic director marked the organization's emergence as a nationally recognized center for poetry. The small press library, founded by former *Coastlines* editor Alexandra Garrett, grew to over 10,000 books and recordings. The NewComp Graphics Center provided the technological muscle needed by aspiring young poets and publishers to put out books and magazines.

When Cooper departed for New York City, Beyond Baroque barely survived. A much-needed National Endowment for the Arts grant failed to materialize, and the institution almost closed down. A concert by the punk band X, whose founding songwriters Exene Cervenka and John Doe met at Beyond Baroque's poetry workshop, raised over $10,000 and provided sufficient funds to keep the doors open. Enough generous individuals have contributed over the years to sustain Beyond Baroque under a series of artistic directors, including Manazar Gamboa, Jocelyn Fisher, Dennis Phillips, D. B. Finnegan, Tosh Berman, and, since the mid-1990s, Fred Dewey. For about a decade, the artistic programming began to favor fiction writing, but under Dewey's gritty leadership, the focus has returned to poetry. In December, 2008, as Beyond Baroque concluded the celebration of its fortieth anniversary, its lease at the Old City Hall in Venice was renewed for another twenty-five years, thus potentially cantilevering the Venice scene well past the lifetime of the founding members of the Wednesday night workshop.

Page and stage: Stand Up and spoken word

Almost simultaneously with the development of Beyond Baroque, "Los Angeles ... quietly emerged as an important center of West Coast poetry, where a form of populist performance poetry variously called 'Standup Poetry,' 'Easy Poetry,' or 'Long Beach Poetry' has combined stand-up comedy and post-Beat poetry exemplified by Charles Bukowski."[2] California State University, Long Beach poet and professor Gerald Locklin joined forces with Ron Koertge, who taught at Pasadena City College, to form the core of this movement, which is often misapprehended even by those who admire it. Other core members include Laurel Ann Bogen, Elliot Fried, Ray Zepeda, Austin Straus, Jack Grapes, Eloise Klein Healy, Suzanne Lummis, and Edward Field, whose Lamont Poetry Prize-winning first book, *Stand Up, Friend, with Me* (1963), provided the group with its name. In an introductory essay to the third edition of his anthology *Stand Up Poetry* (2002), Charles Harper Webb warns that while "Stand Up poetry is sometimes lumped with 'street' poetry of an antiliterary bent" or "confused with performance art," both conflations are "a mistake. A good Stand Up poem requires as much literary art as any other good poem... Stand Up poetry is written for the printed page, bearing in mind that poetry has always been an oral art, at its best when read aloud."[3] Webb lists ten aspects that are almost always present in a Stand Up poem, with humor, performability, and clarity being the prime qualities, even in a poem about grim subject matter such as Suzanne Lummis's "Letter to My Assailant." More often, though, Stand Up poems make use of popular culture and subject matter as unpoetic as linoleum or a box of crayons, as in Ron Koertge's "Coloring," whose speaker asks, "Who ever heard of the Nobel / Coloring Prize. Who says, 'This is my son. / He has a Ph.D. in Coloring'?"[4]

The success and continued popularity of the Stand Up poets makes them the most easily accessible LA poets both in a literary sense and in terms of easily obtaining their books. The first two editions of Webb's *Stand Up Poetry* anthology (1990, 1994) are long out of print, but the third edition (2002) provides not only a representative sampling of the work produced by the best-known Stand Up poets in Los Angeles, but a means of comparing and contrasting their work with such other American poets as James Tate, Tom Lux, and Denise Duhamel, whose work occasionally overlaps with Stand Up.

One offshoot of the Stand Up school is the spoken word contingent, which evolved in Los Angeles largely through the efforts of a former pop music producer, Harvey Robert Kubernik. His first ventures were anthologies on vinyl, but by the early 1990s his roster of solo cassette and compact disc recordings on the New Alliance label included poets Holly Prado, Harry Northup, Michael C. Ford, Linda Albertano, Steve Abee, and Michael Lally. Aligned with the spoken word movement, which was often featured on Liza Richardson's "Man in the Moon" radio show on KCRW, were Cervenka, Doe, and Dave Alvin, who were primarily known as punk musicians, and Henry Rollins, the former Black Flag lead vocalist who supplemented his own voluminous self-publication on 2.13.61 Publications with books by neo-Beat poets such as Ellyn Maybe. Many of these poets were as likely to read at McCabe's Guitar Shop in Santa Monica or BeBop Records in the San Fernando Valley as at a bookstore or library.

The most prominent member of these populist poetic communities is Watts native Wanda Coleman, who has described herself as "disadvantaged first by skin, second by class, third by sex, fourth by craft ... fifth by regionality."[5] Nevertheless, Coleman began to publish her poetry in Los Angeles' little magazines and has published a dozen full-length books of poetry and prose to date with Black Sparrow Press and frequently recorded material with Kubernik. Emboldened by Coleman's ability to intermingle performance poetics and a caustic acoustics of street-level prosody, other poets such as Bogen and Kate Braverman also began to meld page and stage. Both Coleman and Bogen appear in all three *Stand Up* poetry anthologies edited by Webb, who moved to Los Angeles after a successful career as a rock musician in the Pacific Northwest.

The bookstore scenes and the maverick avant-garde

Essential to the survival of all these scenes and communities is the fact that, by the late 1970s, Los Angeles had a set of independent bookstores willing to stock and restock poetry books and magazines, including a favorite Stand Up hangout, *Pearl*, edited by Long Beach poets Joan Jobe Smith, Barbara Hauk, and Marilyn Johnson, and Doren Robbins and Uri Hertz's *Third Rail*. One store was central to this development; Papa Bach in West Los Angeles, originally known for its willingness to stock Marxist literature and the availability of draft counseling in its back loft, launched its own literary magazine with a diminutive nickname of a title, *Bachy*, that ran from 1972 until 1981. Lee Hickman became its poetry editor in 1977 and then established *Temblor*, which achieved national stature before he left after ten issues due to the onset of AIDS. Hickman's primary focus in *Temblor* was on poets whom he characterized as the maverick avant-garde, and he shared this interest with Paul Vangelisti, a poet and editor who had moved to Los Angeles in the late 1960s from his city of birth, San Francisco. Viewing himself as an artist in exile, Vangelisti edited *Invisible City* throughout the 1970s and has published several dozen volumes of vitally experimental poetry through his imprint, Red Hill Press, in addition to being a major translator of Italian poetry and editing a series of literary magazines, including *New Review of Literature* and *Or*. Although the first half-dozen issues of *Invisible City* featured such poets as Bukowski, the contributors who most epitomized the freewheeling approach of Vangelisti and his co-editor, John McBride, were Amiri Baraka and Jack Hirschman, the latter of whom translated Antonin Artaud, René Depestre, and Vladimir Mayakovsky. Hirschman moved to San Francisco in the mid-1970s, but returns frequently to Los Angles to give readings.

By the mid-1980s, the majority of the important independent bookstores had closed or was barely surviving. One publisher who managed to soldier on despite the dwindling outlets was Douglas Messerli, a poet-editor who arrived in Los Angeles in the mid-1980s and turned his Sun & Moon imprint into one of the most eclectic publishers of avant-garde poetry in the United States. His largest anthology, *From the Other Side of the Century* (1994), barely recorded the presence of the poets of his adopted home, but Messerli's anthology of *Innovative Poetry* blends together disparate LA experimentalists such as neo-surrealist Will Alexander, Dennis Phillips, and Language poets, such as Diane Ward, who also had settled in Los Angeles. Messerli has proved to be particularly supportive of poets who experiment with long, serial poems.

If Messerli operated free of any potential constraints from sponsoring institutions, other editors in Los Angeles with equivalent avant-garde credentials were less fortunate. With his scintillating translations of Cesar Vallejo and a vigorous network of experimental poets created around his first poetry magazine, *Caterpillar*, Clayton Eshleman had established himself as a cultural provocateur with a knack for finding poets who could challenge the orthodoxy of American poetry before intermittently living in Los Angeles. Eshleman's second magazine, *Sulfur*, was started through the largesse of Caltech, where Eshleman taught, but quickly ran into censorship problems, and once again his visionary determination was the main source of its continued publication. Eshleman had little use for poets who made up what he regarded as a local scene, but his magazine had a Pasadena address, and however much Eshleman might have disdained the region, he nonetheless managed to write a considerable number of poems while in residence, and to establish in that grove of rocket scientists the idea that the art of poetry is the most daunting challenge to be posed to the human imagination.

Feminist poetry, multicultural poetry, and the academy

Many women poets aligned themselves with the visual arts and performance community at the Woman's Building, which flourished as a feminist institution in Los Angeles for close to two decades. Housed in a former arts school until it moved to an industrial section of downtown Los Angeles, the Woman's Building eventually included a print center that trained women to typeset and to operate a letterpress machine. Its magazine, *Chrysalis*, was not a literary magazine as such, but a venue for feminist cultural commentary including creative writing by poets like Eloise Klein Healy and Deena Metzger. The single most important literary event at the Woman's Building was the conference of women writers in 1975 recorded in Holly Prado's *Feasts* (1976), an experimental book of prose poetry far more audacious and memorable than contemporaneous texts such as Lyn Hejinian's *My Life* (1987). While Healy, Metzger, and Prado have remained aligned with the West Coast small press movement, other poets associated with the Woman's Building reading series or its in-house Women's Graphic Center explored the alluring archipelago of "cultural exile" that Paul Vangelisti has attributed to an "extreme presence and absence" summed up by Igor Stravinsky's apposition, "splendid isolation."[6]

"Desire in L.A.," by Martha Ronk, who has taught Renaissance literature at Occidental College for many years, is a prime example of this provisional identity:

> Waves turn to go out to sea,
> a whole city expanding like the universe,
> each drive up canyons, each centrifugal wind reaching
> beyond what used to be the limits of a city
> and none of us can stop

pushing beyond our time, our money, the need
for some outskirts of a city already wholly outskirts,
reaching for, like erotic desire, the nether parts.
Mannered fingers and necks elongate beyond themselves,
skin hurts drying in the wind,
and waiting to find transparent expansion
into the upper reaches of not even belief,
but craving our own unbelief
and that image of another's skirt
lifted by the warm, slightly soiled air of an open grate.[7]

For other poets, the exile is more literal. Bertolt Brecht was able to return to Germany after spending over half a decade in Santa Monica, but Aleida Rodríguez, who was born in Cuba, entitled her first collection of poems *Garden of Exile* (1999) as a declaration of ineluctable fate. In "My Mother's Art," she examines the aftermath of banishment, and focuses on how exile impacts generational social transformation.

In my dream, my mother sat on the floor,
painting several small pictures of Los Angeles.
I recognized City Hall, poking up like a giant Rapidograph pen
behind some low yellow buildings
on which the sun burned fiercely.
And the Ambassador Hotel,
its long awnings and withered glamour,
a bluish evening seeping up its faded façade.
The paintings lay around her on the floor
and she was clearly enjoying herself.
...
How had I never known this?
That my mother was a great artist?
And that she did it so naturally,
so casually, just sitting there on the floor,
her work, the obvious product of her delight,
all around her?[8]

Almost all of the poets I have mentioned subsequent to the sketch of Venice West and the Watts Writers Workshop appear in one or the other of two anthologies I edited, *The Streets Inside* (1978) and *"Poetry Loves Poetry"* (1985), which features more than five dozen poets. Michelle T. Clinton, an African-American poet who, like Coleman, had attended the weekly workshops at Beyond Baroque, and Suzanne Lummis, who had moved to Los Angeles in the late 1970s from California State University, Fresno's MA program, segued during the next decade from my second anthology to working as anthologists. Clinton's anthology, *Invocation L.A.: Urban Multicultural Poetry* (1989), co-edited with Sesshu Foster and Naomi Quiñonez, focuses on the rapidly expanding community of Third-World poets in Los Angeles, including Manazar Gamboa, Gloria Alvarez, Rubén Martinez, Russell Leong, Victor Valle, Amy Uyematsu, and Lynn Manning, but also includes Anglo poets Karen Holden and Fred Voss. Drawn from a series of city-wide poetry festivals, Lummis and Webb's anthology, *Grand Passion: The Poetry of Los Angeles and Beyond* (1995), incorporates a broad array of ethnically identified poets. In recent years poets such as Marisela Norte, Ramon Garcia, Max Benavidez, and the late Gil Cuadros have collaborated with a multitude of other communities.

The universities and colleges ensconced in their various purlieus of Southern California enable academically inclined poets to make their livings as professors while coming to terms with the singular environment provided by the cultural climate of Los Angeles. If the professor-poets were initially bemused by what struck many of them as a provincial fervor, they also eventually discovered the providential aspect of the region's contradictions. The apparent anti-intellectualism of the performance poets concealed a profound respect for any poet who was willing to concede the advantages of tradition and experimentation sharing the same bookshelf. In the early 1970s, only a handful of academic poets, such as Ann Stanford, Jascha Kessler, Charles Gullans, and Henri Coulette, seemed to be at work in the city. By the final decade of the twentieth century and into the first decade of the twenty-first, one could assemble a tantalizing anthology comprised only of university-affiliated poets: Gail Wronsky, Tim Steele, Ralph Angel, David St. John, Steven Yenser, Sarah Maclay, Cecilia Woloch, Harryette Mullen, B. H. Fairchild, Christopher Buckley, Dorothy Barresi, the late Dick Barnes, Robert Mezey, Molly Bendall, Patty Seyburn, Carol Muske-Dukes, Robert Peters, James McMichael. While readers in other cities may not have an initial impulse to identify these poets with Los Angeles, almost all of them write poems in which specific streets of Los Angeles imbue the images and themes. It is quite simply impossible to imagine David St. John writing a poem such as *The Face: A Novella in Verse* (2004) except as a direct consequence of years of working in Los Angeles. Indeed, perhaps one of the most surprising aspects of poetry in Los Angeles is not simply its resiliency, but that the poets have an interest in long poems, whether it be Hickman's unfinished, but masterful "Tiresias" or Steven Yenser's *Blue Guide* (2006) or Mark Salerno's *Odalisque* (2007). James McMichael's book-length meditation on the city of Pasadena, *Four Good Things* (1980), served as an early model for many of these projects.

In looking back on the diverse communities of poets who have inhabited the canyons, side streets, boulevards, and beaches of Los Angeles, one can wonder how so much diversity could adapt to a literary congestion akin to its notorious freeway. In my introduction to "*Poetry Loves Poetry*," I suggested that one of the elements that attracted poets to Los Angeles, and continues to sustain them, was the same thing that brought the film industry here: the quality of light, which possesses more variety in intensity and tones than any other place in the United States. Almost all of the poets who continue to work in this city find strength not just in the light, but in the open acceptance of each community's visibility to the others, and in the fruition that awaits their patient labor.

NOTES

1. Lawrence Lipton, *The Holy Barbarians* (New York: Julian Messner, 1959), p. 15.
2. Christopher Beach, *Poetic Culture: Contemporary American Poetry between Community and Institution*, Avant-Garde and Modernism Studies (Evanston, Ill.: Northwestern University Press, 1999), p. 36.
3. Charles Webb, *Stand Up Poetry: An Expanded Anthology* (Iowa City: University of Iowa, 2002), p. xvii.
4. Suzanne Lummis, "Letter to My Assailant," *ibid.*, pp. 210–11; Ron Koertge, "Coloring," *ibid.*, p. 185.
5. Wanda Coleman, "Clocking Dollars," *African Sleeping Sickness: Stories and Poems* (Santa Rosa, Calif.: Black Sparrow, 1990), p. 218.
6. Paul Vangelisti, "Introduction: Being Elsewhere," *L.A. Exile: A Guide to Los Angeles Writing, 1932–1998*, ed. Vangelisti with Evan Calbi (New York: Marsilio Publishers, 1999), pp. 13, 17; Stravinsky, cited *ibid.*, p. 7.
7. Martha Ronk, "Desire in L.A.," *Desire in L.A.* (Athens: University of Georgia Press, 1990), p. 69.
8. Aleida Rodríguez, "My Mother's Art," *Garden of Exile* (Louisville, Ky.: Sarabande Books, 1999), p. 23.

14

J. SCOTT BRYSON

Surf, sagebrush, and cement rivers: Reimagining nature in Los Angeles

> Here in California what you've got is an instant megalopolis superimposed on a
> background which could almost be described as raw nature. What we've got here is the
> twentieth century right up against the primitive.
> Ross Macdonald, "Ross Macdonald in Raw California" (1972)

The terms *urban* and *nature* have been set up in our cultural imagination as opposites that necessarily deny each other. The average person has probably never heard them joined in the phrase *urban nature*, even though examples of it – New York's Central Park, Chicago's Lakefront, a Houston bayou – spring to mind easily enough. People may be especially unlikely to think of concrete-laden and smog-burdened Los Angeles in relation to a dynamic and thriving natural world. This, despite the region's well-known beaches, mountains, arroyos, gardens, and even natural disasters. Angelenos would quickly add to this list wild parrots haunting Pasadena, deer meandering through the lawns of Brentwood mansions, wild coyotes preying on pets in various gated communities, and even farm animals grazing, braying, and neighing in backyards all across different regions of the city. As I write this chapter, it's been raining for the last few days, and I just returned from hiking with my young sons in Eaton Canyon, where they learned about the sting of a yucca plant, found their feet stuck in a boglike mud pile, and crossed a rushing stream by "climbing" a downed sycamore that had fallen across the water. Clearly, it's not stretching credulity to speak of a flourishing urban nature in Los Angeles where, as Gary Snyder has written, the "Los Angeles basin and hill slopes" are "checkered with streetways."[1]

As surprising as it may be to many readers, the natural world pervades the city's literature as well, with authors posing infinitely more important and interesting questions than Is there nature in Los Angeles? They ask, instead, How do people in Los Angeles interact with and depend on the natural world? To what degree are we a part of that world? What results from ignoring or honoring this symbiosis? And how, from this point forward, do we protect the beauty and vitality of the world around us? By examining these questions and others like them, we can begin to appreciate the intricate role nature plays in LA literature, and in the city itself.

One of the most traditional ways that LA authors have used nature is to create a mood or to convey the feel of a scene. Think, for example, of the relentless rain in *The Big Sleep* (1939). As opposed to the sunshine that actually dominates most days in Southern California, the novel's ubiquitous rain helps Chandler establish a mood that we now call *noir*. He does something similar in *The Long Goodbye* (1953), where he writes, "The weather was hot and sticky and the acid sting of the smog had crept as far west as Beverly Hills."[2] Here again, meteorological facts serve to render a bleak and even ominous ambience. As Philip Marlowe moves through the depravity of LA venues high and low, the climate, along with the dark days and nights it so often produces, serves as an emblem of a social world bereft of goodness and light.

A more evocative use of nature that Chandler introduced has become one of the most dominant and long-lasting concepts in all of LA writing. In his short story "Red Wind" (1938), he depicts nature – and in particular the gale-force winds known as Santa Anas – as a bio-mystical force that compels humans toward mania and violence. Perhaps the most quoted lines from Los Angeles literature come from Chandler's take on the fierce autumn winds: "It was one of those hot dry Santa Anas that come down through the mountain passes and curl your hair and make your nerves jump and your skin itch. On nights like that every booze party ends in a fight. Meek little wives feel the edge of the carving knife and study their husbands' necks. Anything can happen."[3] Joan Didion takes this theme even further, explaining that when the Santa Anas appear, they initiate "the season of suicide and divorce and prickly dread, wherever the wind blows." In the opening paragraphs of "Los Angeles Notebook," she writes of "something uneasy in the Los Angeles air this afternoon, some unnatural stillness, some tension":

> What it means is that tonight a Santa Ana will begin to blow, a hot wind from the northeast ... I have neither heard nor read that a Santa Ana is due, but I know it, and almost everyone I have seen today knows it too. We know it because we feel it. The baby frets. The maid sulks. I rekindle a waning argument with the telephone company, then cut my losses and lie down, given over to whatever it is in the air. To live with the Santa Ana is to accept, consciously or unconsciously, a deeply mechanistic view of human behavior.[4]

With their emphasis on the mysterious power of the Santa Anas, Chandler and Didion create one of the most representative and abiding themes in all of LA literature, underscoring the intensely intimate connection between the human and nonhuman worlds.

Another perspective on nature, one that has pervaded LA literature for decades across multiple genres, works from a decidedly environmentalist perspective. Countless writers have been taken by the beauty of the region – Vladimir Nabokov is said to have claimed that he could live in Los Angeles simply for the jacarandas – but even more often the texts portray the nonhuman world as a victim of the city that has sprawled and spawned destruction across Southern California.

Ross Macdonald, one of the most ecologically aware writers in the Los Angeles literary canon, highlights throughout his fiction the notion that human shortsightedness comes with harsh environmental consequences. In *The Underground Man* (1971), a discarded cigarette ignites a wildfire that, after wreaking havoc itself, helps produce mudslides following heavy rains. As David Fine explains, the fire in Macdonald's novel "functions as metonymy for, and ecological counterpart to, human transgression... It signals man's violation both of the landscape and of his fellow man... The drive for power over others is reflected in the drive to transform the landscape, to commodify and exploit it for what it will bear." Two decades later, T. C. Boyle would borrow these natural disasters, along with Macdonald's theme of what Fine calls the "nexus of nature and man, the place where the natural world confronts human desire and the ability to transform it." In *The Tortilla Curtain* (1995), Boyle initiates his novel's climax by sending fire and floods raging through the elite subdivision where the characters live. In Boyle, as in Macdonald, "Nature and human nature bear a correspondence; the harm done to the fragile ecology ... is the consequence of, and counterpart to, violations inflicted on other people."[5]

Another archetypal symbol chosen by LA writers to highlight the degradation of the natural world is the Los Angeles River, often used as a metaphor for city leaders' historic myopia and mismanagement. Visitors to the city can hardly be blamed if they aren't aware of the LA River. Its very existence has become the butt of many a local joke: Mark Twain once said that he had fallen into a California river and "come out all dusty."[6] The huge concrete aqueducts running through the city might look familiar from Hollywood car races and chase scenes, but they don't exactly scream Huck Finn.

In a decision that in hindsight appears a colossal blunder, the river was "channelized" in the 1930s and 1940s to control flooding. Mike Davis, the current godfather of social criticism about Los Angeles, has recounted this story with his characteristic wrath and venom in the chapter "How Eden Lost Its Garden," in *Ecology of Fear* (1998). Davis decries the selfish, profit-driven "presentism" that drove city leaders to sacrifice the Los Angeles River, "the defining landscape of the nineteenth century ... for the sake of emergency work relief, the preservation of industrial land values, and temporary abatement of the flood problem."[7] Instead of the greenbelts and parks envisioned by early urban planners Frederick Law Olmsted, Jr., and Harlan

Bartholomew, the river is now restrained by a series of giant concrete troughs that lead it through the city. Even the name has been industrialized, so that instead of "the Los Angeles River," the graffiti-shrouded cement gutters have now been dubbed "the Los Angeles River Flood Control Channel."

LA authors have made frequent symbolic use of the river, sensing in it a modern-day Greek myth about a whimsical and powerful water-god shackled by humanity and its technology. Blake Gumprecht laments that what was once a "beautiful stream, wandering peacefully amid willows and wild grapes" has since been rendered "an ugly, concrete gutter."[8] Jenny Price, who nevertheless acknowledges that the river is her favorite part of the city, agrees that it "looks like an outsize concrete sewer" or "a *Blade Runner* set that a crew disassembled and then put back together wrong."[9] And Luis Rodriguez eulogizes the river in his book of poems *Concrete River*, describing "Spray-painted outpourings / On walls" that "offer a chaos / Of color for the eyes."[10] Rodriguez implicitly connects the blight of the river to the plight of young Latinos who feel that drugs and gangs are their only viable futures.

For writers in Los Angeles, the destruction of the LA River emblematizes the broader desecration of the natural world in and around the city. Not surprising is the fact that urban sprawl, especially in the form of suburbanization, is one of the most frequent targets. Olmsted, writing in 1930, offered a clear warning regarding the dearth of public space in Los Angeles: "Continued prosperity will depend on providing needed parks... In so far ... as the people fail to show the understanding, courage, and organizing ability necessary at this crisis, the growth of the Region will tend to strangle itself."[11] Authors following Olmsted have indeed pointed to the "strangulation" of the region and condemned public leaders for their myopia. In *A Single Man* (1964), Christopher Isherwood's protagonist wants to enjoy the rural world surrounding the city, but finds it impossible because "he is oppressed by awareness of the city," which has "spawned and spread itself over the entire plain," eating up "the wide pastures and ranchlands and the last stretches of orange grove."[12] Davis goes so far as to name this type of sprawl and suburbanization "another one of Southern California's natural disasters."[13]

In his memoir *Holy Land* (1996), D. J. Waldie offers a much more complex take on suburban living, yet he also offers harsh criticism of a way of life whose greatest sin is "a defection from predictability." He goes on to say that "In the suburbs, a manageable life depends on a compact among neighbors. The unspoken agreement is an honest hypocrisy."[14] Price goes further with her criticism, investing her words with a Davis-like acidity as she seethes against the "personal liberty" argument used to justify irresponsible over-production and overconsumption. She stresses that grand ideals like "individual freedom" can serve a range of agendas. And the conviction that it should mean you can do whatever the hell you want cannot possibly have found more extreme expression than in the traditional refrain here that L.A. is, in reality, exactly whatever you want it to be... And this pushes the ideal of individual liberty well beyond the outer edge. It's the American dream on a shooting rampage.[15]

For Price, and for many other LA writers, a primary victim of this rampage is the very world we live in.

Some writers move well beyond the claim that nature is merely damaged by urban growth and overconsumption. They follow the point to what they see as its "natural" conclusion: apocalypse and dystopia. In his essay "The Literary Destruction of Los Angeles," Davis has documented and catalogued the myriad examples of the city's destruction in fiction, stating that "the biological unsustainability of the giant city is now firmly lodged in contemporary doom consciousness." And "Los Angeles, of course, is perfectly cast in the role of environmental suicide."[16] As a result, then, a novel like Octavia Butler's *Parable of the Sower* (1993), where apocalypse results from global warming, pollution, and racial discord, feels less like a sci-fi fantasy, and more like a potential prophecy. The same goes for Carolyn See's *Golden Days* (1987) and Cynthia Kadohata's *In the Heart of the Valley of Love* (1997), each of which presents a post-apocalyptic vision that is both prototypical LA literature and a cautionary tale of what might be wrought by fundamental injuries to the planet.

But as writer after writer proclaims, the nonhuman world is willing to play the role of victim only to a certain extent. LA authors repeatedly remind us that nature is chaotic and wild; even within the "civilized" city there exists a nonhuman world that refuses to be tamed. Far from being just a mood-setter or a metaphor of some sort of social criticism the author wants to offer, these writers depict nature in all its force and power. The classic example can be found in John McPhee's *The Control of Nature* (1990), which details various attempts to achieve mastery over the natural world. The book concludes with an essay, "Los Angeles Against the Mountains," about debris flows that periodically stream down the San Gabriel Mountains, taking with them boulders, trees, and eventually even cars and small buildings. City and county leaders have dealt with this threat to the people living in the canyons at the base of the mountains by creating what McPhee describes as an "elegant absurdity": a series of dams and catch-basins that collect the debris so that it can then be trucked back into the hills. His essay highlights the power of the nonhuman world as well as the intensely intimate relationship humans share with it. What comes through in McPhee's elegant and nonjudgmental rendering of the situation is that to a significant degree the local strategies make sense. But at no point in the essay does the reader get the sense that humans will eventually be successful in their attempt to achieve "the control of nature." It is wild and chaotic, even as it butts up against the city. We are left with a clear awareness of humanity's ignorance and hubris as it attempts to control what will not be tamed. As David L. Ulin has written, "California ... has always been an elemental landscape, where we don't so much master nature as coexist uneasily with it, waiting for the next fire, flood or earthquake to destabilize our lives."[17]

This theme of nature's elemental wildness and mystery, its inability to be fully domesticated even as it interacts with human civilization, appears again and again in Los Angeles writing. As Lionel Rolfe has said, Los Angeles is "a harsh but beautiful place, over which a thin veneer of civilization has been laid."[18] Nathanael West, of course, accentuates how thin that veneer is in *Day of the Locust* (1939). Think, for instance, of the cockfight in Homer Simpson's garage, or the physically and sexually violent campfire scene. Chandler features this concept as well, for example, in the Sternwoods' oil fields in *The Big Sleep*. Only "five or six barrels a day" are still being pumped, we are told, but the image of the "old wooden derricks" and the smell of the "stale sump water" serve as reminders of the primeval power bubbling beneath the city's surface. William L. Fox explores this natural phenomenon in "Tracking Tar," as he walks his readers through a fascinating explanation of the oil basin beneath Los Angeles, and how it has produced the La Brea Tar Pits, mere blocks from the Los Angeles County Museum of Art, where visitors can view prehistoric fossils of animals trapped in asphalt deposits. Fox asserts that the veneer of civilization has blinded Angelenos to the realities by which they are surrounded; energy companies have "camouflage[d] their activities" so that derricks have been "dismantled or covered up to resemble buildings," and landscaping has been designed to screen the pumps from view. "Only in a few instances," writes Fox, "are we reminded that what we're walking around on is not a two-dimensional sheet of paper ... but a planet with three dimensions in space and great depth in time."[19] No matter how much we may try to deny the world around us (or beneath us), it is always there, unable to be completely managed or controlled.

Key in all of these texts focusing on humanity's inability to control nature is the concept that regardless of human hubris, the natural world ultimately pays us no mind and will outlast us. David Quammen, in his essay "To Live and Die in L.A.," features this theme in relation to the stubborn presence of coyotes.[20] William McClung underscores the point in his discussion of a passage from *Farewell, My Lovely* (1940), in which Chandler describes a lonely landscape. McClung quotes the beginning and end of the passage, the two parts of the quote separated by an ellipsis. He then demonstrates how oblivious the nonhuman world is to humans and their problems, pointing out that "within the ellipsis, a man is murdered and Marlowe is knocked unconscious." But even as these dramatic human events unfold, the natural world around them remains essentially unchanged: "The charms of the setting, delicately rendered, neither reinforce nor contradict the evil that occurs; what irony attaches to it arrives with human expectations and sensitivities and departs, leaving the canyon as it was."[21]

John Fante makes a similar move in the elegiac conclusion to *Ask the Dust* (1939), when Arturo Bandini looks across the unknown and unknowable Mojave Desert, seeing "nothing but wasteland for almost a hundred miles." Bandini considers the "supreme indifference" that lay "across the desolation," then concludes that "the casualness of night and another day, and yet the secret intimacy of those hills, their silent consoling wonder, made death a thing of no great importance. You could die, but the desert would hide the secret of your death, it would remain after you, to cover your memory with ageless wind and heat and cold."[22] Again, the greater-than-human world remains after us, and will cover our memory when we are gone.

One final approach to depicting nature in LA literature offers a completely different lens through which to view our relationship with the natural world. Whereas all of the above depictions work from a fairly conventional perspective on nature – defining it primarily as whatever is beyond the realm of the human world – one writer in particular is presently challenging our conceptions of what nature means, in LA or anywhere else. Jenny Price, whose "Thirteen Ways of Seeing Nature in L.A." is must reading for anyone wanting to think about nature in this city or any other, pares down the issue to its most essential question: What is nature? For Price, "What we need in L.A., as elsewhere, is a foundational literature that imagines nature not as the opposite of the city but as the basic stuff of modern everyday life." This means, for example, that if she is to narrate all the encounters with nature involved in one of her hikes, she must write about more than plants and animals. She must also consider "the oil, stone, metals, and animal skins in [her] twenty-first-century hiker gear," as well as how they connect her "to the global transformation of nature," and even "how wealthier Angelenos are more likely to live near L.A.'s mountain parks – and to own cars to get to them."[23] In other words, Price explains, it's too simplistic to define nature as anything that is nonhuman and apart from the world of civilization. Instead, it is where we live, what we eat, what we drive, and even who we are and how we treat each other.

Price's argument has significant implications for how we view nature and its place in Los Angeles literature. From this broadened perspective that asks us to view nature as practically everything we use and interact with, any writing about the city at all could be considered a form of nature writing.

When Chester Himes narrates Bob Jones's quest for racial and social justice in *If He Hollers Let Him Go* (1945); when Yxta Maya Murray examines Echo Park gangs in *Locas* (1997); when Bret Easton Ellis explores the mania, chaos, and destruction of rich, white adolescents in *Less Than Zero* (1985); when we write about any of these interactions, or explore relationships among the different entities within the city, we are writing about nature. "These are nature topics all," Price contends, "about how we live in and fight about nature, and about how we use it more and less fairly and sustainably, and about the enormous consequences for our lives in L.A., as well as for places and people and wildlife everywhere." She goes on to explain that "such topics beg for a literature – for a poetry, for an aesthetics – because to clearly ponder our lives in and out of cities, we have to be able to imagine and reimagine these connections to nature."[24]

That is what we do when we explore a text through the lens of how it depicts the natural world: we "imagine and reimagine our connections to nature." When we raise basic questions about how Chandler, or Didion, or Davis, or McPhee writes about the natural world, we open ourselves up to having some of our most basic assumptions challenged. We may or may not be prepared to redefine "nature," or to expand our perspective to the degree that Price calls for. But simply by examining Los Angeles' relationship with the world around it, and the way that relationship has been depicted in the "literary landscape" of the city, we offer ourselves the opportunity not only to understand Los Angeles texts in wholly new ways, but to achieve a fuller understanding of ourselves and our place in the world as well.

NOTES

1. Gary Snyder, "Night Song of the Los Angeles Basin" (1986), in *Writing Los Angeles: A Literary Anthology*, ed. David L. Ulin (New York: Library of America, 2002), p. 710.
2. Raymond Chandler, *The Long Goodbye*, in *Later Novels and Other Writings* (New York: Library of America, 1995), p. 615.
3. Raymond Chandler, "Red Wind," in *Stories and Early Novels* (New York: Library of America, 1995), p. 368.
4. Joan Didion, "Some Dreamers of the Golden Dream," in *Slouching Towards Bethlehem* (New York: Noonday Press, 1990), p. 3; Didion, "Los Angeles Notebook," *ibid.*, p. 217.
5. David Fine, *Imagining Los Angeles: A City in Fiction* (Albuquerque: University of New Mexico Press, 2000), pp. 132, 133, 132.
6. Quoted in Carey McWilliams, *Southern California Country: An Island on the Land*, American Folkways (New York: Duell, Sloan & Pearce, 1946), p. 6.
7. Mike Davis, *Ecology of Fear: Los Angeles and the Imagination of Disaster* (New York: Vintage, 1999), p. 71.

8. Blake Gumprecht, *The Los Angeles River: Its Life, Death, and Possible Rebirth* (Baltimore: Johns Hopkins University Press, 2001), p. 284.

9. Jenny Price, "Thirteen Ways of Seeing Nature in L.A., Part One," *Believer Magazine*, April 2006, www.believermag.com/issues/200604/?read=article_price.

10. Luis Rodriguez, *Concrete River* (Willimantic, Conn.: Curbstone Press, 1993), p. 38.

11. Olmsted Brothers and Bartholomew and Associates, *Parks, Playgrounds and Beaches for the Los Angeles Region* (Los Angeles: Los Angeles Chamber of Commerce, 1930), p. 23.

12. Christopher Isherwood, *A Single Man* (New York: Simon & Schuster, 1964), p. 111.

13. Davis, *Ecology of Fear*, p. 91.

14. D. J. Waldie, *Holy Land: A Suburban Memoir* (New York: Norton, 2005), p. 20.

15. Price, "Thirteen Ways of Seeing Nature in L.A., Part Two," *Believer Magazine*, April 2006, www.believermag.com/issues/200605/?read=article_price.

16. Davis, *Ecology of Fear*, p. 318.

17. John McPhee, "Los Angeles Against the Mountains," *The Control of Nature* (New York: Farrar, Straus & Giroux, 1990), p. 271; David L. Ulin, "Unshakeable Memories," *Los Angeles Times*, April 16, 2006, M1.

18. Lionel Rolfe, "Words Are Powerful Still," *Notes of a California Bohemian*, www.dabelly.com/columns/bohemian10.htm.

19. William L. Fox, "Tracking Tar," *Orion*, January/February 2007, www.orionmagazine.org/index.php/articles/article/93/.

20. David Quammen, "To Live and Die in L.A.," *Wild Thoughts from Wild Places* (New York: Scribner, 1999), pp. 90–9.

21. William A. McClung, *Landscapes of Desire: Anglo Mythologies of Los Angeles* (Berkeley: University of California Press, 2002), pp. 68, 68–9.

22. John Fante, *Ask the Dust* (New York: HarperCollins, 2006), p. 164.

23. Price, "Thirteen Ways of Seeing Nature in L.A., Part One."

24. *Ibid.*

15

ERIC AVILA

Essaying Los Angeles

After several decades of inquiry, scholars agree that Los Angeles defies the conventions of urban theory. To some, it models a new paradigm of decentralized development, although others find in the city's sprawl extremes of the excess and deprivation characteristic of capitalist cities. Still others depict Los Angeles as the immigrant entrepôt of the twenty-first century. While detractors still dismiss it as one big movie set, recycling the myth of Tinseltown, in *America* (1988), Jean Baudrillard extends the notion of Los Angeles as a land of simulation beyond Hollywood by noting the effects on the regional life and landscape of such signature Southern California industries as informatics, genetics, the fitness industry, and New Age therapies. Like all cities, Los Angeles excites a range of emotions, but as the twelfth-largest urban area in the world, brimming with almost eighteen million inhabitants, Los Angeles remains fixed in the urban imagination.

How do we know Los Angeles and where does that knowledge come from? This is a complicated question with too many easy answers. It has become a cliché, for example, to implicate Hollywood in spinning a marketable identity of Los Angeles through a century of film and television production. That "knowledge," prone to distortion, hyperbole, and much mythology, is suspect, but the images rendered on television and movie screens nonetheless continue to shape popular understandings of the city. Yet the idea that movies and stars inspire people from the world's pockets of desperate poverty to undertake treacherous journeys across oceans and borders to this city of immigrants is fatuous. Immigrant understandings of the city rely upon the concrete aspects of urban growth: labor markets, employment opportunities, housing availability, and preexisting networks of family and community. The Los Angeles that immigrants know is infrequently featured in films and television shows.

Many scholars have studied Los Angeles from their various disciplinary perspectives, but only a few authors, among them Carey McWilliams, Reyner Banham, Joan Didion, and Mike Davis, have reached a general audience. In both inspiring and unsettling ways, these thinkers brought Los Angeles into an ongoing debate about the future prospects of city life.

Anyone writing about Los Angeles since the mid-twentieth century owes an intellectual debt to Carey McWilliams. A prolific essayist, progressive journalist, longtime editor of *The Nation*, and civil rights attorney, McWilliams was unfettered by the conventions of disciplinary scholarship. Synthesizing sociological and historical insights into a distinctive vision of his adopted city, the Colorado native retained his fascination with California's rise over many decades. During the 1920s, McWilliams's relations with a coterie of Southern California intellectuals that included book-dealer and publisher Jake Zeitlin, Lloyd Wright, son of Frank Lloyd Wright, the author Louis Adamic, the architect Richard Neutra, and Paul Jordan Smith, literary editor of the *Los Angeles Times*, deepened his interest in the region's history. During the early 1930s he began writing a monthly column on Southern California, which became the basis for *Southern California Country: An Island on the Land* (1946), an overview of Los Angeles' development from the US conquest of Alta California in 1848 to the 1940s. Reflecting on *Southern California Country* toward the end of his career, McWilliams commented in a new introduction to the book, "I did not just happen to write this book: I lived it." The history is rich with detail, at times anecdotal, but always designed to explain how and why Los Angeles "began to make a real impact on world opinion."[1]

Nothing escaped McWilliams's purview. He begins with the physical setting, the region's unique topographic and climatologic features. At first this discussion seems abstract, but the rest of the book reads like a subtle case for ecological determinism: the distinctive features of the natural landscape delimit the region's social, political, and cultural boundaries. The climate, for example, attains a rich folklore of its own: Southern California's Mediterranean climate – its fabled warmth and sunshine – confers a powerful celebrity upon the region, which, like all forms of modern celebrity, proves highly marketable. In fact, much of McWilliams's analysis dwells upon the centrality of the climate to the growth of the region, particularly as the boosters capitalize on the climate to make fantastic claims for the region's tonic powers.

Like the climate, the Pacific Ocean also plays a conspicuous role in McWilliams's narrative. Aside from the quirky culture of beachside communities like Venice, McWilliams detected a certain finality in the air where the ocean brings a decisive end to the lingering hopes of the downtrodden, the internal migrants who vainly drifted to the continent's far southwestern corner seeking new beginnings. Even Southern California's unique topography plays some part in McWilliams's explanation of the regional sociology.

The slopes of the Santa Monica and San Gabriel Mountains shape the socio-economic geography of Southern California – the higher the ground the higher the income – and the Tehachapi Mountains, which mark a dramatic border between Southern and Central California, set the stage for the flowering of a unique regional culture, sealed off from the rest of the continent.

McWilliams's prescient analysis of Southern California's natural landscape is sharpest as he recounts how Los Angeles fulfilled its destiny by commandeering distant sources of fresh water. Like most accounts of this episode, McWilliams's dwells upon the means, not the end, emphasizing the shady dealings of a secret cabal. It's *Chinatown* before *Chinatown*: a lurid tale of conspiracy, greed, and urban growth in which a handful of wealthy and powerful men conspire with federal and municipal insiders to rob poor Owens Valley farmers of their livelihood to ensure Los Angeles' steady and limitless supply of runoff from the Sierra Nevada Mountains. Nevertheless, McWilliams recognized that Los Angeles could never have exceeded the size of Bakersfield and Modesto – two Central Valley cities whose population remained below 200,000 through much of the twentieth century – without water supplied by the Owens Valley Aqueduct.

The Owens Valley episode substantiated McWilliams's claims about the contrived nature of the region's "natural" landscape, but he was equally interested in the cultural landscape as a fantastic improvisation premised on the reinvention of the Spanish, Indian, and Mexican pasts. Though the cultures themselves had been conquered, marginalized, or exterminated, these pasts, especially the Mission–Spanish fantasy past – which incorporated the disparate elements of the Spanish and Mexican past into a regional fantasy of romance, exoticism, and nostalgia – were perpetuated by Anglo boosters and writers. In John Steven McGroarty's *Mission Play*, Helen Hunt Jackson's *Ramona*, Charles Fletcher Lummis's Southwest Museum, and Christine Sterling's faux-pueblo past on Olvera Street, the seductive combination of "exotic" ingredients created a usable past that suited the ambitions and aspirations of the Anglo-American settlers and developers. McWilliams recognized the profitability of this scheme, but he also saw its appeal to the Midwestern migrants flocking to the region.

McWilliams was the first to note the city's ethnic masquerade, but he also recognized the racial inequality that lurked behind the Spanish-colonial facades. Half a century before the first utterances of "multiculturalism," McWilliams acknowledged the diverse racial and ethnic groups who converged upon the landscape, emphasizing their struggle to make ends meet, often against the tide of white prejudice and nativism. Whether discussing shanty-town *colonias* of Mexican orange pickers in the posh communities of Pasadena and Redlands, the indiscriminate slaughter of Chinese immigrants in downtown Los Angeles, or the utter decimation of Southern California's indigenous population, McWilliams exhibited an atypical degree of sympathy and compassion for people of color, recognizing their plight and their perseverance through cycles of boom and bust.

If McWilliams recognized the racial fault lines that fractured Southern California's fragmented metropolis, he also saw the class war that engendered a set of violent confrontations at the outset of the twentieth century, when Los Angeles was an "open-shop" city that effectively banned union activity. Through every aspect of his account of the region, McWilliams sided with the ordinary men and women and exhibited fascination with, and curiosity about, the tourists, the boosters and hucksters, the displaced Midwesterners, the invalids and convalescents, the fugitives, the Okies and the Arkies, the immigrants from Japan, Mexico, and China. These were the same people whom Nathanael West described as "locusts" in *Day of the Locust* (1939), but McWilliams did not condescend. He never mocked their taste, insulted their intelligence, or lost his empathy. In his compassionate sense of history, McWilliams understood why Iowans, Indianans, and Kansans organized around their state societies in the 1880s; why people flocked to the Angelus Temple to marvel at the showmanship of Sister Aimee Semple McPherson; and why people crowded at movie premieres to gawk at Hollywood celebrities. He delivered his understanding without recourse to the theories of mind control or false consciousness that often shape accounts of Los Angeles' history and culture.

McWilliams's account of Los Angeles, critical and nuanced, yet fair and empathetic, preceded a much darker critique of the civilization that materialized in Southern California toward the middle of the twentieth century. If *Locust* dramatized how Hollywood could tap into the very core of the collective psyche, ruthlessly exploiting popular desires, fantasies and anxieties for corporate profit, Theodor Adorno and Max Horkheimer elevated the "locusts" to the realm of theory in "The Culture Industry: Enlightenment as Mass Deception" (1944), written in the shadow of Hollywood during World War II. Adorno and Horkheimer insisted upon the homogenizing influences of mass culture, arguing that its standardized and predictable formulas disseminate the false consciousness that reconciles the public to the prevailing inequalities of the status quo. Mass domination, in other words, entails mass deception, and therein lies the parallel between *The Day of the Locust* and the Frankfurt School: both emphasize the shallow conformity of the modern public and its stunted capacity to realize the limits of their freedom. In this context, Los Angeles – the city of mass-produced homes, accessories, and entertainment – is the tragic realization of Enlightenment civilization. Lest anyone doubt the "LA-centeredness" of this mid-century Marxist critique, Adorno and Horkheimer spell it out in their famous opening to the essay:

Even now the older houses just outside the concrete city center look like slums, and the new bungalows on the outskirts are at one with the flimsy structures of world fairs in their praise of technical progress and their built-in demand to be discarded after a short while like empty food cans. Yet the city housing projects designed to perpetuate the individual as a supposedly independent unit in a small hygienic dwelling make him all the more subservient to his adversary – the absolute power of capitalism.[2]

Adorno further developed the critique in "The Stars Down to Earth," (1953), which probes the appeal of the *Los Angeles Times* horoscope column. In a society where social relations are abstract and individuals are alienated from experience, he proposed, advice is valued simply because it exists. Few people consider the source or the interests that produce it. They want knowledge without the hard work of thinking, so they accept a hash of bygone super-stitions and tips for attaining fulfillment that subtly but decisively negate the possibilities for real social change.

Adorno may have sensed that Western civilization ended in Los Angeles, but postwar Southern California kept growing, as if the masses flocked to deception. By the 1950s, Los Angeles was the place you wanted to be: where Disneyland opened in 1955, where the Brooklyn Dodgers migrated to in 1957, where freeways integrated suburban idylls into a sprawling region, and where you could find Annette Funicello and Frankie Avalon frolicking on Malibu's beach. The Beach Boys delivered the winning narrative: Southern California as a land of eternal sunshine, killer waves, and heavy petting in the back of a T-bird convertible. The "it" city of postwar America, Los Angeles commanded national resources and attention; it also demanded a new narra-tive, one that would rescue the city from the dire assessments of highbrow Marxism.

The 1960s asserted radical new ideas that profoundly altered the percep-tion and experience of Los Angeles. Two intellectual developments in parti-cular, which, ironically, originated in New York, opened the door to a new understanding of Los Angeles. First, in the nooks and crannies of lower Manhattan, a full-time mother and housewife used the power of her pen to launch a full-scale assault upon the tenets of modernist city planning. In *The Death and Life of Great American Cities* (1961), Jane Jacobs took the planning establishment to task for its seeming eagerness to replace the home-grown spaces of urban social life with lifeless labyrinths of concrete and elevated highways. The paragon of good city form, Jacobs argued, was a bustling sidewalk. In *Death and Life*, she celebrated the "street ballet" of children, parents, shopkeepers, policemen, and passers-by. From her stoop in Greenwich Village, Jacobs judged other American cities according to the extent to which they mirrored the pedestrian vitality of her own neighborhood. She praised Boston's North End and Washington, DC's Georgetown, for example, but she made no secret of her disdain for Los Angeles. Although it was not a victim of modernist planning in the same way as Chicago or New York, Jacobs dismissed Los Angeles as a parking lot whose residents had sacrificed intimacy and vital spaces to satisfy their addiction to the automobile. But despite her trenchant criticism of Southern California's car culture, *Death and Life* ultimately enabled a new appreciation of Los Angeles. Its revulsion toward centralized state planning, its validation of vernacular spaces and commercial activity, and its celebration of "messy vitality" and "complex diversity" provided the tools with which the terms for understanding Los Angeles were remade at the end of the decade.

Second, in another sphere of 1960s New York, a new aesthetic sensibility forever changed Americans' relationship to consumer culture. In a Midtown loft, Andy Warhol launched his Factory, producing canvases that celebrated the commodities of everyday life. Campbell's Soup cans, Spam tins, and Brillo boxes: these objects captivated the art world of 1960s New York and suddenly a visit to the supermarket might become a transcendent aesthetic experience. Actually, Pop Art found even more vibrant expression in Los Angeles, which had nurtured its own avant-garde art scene since the 1950s. In the 1960s, artists like Ed Ruscha and the British expatriate David Hockney elaborated on the Pop sensibility, turning their eyes toward the city's sprawling commercial landscape and rendering its portrait on canvas and in photographs. Parking lots, apartment complexes, gas stations, and swimming pools debuted in the hip galleries. Whether low became high or high went low, the progenitors of Pop Art recast the perception and experience of ordinary landscapes, vaporizing the distinction of fine art from everything else.

Amidst this cultural ferment, Reyner Banham, another British expat with roots in the Pop Art movement, delivered a radically new interpretation of Los Angeles. Unlike his Frankfurt predecessors, Banham surrendered his familiarity with classical models of European urbanity to understand Los Angeles on its own terms by "learning the local language," which he discovered was the "language of movement." By "learn[ing] to drive in order to read LA in the original," Banham discovered a "comprehensible, even consistent quality to its built form."[3] Banham had studied under the architectural historians Sigfried Giedion and Nikolaus Pevsner. In *Los Angeles: The Architecture of Four Ecologies* (1971), he did for Los Angeles what Robert Venturi, Denise Scott Brown, and Steven Izenour's *Learning from Las Vegas: The Forgotten Symbolism of Architectural Form* (1972) was to do for that city the following year. Both tracts scold establishment academics for failing to take seriously auto-scaled landscapes that cater to popular sensibilities. In both cities, civic plazas and temples of high art were afterthoughts; the car washes, gas stations, and parking lots came first, and then came the drive-ins, billboards, and freeways. The car culture of the urban West deserved appreciation on its own terms, or so argued this younger generation of architects who embraced a more popular, and, they argued, more democratic model of urban design driven by market demand.

Banham found order where others saw chaos. The sprawling freeway network of Southern California was not imposed willy-nilly, but followed historic patterns of movement. Thus, the footpaths of Indians and Spaniards set patterns for the railroad tracks that followed in the mid-nineteenth century. Railroads, in turn, dictated the placement of streetcar lines, which further guided development and subsequently shaped the twentieth-century system of streets, boulevards, and freeways. Explaining this vital aspect of urban development, Banham emphasizes the interplay between past and present, finding historical continuity and logical progression. A similar recovery of lost traces frames Banham's discussion of Los Angeles' built environment. European architectural traditions cannot explain the rich and distinctive architectural culture of Southern California because the region's geographic isolation from the East Coast establishment left it open to other, non-European influences. Banham thus turns to the city's Mexican past to explain the significance of Irving Gill's architecture, noting the mutual emphasis upon open air porches, exposed rafters, broad surfaces, and a fluid interplay of interior and exterior. That Los Angeles' culture is shaped by non-European influences is a commonplace today; it was considerably more radical in the overwhelmingly white Los Angeles of some forty years ago.

Like McWilliams, Banham also stressed the primacy of the natural landscape. His analysis of the four "ecologies" combines topography with sociology to explain the realms of "Surfurbia," the culture of the coastline, which marks "a symbolic rejection of the values of the consumer society"; "Autopia," the freeways and architectural innovations (especially the strip and the drive-in) that support the city's infamous car culture; "the Plains of the Id," or middlebrow landscapes of Southern California's basins; and "the Foothills," home to the elites and their often experimental domestic architecture. Throughout each chapter, Banham emphasizes his new set of imperatives for twentieth-century urbanization: innovation, experimentation, accessibility, mobility, and convenience, as he imposes an order upon a city that had been a longstanding stereotype of chaos.

Banham's book inspired a generation of urbanists to stop comparing every undiscovered city to Paris or New York, and to try instead to understand it on its own terms. Many of us still write about Los Angeles under the influence of

Banham's vision, even if it's difficult wholly to subscribe to his "I Love LA" school of urban theory. After all, Banham glossed over the extremes of inequality that festered in postwar Los Angeles, confusing spatial mobility with social mobility. Thus he could read the Watts Rebellion, one of the bloodiest and most destructive urban uprisings in US history, as but a "sporadic flare[] of violence" in a "fashionable venue for confrontations." For all its insight and impact, *Los Angeles: The Architecture of Four Ecologies* ultimately wrote another myth of Los Angeles. A paean to a city where "all its parts are equal and equally accessible from all other parts at once,"[4] *Los Angeles* birthed a sun-drenched fantasy of democratic equality, premised upon convenience, mobility, and consumer choice.

Joan Didion saw a very different Los Angeles. In several collections of essays and her 1970 novel, *Play It As It Lays*, she produces her own idiosyncratic version of Los Angeles and California, a place she renders as the paranoid capital of the world. Many of Didion's essays are refracted through her own paranoia, alienation, and belief that people are "moved by strange, conflicted, ... and, above all, devious motivations which commit them inevitably to conflict and failure,"[5] characteristics noted in a 1968 psychiatric report that she cites in the title essay of *The White Album* (1979). Unsettling perhaps, but this distance is nonetheless central to her typical, deeply skeptical and ironic perspective on Los Angeles. In the maelstrom of brutal murders, brush fires, riots, and the floating world of celebrity happenings, Didion keeps her head cool and her prose taut, writing about the city as if it were an alien world. With a deadpan eye toward the local mix of sex, violence, and celebrity, and the desperations and more than occasional delusions of the strivers on its fringes, Didion homes in upon the dark side of the California dream.

Where some saw affluence and mobility, Joan Didion saw decadence. Herself descended from early Anglo settlers of Northern California (her great-great-great grandmother's family parted ways with the legendary Donner Party before it resorted to cannibalism in the Sierra Nevadas), Didion sees Los Angeles as arriviste. In its paradoxical mix of lush greenery and harsh desert winds, "time was never of the essence"[6] and late night radio programs air the rants of anonymous callers who confess their anxieties about rattlesnakes and the nation's declining morals. Homosexuals lurk in Hollywood's skewed moral universe; knife-brandishing strangers stalk the city's isolated canyons; neighborhoods erupt in spontaneous combustion; and women shop for groceries in bikinis and high heels. The preponderance of mansard roofs and Greek columns signals the social arrival of the nouveaux riches, while Scientologists and Seventh Day Adventists preach the end of the world, and teenage girls place advertisements in trade magazines announcing their intentions to become stars. In many ways, Didion's Los Angeles is the very image of the society critiqued by Daniel Bell's *The Cultural Contradictions of Capitalism* (1976). The city symbolizes a moral dead end, where the underlying values of industrial capitalism – hard work, thrift, diligence, and delayed gratification – have given way to the hedonism and narcissism of twentieth-century consumer capitalism.

Thus Didion recalls that *"no one was surprised"* when Sharon Tate and four others were found stabbed to death at 10050 Cielo Drive in Benedict Canyon on the morning of August 9, 1969. The Manson murders marked the gory climax of a "demented and seductive tension" that was building in a city where "everything was unmentionable but nothing was unimaginable," and where people had been going "'too far.'" The Manson murders were but one of many slayings that caught Didion's attention. She recounts the 1968 murder of Ramon Navarro, the aging silent film star who was murdered in his Hollywood Hills home by two teenage hustlers. She drives to Rancho Cucamonga, on the eastern fringe of Southern California's swelling metropolis, to attend the trial of Lucille Miller, convicted of murdering her husband, Cork, and making it look like an auto accident. And she befriends Linda Kasabian, former member of the Manson Family and star prosecution witness in Manson's murder trial. (Didion picks out the dress Linda wears at the trial.) Los Angeles harbors a chilling version of urban anonymity, where strangers lurking in the city's canyons and hillsides stalk the rich and famous. In a city of "'senseless killing neighborhood[s],'"[7] murder is as commonplace as palm trees, brush fires, and automobiles.

Nature wreaks its own brand of violence upon the city. Santa Ana winds induce murder, suicide, and the season of "prickly dread."[8] They ignite canyons and coastal neighborhoods, leaving behind a wake of ash and desolation. Didion recalls leaving Los Angeles after a brutal fire storm in Malibu in 1978 in which "horses caught fire and were shot on the beach, birds exploded in the air. Houses did not explode but imploded, as in a nuclear strike." The fires are the city's "deepest image of itself,"[9] and could be a metaphor for a society spiraling out of control.

Control is a central theme of Didion's writing, in part for reasons outlined in her psychiatric report. She is fascinated with the vast technologies that control the basic functions of the city. She visits the Operations Control Center for the California State Water Project to watch "the system work on the big board with the lighted checkpoints." She harbors a "passion for seeing the water under control," and she explains that a swimming pool, "for many of us in the West," is less a luxury than a promise of "control over the uncontrollable": the supply of water in an arid land. Traffic, too, is always under surveillance and control. She visits the Operations Center for the

California Department of Transportation in downtown Los Angeles, where again men at consoles watch a huge board of flashing colored lights. They are watching traffic flow on "'the 42 mile Loop"[10] of freeways, monitored by the Xerox Sigma V computer, which communicates with sensors embedded every half-mile in the pavement itself. The paradox of Joan Didion's Los Angeles is that it is a society teetering between the extremes of chaos and control. While brush fires, earthquakes, and random killings threaten social stability and moral order, men watching the city behind immense consoles manipulate switches and flashing buttons to preserve order.

There is no struggle, only enervation in Joan Didion's Los Angeles. Her early writings anticipated a rising conservative critique of cultural decline in the United States, although her politics have drifted steadily leftward over the course of her career. Thanks in part to Didion, but also to contemporary films like *The Graduate* and *Chinatown*, Los Angeles had come to symbolize the moral turpitude of a society awash in affluence – the culmination of an age of excess and hedonism that defined the anything-goes culture of America in the 1960s. But if the Right claimed a stake in shaping collective understandings of Los Angeles and its historic significance, the Left issued a stinging retort toward the end of the century.

Deindustrialization, racial segregation, class polarization, and environmental degradation shifted the terms of the LA debate in the 1980s away from the city's quirky originality to its place in age-old class wars. Mike Davis's *City of Quartz: Excavating the Future in Los Angeles* (1990), the best known book by a member of the so-called LA School of urbanists, sparked a cottage industry (and some controversy) around the analysis of Los Angeles' history and future. Timing was a key to its success. After yet another explosion of racial violence, the 1992 Justice Riots, *City of Quartz* was hailed for having predicted the urban uprising, and as the crystal ball for a city's dark future.

Like Carey McWilliams, Davis crosses disciplinary boundaries. The son of working-class internal migrants from Ohio, Davis combines intellectual history, cultural history, and architectural criticism with political and economic analysis of the region, but the book's brilliance derives from its ability to render transparent the hidden relationships between disparate events and processes within twentieth-century Los Angeles. Davis makes no secret of his Marxist orientation. In some ways, *City of Quartz* reads as a geographically bounded recapitulation of the arguments Davis made in *Prisoners of the American Dream: Politics and Economy in the History of the US Working Class* (1986), which narrates the bitter history of labor exploitation and oppression in the United States. *City of Quartz*, however, infuses this history with an urban sensibility, as if narrating the "spatialization" of class war in

Southern California – that is, the way the city's geography and architecture, as well as its culture and history, were wrought by a century of bitter class conflict. In his take-no-prisoners approach to urban analysis, no one is immune from attack. Architect Frank Gehry becomes "Dirty Harry" for foisting his own brand of "design terror"[11] on the city's outcasts, David Hockney spreads a pop veneer upon Southern California's development juggernaut, and even Reyner Banham enlists as a mercenary in the class war, a booster who celebrates capitalism run amok. All three men are agents of Southern California's historic war of the haves on the have-nots; all of them assist capitalism on its path toward global domination. There is little room for dialogue, let alone debate. Davis's narrative is so airtight, so comprehensive, and so unabashedly polemical that it's hard even to question the terms of the argument. Class war is not *a* means, but *the* means of understanding Los Angeles' history. Other factors – race, ethnicity, geography, language, gender, religion, and the many other elements that mediate social relations – are secondary iterations.

The analysis deploys a set of binaries that frames Southern California culture and politics. The first chapter, "Sunshine or Noir?," delivers an intellectual history of Los Angeles predicated upon a stark opposition between the critics of urbanization in Southern California and its champions. In this schematic compression of the history of writing about Los Angeles, authors are lovers or haters, boosters or debunkers, purveyors of either "Sunshine" or "Noir." Davis thus traces the successive generations of boosters in Los Angeles, from Charles Fletcher Lummis and the "Arroyo Set" to Reyner Banham, developer Eli Broad, and architect Richard Meier, as well as their noir antagonists, from Carey McWilliams to the Frankfurt School to presumably the author himself, who use the language and narrative devices of noir fiction throughout the text. There is a rigorous adherence to this binary: no in-betweenness, no ambivalence. The rest of the book exploits this either/or framework, pitting homeowners against developers, labor against capital, law enforcement against immigrants and minorities.

Davis brackets these binaries with a wistful meditation upon what was and what might have been. The prologue visits the ruins of Llano del Rio, an experimental colony established on the desert frontier of Los Angeles by the Young People's Socialist League in 1914. Today, developers look past the ruins to plan the latest extension of Southern California's infinite suburban grid, obliterating both the indigenous Joshua trees and the memories of a bygone utopia. The final chapter explores Fontana, the "junkyard of dreams" that began its existence as a development of farm tracts and became home to Henry Kaiser's steel plant in 1942, which provided well-paying union jobs with health plans. The plant closed during the 1970s wave of deindustrialization, leaving Fontana to salvage yards, biker hangouts, and meth labs. Lesson: Hope is futile. Mike Davis's Los Angeles devours our aspirations, consuming our collective dreams along with the desert land.

Between the stories of Llano and Fontana lies the story of a city that nurtures its own heavens and hells. Invoking the municipal slogan that "it all comes together in Los Angeles," Davis weaves the disparate strands of the city's history into an image of what advanced capitalism entails for all of us: a nightmarish world where suburban enclaves of privilege are fortified against internal colonies of desperate poverty. But the primacy of class conflict in *City of Quartz* obscures the salience of race, which continues to divide Los Angeles, as it did in deadly ways in 1943, 1965, and again in 1992. Unlike McWilliams, who acknowledged the racial fault lines that fractured Southern California's social landscape, in *City of Quartz* Davis tends toward Banham's two-toned view of race in Los Angeles, even though few American cities have the kind of racial diversity that Los Angeles has sustained throughout its history. As a point of contact among people moving north, east, and west, Los Angeles brings together a racial mix that produces a regionally distinct set of problems and possibilities. Whites now comprise a demographic minority in Los Angeles County, outnumbered by people from Asia and Latin America. At the outset of the twenty-first century, Los Angeles is, once again, a Latino metropolis. Indeed, it is also a Korean metropolis, with a greater concentration of Koreans than anywhere in the world outside of Seoul. The same could be said for Thais, Filipinos, and Armenians. Yet as a basis of social conflict and as an arbiter of social relations, race plays a secondary role in *City of Quartz*. African Americans are almost monolithically poor, most frequently the gangbangers patrolling South Central Los Angeles. Likewise, Asians and Latinos, especially immigrants, are virtually absent from *City of Quartz* except in the Latino community's role as pawns in the internal power struggles of the Catholic Church. For all its insight and depth, *City of Quartz* proffers an analysis that remains bounded by the subjective limitations of a white-male Marxism that slights the salience of race in a deeply racialized metropolis.

Despite its limitations, however, *City of Quartz* heralded a new interest in Los Angeles' history and culture. Since the early 1990s, new studies of Los Angeles that cross academic disciplines, social theories, and political ideologies have promulgated a far more complex and nuanced portrait of the city. The "LA School" of urban theory is well established, although its influence upon broader understandings of the city remains limited by disciplinary jargon and over-theorization. At the end of the day, Los Angeles still defies conventional categories of urban knowledge. It remains an unknown quantity. Is it the future of capitalist urbanization? Is it anomalous in the annals of urban history? Is it the exception at the end of American expansion? These questions still frame contemporary debates about the meaning of the city, and they remain a fruitful basis for further inquiry at the outset of the twenty-first century.

NOTES

1. Carey McWilliams, *Southern California: An Island on the Land* (Layton, Utah: Gibbs Smith, 1973), p. xxi.
2. Cited in Mike Davis, *City of Quartz: Excavating the Future in Los Angeles* (New York: Verso, 1990), pp. 48–9.
3. Reyner Banham, *Los Angeles: The Architecture of Four Ecologies* (Harmondsworth, UK: Penguin, 1971) pp. 23, 21.
4. *Ibid.*, pp. 25, 36.
5. Joan Didion, "The White Album," in *The White Album* (New York: Noonday Press, 1990), pp. 14–15.
6. *Ibid.*, p. 26.
7. *Ibid.*, pp. 42, 41, 15.
8. Didion, "Some Dreamers of the Golden Dream," in *Slouching Towards Bethlehem* (New York: Noonday Press, 1990), p. 3.
9. Didion, "Los Angeles Notebook," *ibid.*, p. 220.
10. *Didion*, "Holy Water," in *The White Album*, pp. 66, 65, 64; Didion, "Bureaucrats," *ibid.*, p. 79.
11. Davis, *City of Quartz*, pp. 236, 73.

Abbott, Carl. *Frontiers Past and Future: Science Fiction and the American West.* Lawrence: University Press of Kansas, 2006.

Abelmann, Nancy, and John Lie. *Blue Dream: Korean Americans and the Los Angeles Riots.* Cambridge, Mass.: Harvard University Press, 1995.

Avila, Eric. *Popular Culture in the Age of White Flight: Fear and Fantasy in Suburban Los Angeles.* American Crossroads 13. Berkeley: University of California Press, 2004.

Avril, Chloé. "'Burn, Baby, Burn!': Walter Mosley's *Little Scarlet* and the Watts Riots." In *Riots in Literature*, ed. David Bell and Gerald Porter, pp. 129–50. Newcastle upon Tyne: Cambridge Scholars Press, 2008.

Bahr, Ehrhard. *Weimar on the Pacific: German Exile Culture in Los Angeles, and the Crisis of Modernism.* Weimar and Now: German Cultural Criticism 41. Berkeley: University of California Press, 2007.

Bahr, Ehrhard, and Carolyn See. *Literary Exiles and Refugees in Los Angeles: Papers Presented at a Clark Library Seminar, 14 April 1984.* Los Angeles: William Andrews Clark Memorial Library, University of California, Los Angeles, 1988.

Baldassare, Mark, ed. *The Los Angeles Riots: Lessons for the Urban Future.* Boulder, Colo.: Westview Press, 1994.

Banham, Reyner. *Los Angeles: The Architecture of Four Ecologies.* Harmondsworth, UK: Penguin, 1971.

Baudrillard, Jean. *America.* Tr. Chris Turner. New York: Verso, 1988.

Berg, James J., and Chris Freeman, eds. *The Isherwood Century: Essays on the Life and Work of Christopher Isherwood.* Madison: University of Wisconsin Press, 2000.

Brodsly, David. *L.A. Freeway: An Appreciative Essay.* Berkeley: University of California Press, 1981.

Bryant, Clora, *et al. Central Avenue Sounds: Jazz in Los Angeles.* Roth Family Foundation Music in America Imprint. Berkeley: University of California Press, 1998.

Bryson, J. Scott. "Los Angeles Literature: Exiles, Natives, and (Mis)Representation." *American Literary History* 16 (2004), 707–18.

Bullock, Paul. *Watts: The Aftermath – An Inside View of the Ghetto by the People of Watts.* New York: Grove Press, 1969.

Carby, Hazel V. "Figuring the Future in Los(t) Angeles." *Comparative American Studies: An International Journal* 1 (2003), 19–34.

Cheung, King-Kok. "(Mis)Interpretations and (In)Justice: The 1992 Los Angeles 'Riots' and 'Black-Korean Conflict.'" *MELUS* 30.3 (2005), 3–40.

Chipman, Bruce L. *Into America's Dream-Dump: A Postmodern Study of the Hollywood Novel*. New York: University Press of America, 1999.

Clinton, Michelle T., Sesshu Foster, and Naomi Helena Quiñonez, eds. *Invocation L.A.: Urban Multicultural Poetry*. Albuquerque, N.M.: West End Press, 1989.

Comer, Krista. "Revising Western Criticism through Wanda Coleman." *Western American Literature* 33.4 (1999), 357–83.

"Western Literature at Century's End: Sketches in Generation X, Los Angeles, and the Post-Civil Rights Novel." *Pacific Historical Review* 72 (2003), 405–13.

Cooper, Stephen, and David M. Fine, eds. *John Fante: A Critical Gathering*. Madison, N.J.: Fairleigh Dickinson University Press, 1999.

Davis, Mike. *City of Quartz: Excavating the Future in Los Angeles*. New York: Verso, 1990.

Ecology of Fear: Los Angeles and the Imagination of Disaster. New York: Vintage, 1999.

Magical Urbanism: Latinos Reinvent the U.S. City. New York: Verso, 2000.

de Graaf, Lawrence B., Kevin Mulroy, and Quintard Taylor. *Seeking El Dorado: African Americans in California*. Seattle: Autry Museum of Western Heritage-University of Washington Press, 2001.

Dear, Michael J., H. Eric Schockman, and Greg Hise. *Rethinking Los Angeles*. Thousand Oaks, Calif.: Sage, 1996.

DeLyser, Dydia. *Ramona Memories: Tourism and the Shaping of Southern California*. Minneapolis: University of Minnesota Press, 2005.

Deverell, William. *Whitewashed Adobe: The Rise of Los Angeles, and the Remaking of Its Mexican Past*. Berkeley: University of California Press, 2004.

Deverell, William, and Greg Hise. *Land of Sunshine: An Environmental History of Metropolitan Los Angeles*. Pittsburgh: University of Pittsburgh Press, 2005.

Didion, Joan. *Slouching Towards Bethlehem*. 1968. New York: Noonday Press, 1990.

Where I Was From. New York: Knopf, 2003.

The White Album. 1979. New York: Noonday Press, 1990.

Dunaway, David King. *Huxley in Hollywood*. New York: Harper & Row, 1989.

Field, Edward, Gerald Locklin, and Charles Stetler, eds. *A New Geography of Poets*. Fayetteville: University of Arkansas Press, 1992.

Fine, David M. *Imagining Los Angeles: A City in Fiction*. Albuquerque: University of New Mexico Press, 2000.

Fine, David M., ed. *Los Angeles in Fiction: A Collection of Critical Essays*. Rev. ed. Albuquerque: University of New Mexico Press, 1995.

Flamming, Douglas. *Bound for Freedom: Los Angeles in Jim Crow America*. Berkeley: University of California Press, 2005.

Fogelson, Robert M. *The Fragmented Metropolis: Los Angeles, 1850–1930*. Rev. ed. Classics in Urban History vol. 3. Berkeley: University of California Press, 1993.

Friedman, Ellen G., ed. *Joan Didion: Essays and Conversations*. Princeton, N.J.: Ontario Review Press, 1984.

Gabler, Neal. *An Empire of Their Own: How the Jews Invented Hollywood*. New York: Crown Publishers, 1988.

George, Lynell. *No Crystal Stair: African-Americans in the City of Angels*. New York: Verso, 1992.

Gottlieb, Robert. *Reinventing Los Angeles: Nature and Community in the Global City*. Cambridge: MIT Press, 2007.

Griswold del Castillo, Richard. *The Los Angeles Barrio, 1850–1890: A Social History*. Berkeley: University of California Press, 1979.

Gumprecht, Blake. *The Los Angeles River: Its Life, Death, and Possible Rebirth*. Baltimore: Johns Hopkins University Press, 2001.

Haas, Lisbeth. *Conquests and Historical Identities in California, 1769–1936*. Berkeley: University of California Press, 1995.

Hausladen, Gary J., and Paul F. Starrs. "L.A. Noir." *Journal of Cultural Geography* 23 (2005), 43–69.

Heilbut, Anthony. *Exiled in Paradise: German Refugee Artists and Intellectuals in America, from the 1930s to the Present*. New York: Viking Press, 1983.

Hermanson, Scott. "Fear and Loathing in Los Angeles: Mike Davis as Nature Writer." *Western American Literature* 37.3 (2002), 293–317.

Hicks, Heather J. "On Whiteness in T. Coraghessan Boyle's *The Tortilla Curtain*." *Critique* 45 (2003), 43–64.

Hoopes, Roy. *Cain*. New York: Holt, Rinehart & Winston, 1982.

Itagaki, Lynn M. "Transgressing Race and Community in Chester Himes's *If He Hollers Let Him Go*." *African American Review* 37 (2003), 65–80.

Izzo, David Garret. *Christopher Isherwood: His Era, His Gang, and the Legacy of the Truly Strong Man*. Columbia: University of South Carolina Press, 2001.

James, David. *The Most Typical Avant Garde: History and Geography of Minor Cinemas in Los Angeles*. Berkeley: University of California Press, 2005.

Jeneman, David. *Adorno in America*. Minneapolis: University of Minnesota Press, 2007.

Kennedy, Liam. "Black Noir: Race and Urban Space in Walter Mosley's Detective Fiction." In *Diversity and Detective Fiction*, ed. Katherine Gregory Klein, pp. 224–39. Bowling Green, Ohio: Popular Press, 1999.

Klein, Norman. *The History of Forgetting: Los Angeles and the Erasure of Memory*. New York: Verso, 1997.

Kling, Rob, Spencer Olin, and Mark Poster, eds. *Postsuburban California: The Transformation of Orange County since World War II*. Berkeley: University of California Press, 1991.

Leclerc, Gustavo, Raúl Villa, and Michael J. Dear, eds. *Urban Latino Cultures: La vida latina en L. A.* Thousand Oaks, Calif.: Sage, 1999.

Lee, James Kyung-Jin. *Urban Triage: Race and the Fictions of Multiculturalism*. Minneapolis: University of Minnesota Press, 2004.

MacShane, Frank. *The Life of Raymond Chandler*. New York: Random House, 1976.

Madden, David, ed. *Tough Guy Writers of the Thirties*. Carbondale: Southern Illinois University Press, 1968.

Marling, William. *The American Roman Noir: Hammett, Cain, and Chandler*. Athens: University of Georgia Press, 1995.

Raymond Chandler. Boston: Macmillan, 1986.

Mason, Theodore O., Jr. "Walter Mosley's Easy Rawlins: The Detective and Afro-American Fiction." *Kenyon Review* 144 (Fall 1992), 173–83.

Matsumoto, Valerie J., and Blake Allmendinger, eds. *Over the Edge: Remapping the American West*. New York: Oxford University Press, 1995.

McCaffery, Larry, and Takayuki Tatsumi. "An Interview with Steve Erickson." *Contemporary Literature* 38 (1997), 395–421.

McClung, William A. *Landscapes of Desire: Anglo Mythologies of Los Angeles.* Berkeley: University of California Press, 2002.

McNamara, Kevin R. "*Blade Runner*'s Post-Individual Worldspace." *Contemporary Literature* 38 (1997), 422–46.

"CityWalk: Los(t) Angeles in the Shape of a Mall." In *The Urban Condition: Space, Community, and Self in the Contemporary Metropolis,* ed. Dirk De Meyer *et al.,* pp. 186–201. Rotterdam: 010 Press, 1999.

"In and out of History: Forest Lawn's Ideal America." In *Dreams of Paradise, Visions of Apocalypse: Utopia and Dystopia in American Culture,* ed. Jaap Verheul, pp. 149–58. Amsterdam: VU Press, 2004.

"Los Angeles, 2019: Two Tales of a City." In *Productive Postmodernism: Consuming Histories and Cultural Studies,* ed. John N. Duvall, pp. 123–36. SUNY Series in Postmodern Culture. Albany: State University of New York Press, 2002.

McPhee, John. *The Control of Nature.* New York: Farrar, Straus & Giroux, 1990.

McWilliams, Carey. *Southern California Country: An Island on the Land.* American Folkways. New York: Duell, Sloan & Pearce, 1946.

Messerli, Douglas, ed. *Intersections: Innovative Poetry in Southern California.* Vol. 5 of *The PIP Anthology of World Poetry of the 20th Century.* Copenhagen and Los Angeles: Green Integer, 2005.

Mitchell, James B. "Cul-de-Sac Nightmares: Representations of Californian Suburbs in Science Fiction During the 1950s and 1960s." *Iowa Journal of Cultural Studies* 3 (Fall 2003). www.uiowa.edu/~ijcs/suburbia/mitchell.htm/.

Mohr, Bill. *Backlit Renaissance: Los Angeles Poets During the Cold War.* Iowa City: University of Iowa Press, 2010.

"Peripheral Outlaws: Beyond Baroque and the LA Poetry Renaissance." In *The Sons and Daughters of Los: Culture and Community in L.A.,* ed. David E. James, pp. 15–38. Philadelphia: Temple University Press, 2003.

Mohr, Bill, and Sheree Levin, eds. *"Poetry Loves Poetry": An Anthology of Los Angeles Poets.* Santa Monica, Calif.: Momentum Press, 1985.

Moylan, Michele. "Reading the Indians: The *Ramona* Myth in American Culture." *Prospects* 18 (1993), 153–86.

Murphet, Julian. *Literature and Race in Los Angeles.* Cambridge: Cambridge University Press, 2001.

Nolan, Tom. *Ross Macdonald.* New York: Scribner's, 1999.

Nolan, William. *The Black Mask Boys.* New York: Morrow, 1985.

Novak, Estelle Gershgoren, ed. *Poets of the Non-Existent City: Los Angeles in the McCarthy Era.* Albuquerque: University of New Mexico Press, 2002.

Nyman, Jopi. *Men Alone: Masculinity, Individualism, and Hard-Boiled Fiction.* Amsterdam: Rodopi, 1997.

Price, Jenny. "Thirteen Ways of Seeing Nature in L.A." *Believer Magazine,* April 2006. www.believermag.com/issues/200604/?read=article_price.

Ramirez, Karen E. *Reading Helen Hunt Jackson's* Ramona. Boise State University Western Writers Series 171. Boise, Idaho: Boise State University, 2006.

Rhodes, Chip. *Politics, Desire and the Hollywood Novel.* Iowa City: University of Iowa Press, 2008.

Rodriguez, Ralph E. *Brown Gumshoes: Detective Fiction and the Search for Chicana/o Identity*. Austin: University of Texas Press, 2005.

Ruiz, Reynaldo, ed. *Hispanic Poetry in Los Angeles 1850–1900: La poesía angelina*. Lewiston, N.Y: Edwin Mellen Press, 2000.

Sánchez, Rosaura. *Telling Identities: The Californio Testimonios*. Minneapolis: University of Minnesota Press, 1995.

Sánchez, Rosaura, and Beatrice Pita. *Conflicts of Interest: The Letters of Maria Amparo Ruiz de Burton*. Houston, Tex.: Arte Público Press, 2001.

Schmidt-Nowara, Peter. "Finding God in a World of 'Leg Breakers' and 'Racist-Shitbirds': James Ellroy and the Contemporary L. A. Crime Novel." *Western American Literature* 36.2 (2001), 117–33.

Schulberg, Budd, ed. *From the Ashes: Voices of Watts*. New York: New American Library, 1967.

Scott, Allen J., and Edward W. Soja. *The City: Los Angeles and Urban Theory at the End of the Twentieth Century*. Berkeley: University of California Press, 1996.

Scruggs, Charles. "'Oh for a Mexican Girl!': The Limits of Literature in John Fante's *Ask the Dust*." *Western American Literature* 38 (2003), 228–45.

Shiel, Mark and Tony Fitzmaurice, eds. *Screening the City*. New York: Verso, 2003.

Sitton, Tom, and William Deverell, eds. *Metropolis in the Making: Los Angeles in the 1920s*. Berkeley: University of California Press, 2001.

Song, Min Hyoung. *Strange Future: Pessimism and the 1992 Los Angeles Riots*. Durham, N.C.: Duke University Press, 2005.

Springer, John Parris. *Hollywood Fictions: The Dream Factory in American Popular Literature*. Norman: University of Oklahoma Press, 2000.

Starr, Kevin. *Americans and the California Dream, 1850–1915*. New York: Oxford University Press, 1973.

    Embattled Dreams: California in War, and Peace, 1940–1950. Oxford: Oxford University Press, 2002.

    Endangered Dreams: The Great Depression in California. New York: Oxford University Press, 1996.

    Inventing the Dream: California through the Progressive Era. New York: Oxford University Press, 1985.

    Material Dreams: Southern California through the 1920s. New York: Oxford University Press, 1990.

Timberg, Scott, and Dana Gioia, eds. *The Misread City: New Literary Los Angeles*. Los Angeles: Red Hen Press, 2003.

Tygiel, Jules. *The Great Los Angeles Swindle: Oil, Stocks, and Scandal during the Roaring Twenties*. New York: Oxford University Press, 1994.

Ulin, David, ed. *Writing Los Angeles: A Literary Anthology*. New York: Library of America, 2002.

Vangelisti, Paul, and Evan Calbi. *L.A. Exile: A Guide to Los Angeles Writing, 1932–1998*. New York: Marsilio Press, 1999.

Villa, Raúl H. *Barrio-Logos: Space and Place in Urban Chicano Literature and Culture*. Austin: University of Texas Press, 2000.

Wasserburg, Charles. "Raymond Chandler's Great Wrong Place." *Southwest Review* 74 (1989), 534–45.

Webb, Charles Harper, ed. *Stand Up Poetry: An Expanded Anthology*. Iowa City: University of Iowa Press, 2002.

Widener, Daniel. "Writing Watts: Budd Schulberg, Black Poetry, and the Cultural War on Poverty." *Journal of Urban History* 34 (2008), 665–87.

Wolverton, Terry. *Insurgent Muse: Life and Art at the Woman's Building*. San Francisco: City Lights Books, 2002.

Wyatt, David. *Five Fires: Race, Catastrophe, and the Shaping of California*. New York: Oxford University Press, 1999.

Cambridge Companions to...

AUTHORS

TOPICS